Enticement
of the Forbidden

Judy Starr

Enticement of the Forbidden

Published by
LifeConneXions
A ministry of Campus Crusade for Christ
375 Highway 74 South, Suite A
Peachtree City, GA 30269

Design and production by Genesis Group

Cover by Larry Smith & Associates

Printed in the United States of America

ISBN 1-56399-220-5

Unless otherwise indicated, Scripture quotations are from the *New American Standard Bible*, © 1960, 1962, 1963, 1968, 1971, 1972, 1973, 1975, 1977, 1995 by the Lockman Foundation, La Habra, California.

Scripture quotations designated NIV are from the *New International Version*, © 1973, 1978, 1984 by the International Bible Society. Published by Zondervan Bible Publishers, Grand Rapids, Michigan.

Scripture quotations designated TLB are from *The Living Bible*, © 1971 by Tyndale House Publishers, Wheaton, Illinois.

Scripture quotations designated RSV are from *The Holy Bible: Revised Standard Version*, © 1946, 1952, 1959, 1973 by the Division of Christian Education of the National Council of the Churches of Christ in the United States of America.

To Stottler

Words are inadequate to convey my overflowing love. You're simply the best!

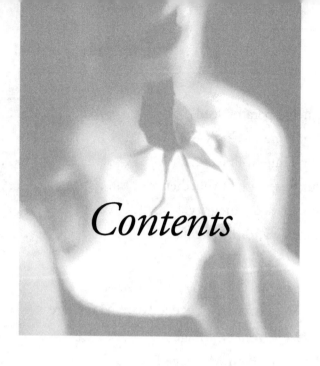

Contents

Acknowledgments 7

Part One
How Small, Poor Choices Made One Big Problem
1. Sunset in the Caribbean 11
2. We Have a Problem 13
3. What Does God Say? 23
4. How Could This Happen? 35
5. Stay or Leave? 43
6. Rebuilding Our Marriage 51

Part Two
How Our Relationship with God Affects Our Marriage
7. Our Relationship with God 65
8. Transparent Repentance .77
9. The Spirit-Controlled Life 91

10. Our Desperate Need 103
11. Our Time in God's Word 117
12. Our Time in Prayer 135
13. Our Response of Obedience 149
14. Our Lives of Integrity 163
15. Integrity and the Media 177

Part Three
How to Protect Your Marriage

16. Love and Your Marriage 195
17. Caring for Your Marriage 213
18. Establishing Accountability in Your Marriage 227
19. Building Walls to Protect Your Marriage 241
20. Responding to Marital Temptations 257
21. View from the Top 271

Resources 275

Notes 279

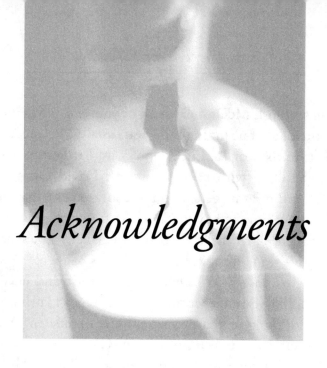

Acknowledgments

T his book never could have been written without the constant love, support, and encouragement of my precious husband, Stottler. Thanks for praying through every moment with me, for telling me when to rest, for encouraging me to keep on. You are incredible!

Many of the names have been changed throughout the book —but not those listed here. These are special people indeed:

A special thanks goes to my dear friends, Bonnie Lang and Holly Elliff. You have stood with me my entire adult life, and I owe so much to both of you for your prayers, wisdom, guidance, and especially your love. I love you.

What would I have done without my prayer team? You have upheld this entire writing from day one, and only the Lord knows the impact of your faithful prayers. Thanks Stottler, Bonnie, Holly, Erin and Jason Rehard, Cindy and Steve Antosh, Jeanie Euler, Donna Backus, and Carol Culbertson.

Thanks to Diana Kelly for all of your invaluable research. I would probably *still* be doing Internet searches without your help and patience in finding those elusive articles and footnotes. Thanks to Tisha Thompson for jumping in and helping as well.

Thanks to Josh McDowell for all of your encouragement, not only for the book, but through the years as a leader and a friend.

Thanks to the team at LifeConneXions: Pat Pearce, who started the ball rolling with my manuscript; David Orris for your wonderful enthusiasm, belief, and encouragement that kept me going; Joette Whims and Lynn Copeland for your invaluable editing (and patience); Michelle Treiber; Karl Schaller; Marlene Kopp; and the whole team. Thanks for making this happen!

Thanks to those who have come alongside and encouraged me at various points in the writing process: Nancy Hawblitzel (God brought you along at the perfect moment!), Helen Davidson, Shirley Alexander, Pat Peterson, Ruby Crosthwaite, Jacqueline Porter, Amy Wolcott, Janell Searles, and everyone at The JESUS Film Project—you have been so kind and supportive. You are my California family, and I love you tons!

And speaking of family, I owe my family a huge thank you! You are always there for me. My very special thanks to my precious Mom, Dottie Antosh, whose love of life, laughter, and adventure spilled over into mine the moment I was born. I love you *so much!* Also, thanks and lots of hugs to my mother-in-law, Elsa Starr; to my brothers and their wives, Jim and Nancy Antosh, Steve and Cindy Antosh; and to my dad, Ed Antosh.

Above all, my deepest thanks goes to my awesome Lord and Savior, Jesus Christ. I owe You everything! I am a work of Your grace from beginning to end. My greatest joy will be the day I can fall at Your feet in gratitude, then leap into Your arms in love. I pray that You will use this book to draw women to an understanding of our desperate, moment-by-moment need of Your grace and transforming work in our lives, and that as we live in holiness, we'll see transformation in our marriages and in the lives of all those around us. To You goes all praise and glory!

Part One

How Small, Poor Choices Made One Big Problem

"Call upon Me in the day of trouble; I shall
rescue you, and you will honor Me."
PSALM 50:15

1

Sunset in
the Caribbean

This had to be paradise. Absolute contentment enveloped
me as I melted into the deck cushions of our 39-foot
catamaran. The vessel rocked lazily against the wooden
pier of a secluded Caribbean bay as I reflected on the beguiling
issue of love. I had always loved the sea. As children, my brothers
and I would argue over which was better—the mountains or the
ocean. I *always* said the ocean. But it wasn't these crystal waters
that had my pulse elevated.

Any woman would have been affected by the bronze sun,
white sand, and translucent ocean that lapped against our boat.
Life was slower along these balmy shores. The islanders were
friendly and easygoing, and my seven-page "To Do" list seemed
utterly irrelevant here. This setting affected me like a narcotic.

It also affected my emotions. Our captain's kind blue eyes
and lilting British accent mesmerized me. We had been sailing
among the islands for almost four weeks, and I had fallen for this
tanned seaman. We shared so much in common and had spent
many long afternoons discussing everything from music and sailing to family and faith, life and death. Although our lives had

taken different paths up to now, we understood each other com-pletely. My heart yearned to be with him every moment.

This special evening, we sat alone on the boat. I had been help-ing to lead ministry teams throughout the islands, showing a film about the life of Christ. But this particular, fateful night, I had chosen to let the team go on without me.

As the sun slipped below the horizon, pink fingers of fading light danced across the water. Along the shore, towering palm fronds waved blessings of peace and serenity over this magical moment. I envisioned what it would be like to spend the rest of my life with this man, sailing to remote corners of the world, liv-ing this peaceful pace of life. Paradise couldn't be any better.

A warm Caribbean breeze played gently with my hair. Al-though serenity blanketed the evening, my knees shook ever so slightly, and I could hear the drumming of my own heartbeat. As I sat next to Eric, talking softly under the waning light, an elec-tric current of excitement surged through me. My attention was fastened solely upon this intriguing sailor. As we edged closer to-gether, I was aware of nothing else around me—until my husband came around the corner with the returning team.

Paradise had just sprung a leak.

Here I was, in full-time ministry, supposedly a mature Chris-tian woman. In the span of four weeks, how could I go from being a loving, adoring wife to someone who was thinking of leaving her husband? How on earth did I ever get to this point?

As I look back, I see how easy it was! And I'm not alone.

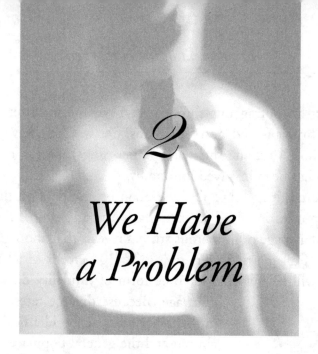

2

We Have a Problem

ffairs are happening all around us. Yet most married women in America's churches probably believe that they will never be attracted to another man—and *certainly* never involved in an affair. How could we be? Don't we go to church? Aren't we known for being spiritual? Don't we have "Christian" marriages? Most of us faithfully declare, "I would *never* divorce my husband!" But reality begs us to open our eyes.

A full 50 percent of all marriages in the U.S. will end in divorce. And according to recent research, wives are twice as likely to first suggest the divorce![1] Sadly for the church, Christian researcher George Barna has found that "born again Christians are just as likely to get divorced as are non-born again adults."[2] Ouch!

These divorce rates in our churches are not a recent phenomenon; they have been stable across the past half decade.[3] And 90 percent of the divorces among born-again Christians actually happened *after* the partners became Christians![4] As if that's not bad enough, Barna adds that the group's researchers "'rarely find substantial differences' between the moral behavior of Christians and non-Christians."[5]

What an outrageous thing to say! No moral difference between Christians and non-Christians? Yet we don't have to look hard to find a recent Christian speaker, singer, pastor, or layperson who has been involved immorally.

Although it is impossible to obtain precise data on the number of spouses involved in extramarital relationships, a realistic statistical average of numerous studies reveals that about 35 to 40 percent of all married men and 25 to 30 percent of all married women will be involved in some form of infidelity during their marriage. Because divorce rates and moral behavior seem to be identical for the church and the general populace, the rate of infidelity among believers is likely the same as that for nonbelievers. This means that approximately one out of every three or four married women will be involved in some sort of extramarital affair during their lives!

Approximately one out of every three or four married women will be involved in some sort of extramarital affair during their lives!

Extramarital affairs have traditionally been viewed as "a man's problem." Most people assume that it is the men who are out there "sowing their oats." But times have changed. With more women in the work force, looser morals in society, and equal rights to sin for women, infidelity has become a significant issue for the female population as well.

Everywhere we go we hear about "a new paradigm," including what's happening in our homes. No longer is it the traditional he-left-his-wife-for-his-secretary scenario. Popular speaker and author Josh McDowell told me that he now hears of more women who are contemplating leaving their husbands than men leaving their wives! In fact, Christian psychologist Dr. James Dobson writes, "At least one secular poll reportedly found that among those under twenty-nine years of age, 'significantly more married women are having affairs than married men.'"[6]

In my own church, one young mother decided that her life needed more excitement, so she left her husband and four children under the age of twelve to sleep with another man and to hang out in bars. I know of another woman who struck up a friendship with a man in her ministry group, and they ended up pursuing a devastating affair.

We need to burst the belief that our marriages are immune to temptations. Before disaster strikes, we need to heed the warning signs posted around us. As we begin this journey, let's first look at what defines an affair and who is vulnerable.

God's Moral Standards

The world's definition of an affair tends to be "sexual intercourse between two people not married to one another." However, we must ask, "What violates *God's* standards?" God has made it clear that *"the marriage bed is to be undefiled"* (Hebrews 13:4). He instructs us to *"abstain from sexual immorality"* (1 Thessalonians 4:3). So does that mean everything else is okay? Since the captain and I had no physical contact, was our relationship all right?

Any relationship outside of marriage that involves emotional and/or sexual intimacy exists outside the bounds of God's desires. Infidelity to my husband can be emotional as well as physical. Dennis Rainey, president of FamilyLife ministries, writes:

> Emotional adultery is unfaithfulness of the heart. It starts when two people of the opposite sex begin talking with each other about intimate struggles, doubts, or feelings. They start sharing their souls in a way that God intended exclusively for the marriage relationship. Emotional adultery is friendship with the opposite sex that goes too far.[7]

Debbie Layton-Tholl, a Florida psychologist who conducted an Internet survey on infidelity, says, "The minute a relationship goes from being public knowledge to becoming a secret—the minute you are feeling as though you can't tell your spouse... about this person—you've crossed the line. It's betrayal."[8]

God has graciously given us guidelines to help us in all of our relationships, both inside and outside our marriage. His love for us is so great that He goes to enormous lengths to protect us from our own destructive tendencies. He tells us to keep our lives pure, not living in lustful passion or defrauding a brother (1 Thessalonians 4:4–7).

Christian speaker and author Bill Gothard defines biblical defrauding as actions that "arouse sexual desires in another which cannot be righteously satisfied."[9] Eric and I shared emotional intimacy during many hours of private conversations. We "connected" emotionally, and my husband, Stottler, was excluded from that bond. Also, the explosive chemistry for sexual intimacy certainly existed between us, though by God's grace we never touched each other. But sexual desires that could not be righteously satisfied were definitely present! Without doubt, my relationship with Eric violated *God's* standards for a relationship outside my marriage.

When I left the Caribbean and returned home, I realized the need to saturate my mind with Scripture and Christian radio. To my amazement, I discovered that no one seemed to be addressing the issue of women's moral struggles. On the radio, I frequently heard guest speakers talking about men and their struggles for purity. I found programs to help men remain faithful to their wives, but I could find no shows to help wives remain faithful to their husbands.

I saw brochures for seminars that helped men deal with their immorality. And there were seminars for women too—to help them deal with their *husbands'* immorality! I browsed the marriage section in a huge Christian bookstore and found many volumes dealing with men's infidelity. But what about the wives' struggles with marital faithfulness? What about women who find themselves attracted to the attention of other men? Who is addressing that?

Christian magazines also frequently run advertisements to help women deal with their husbands' sexual addictions, but almost never do they mention that "nearly one in three visitors to adult Web sites is a woman"![10] Women may not visit pornographic stores like men, but our own romantic tendencies, fueled by daytime soap operas, nighttime dramas, romance novels, and Internet pornography, help create immoral fantasies that are often carried out in our actions.

When I began to ask pastor friends about Christian women having affairs, every one of them admitted that women leaving their husbands is a major issue and a growing problem in the church. Yet most women blindly choose to believe it will never happen to them. And those who do get involved in an extramarital relationship often struggle silently because this issue is rarely addressed.

Who Has Affairs?

It's not just *bad* people who are having the affairs. It's not even necessarily the people who have rocky marriages. I believed I had a wonderful marriage right up until the time my heart began to stray. Christian author and clinical psychologist Dr. Willard Harley says, "We are all wired to have an affair. We can all fall in love with someone of the opposite sex if that person meets one of our emotional needs. If you don't think it can happen to you because of your conviction or will power, you are particularly vulnerable to an affair."[11] For example:

- A husband spends long hours building his career while his wife is at home cleaning spaghetti off the baby's head and running a perpetual-motion carpool. By the time he arrives home each evening, they are both exhausted. As this continues day after day, she feels empty and neglected. She begins to look forward to her child's soccer practice where she has been sharing her frustrations with an understanding father she frequently meets there...

- A woman finds herself in a difficult marriage where her husband's words often penetrate like poison darts. A kind word from some tenderhearted man would feel like a cup of cool water to her parched soul. One defeated afternoon, she flops down in front of the computer and enters a chat room where she begins conversing with a sympathetic man who also struggles in his marriage...

- A military woman gets called to overseas duty, away from her family. Day after day, she encounters men in uniform who are attracted to her strength and abilities. After being apart from her husband for several months, she longs for his attention and affection. An attractive soldier approaches her...

- A career-driven woman loves the challenges of her corporate job. Each day she looks her best at the office while working side-by-side with professional men. At home, she has a loving, reliable husband, and their marriage is stable as a rock—which has become routine and dull to her. One day she meets a fellow executive who loves the excitement of rock climbing and skydiving...

Due to women's rise in the work force, greater financial independence, their increase in the military, and the easy access of Internet chat rooms, the opportunities for extramarital involvement for women have skyrocketed. Patterns of previous sexual involvement have also opened the door for women to be less inhibited. Many women—both Christian and non-Christian—have had experience with premarital sex. Also, the social stigma against a woman purposefully luring a married man away from his family has become far more lax.

All of us, young or old, are susceptible to temptation. It can come upon us like an earthquake—quickly and unexpectedly. If we are not prepared, our marriages can crumble as easily as a poorly built house. Dr. Willard Harley writes:

> In order to make our marriages affair-proof, we cannot hide our heads in the sand. The spouse who believes his or her partner is "different" and, despite unmet needs, would never take part in an affair may receive a devastating shock someday. Instead, we need to understand the warning signs that an affair could happen, how such liaisons may begin, and how to strengthen the weak areas of a marriage in the face of such a relationship.[12]

How easy it is for us to fall into temptation! I certainly wasn't expecting to be tempted by another man. I had been a Christian since age thirteen and had been in full-time Christian work for twelve years. I have been blessed with a wonderful, godly husband. We had experienced five-and-a-half years of fun and harmony when the unexpected dropped on me like a tsunami. Never in my wildest imagination did I think that I could be tempted by another man.

Thankfully, we have a God who loves to forgive us and to remold our lives when we ask in broken humility. I am living proof that He can transform a life. I am also proof that there are consequences to our actions. I must cling to the Lord each day to keep my mind pure and to stay alert to temptations.

I'm not proud of the choices I made on that boat, or of the pain that I brought to my husband. But I *am* excited about the changes the Lord can make in a heart that comes in desperation to Him, hungry to know Him and to have Him remold her life.

You would not be reading this book if you did not desire to live a more holy life. Therefore, if you find yourself toying with another relationship outside of your marriage, please realize that God will never bless such a relationship. And the longer you stay in that destructive relationship, the harder it is to get out. *It's not worth it!*

Where Do We Go from Here?

My experience with the captain was a wake-up call. When I returned home, I began to spend time in God's presence and to study His Word with an urgency I'd never had before. I learned some basic spiritual principles that transformed my life and marriage, and I also discovered that these biblical principles hold true for anyone's life.

I have proven that when I follow sound instruction, temptation flees, and my marriage remains protected.

Whether you are already compromised by an immoral situation, are tempted to do something you will regret, or just want to prepare yourself for when temptation comes, this book will help guide you to God's plan for resisting immorality. The principles found in this book actually apply to *any* temptation and to establishing a consistent, victorious walk with Christ in *all* areas of your life.

The first section of this book addresses the problems of infidelity. We will look at questions such as: How did I get into this situation? What are the consequences? What is God's perspective? In the second part of the book, we will see how to restore and maintain intimacy with God to rebuild a damaged marriage or to prevent future problems. The third section, then, will guide us in constructing spiritual walls that protect our marriages from the onslaught of temptation.

We cannot fight temptation and immorality alone. We are all vulnerable. But God gives us His strength and wisdom so that we *can* stand firm.

When I returned from the Caribbean and began to devour books on Christian marriage, I found myself skimming over the Bible verses so I could get to "the good stuff." (Come on, I know you do the same thing.) Suddenly, it was as if God switched on a light over my head, and I realized that the Bible verses *are* the "good stuff"! It is *Scripture* that has the power to transform my life far more than the thoughts of some fallible person. *Scripture* is God Himself speaking to me, not the thoughts of a mere human. So I chose to slow down and ponder the verses, memorizing those that spoke to my heart. In doing so, God's Word began to permeate my life, change my entire perspective, and remold my thoughts.

As you go through these pages, *please focus particularly on the Scriptures.* They have God's supernatural power to transform our lives and to change us into consistent, faithful women of God. His Word is the manual that tells us how we were designed to function and live. Through His Word we also learn about Him—His overwhelming love, His awesome glory, and His wonderful grace. His Scriptures must form the basis for everything we stand upon and believe.

As you read, I encourage you to particularly study the verses and ask God to help you apply His principles to your life. I know they work. Since returning from the Caribbean, I have had the opportunity to be tested again and have proven that when I follow sound instruction, temptation flees, and my marriage remains protected.

As we go through this journey, I pray that my experience will spare you from the heartache I chose. I also pray that what you find here will help arm you to meet the inevitable temptations of life and to walk through them victoriously.

Let's begin by laying the groundwork of God's perspective.

3

What Does God Say?

People love to tease us about Southern California not having varied seasons. They obviously haven't lived here because we *do* have seasons: the earthquake season, the drought season, the fire season, and the flood season.

Recently after one particularly heavy rain, the sun finally broke through and began to dry up some of the flooded areas around our home. I felt a need to get outside, so I jumped on my bike and rode down a stretch of the Pacific Coast Highway. It's an amazing area. Million-dollar homes sit on the beach to your right, and million-dollar homes rest on top of a sheer cliff to your left. As I pedaled along, reveling in the sunshine and the beauty, I happened to glance up at the cliff. Hanging precariously over the edge perched the back section of a house! The recent flood had washed away the sandy cliff sediment upon which this expensive home had been built.

Each of our lives is like a house, being built and furnished and decorated by every decision we make. But the most crucial decision we make is where we establish our foundation. In Southern California, we often see houses sliding down hillsides because their foundations were laid on sandy, unstable soil. In a similar way, the foundation for our life house must be immovable and unchangeable—God Himself and His Word. His Scriptures must form the basis for everything we stand upon and believe.

God's Perspective on Marriage

Does God have much to say about marriage? The answer is a resounding "YES"! From the very beginning, He made a unique and special bond between a man and a woman who become husband and wife. God tells us that *"a man shall leave his father and his mother, and be joined to his wife; and they shall become one flesh"* (Genesis 2:24). Bible commentator Charles Ryrie explains: "This verse emphasizes the complete identification of the two personalities in marriage. The passage tells us that God instituted marriage and that it is to be monogamous, heterosexual, and the complete union of the two persons."[1] When Jesus quoted Genesis 2:24, He added, *"What therefore God has joined together, let no man separate"* (Mark 10:9), making it clear that marriage is also to be permanent.

Yet today, what God has joined together *is* being ripped apart at an alarming rate. Is there some "missing link" in our understanding? Dr. Daniel Zink, assistant professor of Practical Theology at Covenant Seminary, explains that "any good Biblical definition of marriage has to include the word 'covenant.' And the word covenant represents more than just a contract. It's a life-long bond that's not intended to be broken—a pledge by a couple that they will work through whatever comes their way, because marriage is a covenant."[2]

Kay Coles James, director of the U.S. Office of Personnel Management, says, "After I realized marriage meant forever, my marriage flourished. Forever is not a ball and chain; it is a concept that enables us to truly enjoy the freedom of commitment. It is the cornerstone of marriage."[3]

Yet our culture has become very self-centered, teaching us to look out for Number One. We tend to focus on fulfilling our *own* desires above all else. We ask, "How is this marriage meeting *my* needs? Is it making *me* happy? Don't I deserve someone who fulfills *me* more?" We have completely forgotten or chosen to ignore God's call to do nothing from selfishness, but to regard one another as more important than ourselves (Philippians 2:3).

"Marriage is something one must work at," writes Dr. Bill Bright, cofounder of Campus Crusade for Christ. "The romance and the bloom of the wedding day soon passes and attempts at adjustments can lead to conflicts and misunderstandings unless both husband and wife take seriously the command of God to enter into the sacred bond of marriage with total commitment."[4]

> *We have completely forgotten or chosen to ignore God's call to do nothing from selfishness, but to regard one another as more important than ourselves.*

Commitment and self-sacrifice are the missing links that build lasting marriages. Yet selflessness and dedication don't come naturally to us. The only way we can consistently live out these attributes is to depend on Christ's transforming work within us. And the only way to experience this transforming work is to have daily time in His Word and in humble, dependent prayer. We'll look more at that in a bit.

God's Perspective on Wives

What is God's call for us as wives? He tells us to love our husband, to be his helper, to show him respect, and to *"be subject to your own husbands, as to the Lord"* (Ephesians 5:22).[5] Our first call is to love and obey the Lord (Matthew 22:37,38). Within that obedience comes our willing submission to the leadership of our husbands.

Christian author Susan Foh writes, "The submission of the wife to her husband is not that of an inferior to a superior. The woman is joint heir (with the man) of God's promises; she, like the man, bears the image of God and as a Christian will be conformed to Christ's image. The different roles husband and wife have are by God's appointment and design. That the woman and man are equal in being is re-enforced by the command to wives. Wives are to *submit themselves* (reflexive); their submission is voluntary, self-imposed. It is part of their obedience to the Lord; the Lord is the one who commands it, not the husband."[6]

We are called to do good, not evil, to our husbands all the days of our life and to give our husbands no reason to distrust us (Proverbs 31:11,12). However, by our choices we can bring trouble to our homes instead of blessings. In the midst of my emotional entanglement with the captain, I sat on the bow of the boat one radiant cloudless day and decided to open my Bible. As only God can do, my eyes fell on Proverbs 12:4: *"An excellent wife is the crown of her husband, but she who shames him is as rottenness in his bones."* God's truth drove a dagger deep into my heart. I was bringing rottenness into Stottler's life, like some putrid disease that was eating away at him from the inside out.

Sarah's attitude toward her husband, Abraham, provides us with a wonderful example of respect and submission (1 Peter 3:5,6). Here is a man who has just reached his retirement years. It's finally time to relax and hang out at the Nomad Golf and Country Club, go watch the camel races, and join in a Saturday night game of Bedouin bingo. It's a time he and Sarah can enjoy one another and chat over a cup of hot goat's milk.

Instead, what does Abraham do? He packs up a caravan with all of his stuff and follows God to a totally unknown land! (See Genesis 12:1–5.) Sarah is torn away from her family, friends, the Sahaira Salon, and everything familiar. Instead of resting, they go traipsing off to a place where they don't even speak the language. What kind of a retirement party is that?

But look at how Sarah responded. She willingly respected and followed her husband and was consequently blessed by God (Genesis 17:15,16). The Lord assures us that we don't need to fear whatever He calls us to do because He will never allow anything into our lives that isn't for our good and His glory—even if it means following our husband to Kabukistan!

Many Christian women have husbands who are less than interested in spiritual things. What do you do if you have a husband who is *disobedient to the word*? Although it can be challenging, we are called to imitate Christ's example of self-sacrificing love. He endured heinous torture for our sake and never responded in anger or with threats. He lived out what it means to consider others as more important than self. We are called to follow His example (1 Peter 2:21—3:4). By doing so, husbands who are *disobedient to the word...may be won without a word by the behavior of their wives*" (1 Peter 3:1). This does not mean we are to be doormats or to ever disobey the Lord. But God does call us to honor and respect our spouse, submitting to his leadership as the church submits to Christ (Ephesians 5:24). Although this doesn't promise a problem-free marriage, I find it quite encouraging.[7]

God's Perspective on Affairs

When I began to study God's perspective on infidelity, a crystal-clear picture emerged. God leaves no doubt about how He feels. Concerning our marriages, He tells us that *the marriage bed is to be undefiled; for fornicators and adulterers God will judge*" (Hebrews

13:4). The seventh commandment states, *"You shall not commit adultery"* (Exodus 20:14). He tells us to *"abstain from sexual immorality"* (1 Thessalonians 4:3) and adds that to reject this command of purity is to reject God Himself (v. 8). Those are *His* words, not mine!

Infidelity of any type leads us away from the Lord. In the end, adultery leaves a person full of regret for the choices, the devastation, and the wasted years. The Bible is very clear on the consequences of adultery. God says we are destroying ourselves (Proverbs 6:32).

In this day and age, to "have an affair" sounds almost romantic and exciting. But God paints a very different picture. He says that adultery leads to death. Proverbs 7 shows us the scene of a woman sneaking behind her husband's back at night to entice a young man into sex. God then gives us a heavenly perspective when He describes them as two oxen proceeding toward a slaughterhouse where their heads will be held in a tight enclosure and their throats slit.

But the temptation of the moment seems so enticing. Knowing your husband will not see you, you secretly rendezvous with some alluring man in a park near your home. Walking hand in hand under a canopy of spreading oak branches, you gaze with rapt attention at one another. But the real picture from God's perspective reveals that as you walk together, every step is *"descending to the chambers of death"* (Proverbs 7:27).

We've all seen grotesque pictures of what happens to a woman's skin when she is caught in a fire. The burns disfigure her so that her features become almost unrecognizable. That's the analogy God uses for adultery. *"Can a man hold fire against his chest and not be burned? Can he walk on hot coals and not blister his feet? So it is with the man who commits adultery with another's wife"* (Proverbs 6:27–29, TLB).

God considers the topic of adultery so important that He mentions it repeatedly throughout the first nine chapters of Proverbs. His descriptions of adultery's consequences are *very* graphic. I wish the entertainment industry would make a film about an adulterous affair based on what *God* says. It would make a terrifying horror movie!

God warns us that unfaithfulness in marriage is one of the most painful experiences a spouse can inflict on her partner. Some spouses have said that they would rather be crippled than experience the pain of infidelity.[8] Dr. Willard Harley writes:

> Those I've counseled who have had the tragic misfortune of having experienced rape, physical abuse, sexual abuse of their children, and infidelity have consistently reported to me that their spouse's unfaithfulness was their very worst experience. To be convinced of the devastating impact of infidelity, you only need to go through it once.[9]

He goes on to say that "almost everyone feels betrayed, used, abandoned, and very angry when they discover that their spouse has had an affair. After all, an affair is hatched with full knowledge of how much pain it will inflict on an unsuspecting spouse after it's discovered. It reflects a wanton disregard for the feelings of someone who was supposed to have been cherished and protected for life."[10]

Unfaithfulness in our marriage also greatly impacts our children. Psychologists report that "once a child reaches the age of 20, give or take a couple years, they generally revert back to their parents' values. They may go through their years of rebellion, but as they mature, they begin to do things the same way mom and dad used to."[11]

Because children imitate what they see in the home, it is crucial for us to confront and end our own negative, destructive behaviors now. Otherwise, we will simply pass the problems on from generation to generation (Exodus 20:5). We must build safeguards for our marriages so our children will experience a loving, Christ-centered home from which to model their values and lives.

You may be saying, "But if my children or my husband never know about my fling, no one will get hurt, right?" First, there is no such thing as a "secret" sin. God warns us, *"Be sure your sin will find you out"* (Numbers 32:23). And He *never* lies. Second, sin in our life affects the very core of our soul and spirit, which in turn affects *all* of our relationships—none more profoundly than our own family! *We never sin in a vacuum.* Everything I think and do affects who I am, and consequently the way I treat others.

It is simply not possible to engage in adultery or to pursue infidelity of any kind and not suffer consequences. What may seem enticing and enjoyable for the moment leaves a *lifelong scar* that will not go away. The consequences will resurface in your relationship with your spouse, or in the effects on your children. You can have recurring dreams and flashbacks, continue to struggle with your thoughts, and be vulnerable to further temptations.

Many times I've heard Christian women justify their pursuit of another man by saying, "God brought him into my life." So often we pitch blame onto God to justify our own disobedience. Nowhere in His Word does God *ever* sanction leaving your spouse for someone else, regardless of the reason. God will never, never, never lead you to do something that is contrary to His Word. Never. Not once. Not ever.

God's Perspective on Divorce

What do you do when infidelity has already occurred? Dealing with infidelity is one of the most difficult challenges any marriage can face. Many couples work through the horrific effects of an affair; others choose to divorce.

What is God's perspective on divorce? In Malachi 2:13–16, the Jewish people had returned from captivity in a foreign nation and had rebuilt the walls around Jerusalem. But once again, they grew lax in their obedience to the Lord. When they complained that He wasn't blessing their offerings, God clearly rebuked them and pointed out why He was withholding blessings. The reason? Their refusal to face their sin of divorce. *"'I hate divorce,' says the LORD, the God of Israel... 'So take heed to your spirit, that you do not deal treacherously'"* (Malachi 2:16). According to God, to divorce is to "deal treacherously" with your spouse. Divorce clearly violates the standard for marriage that He established at creation.

Two-thirds of unhappily married spouses who stayed married reported that their marriages were happy five years later.

When the Pharisees confronted Jesus about the fact that Moses permitted divorce, He pointed out that divorce was only *permitted* because of the hardness of our hearts. Clearly, divorce is not God's plan for marriage. Jesus' answer reveals that divorce is an indication of sin in the life of one or both partners (Mark 10:2–9).

Christian speaker and author Charles Colson writes, "Even under the worst of circumstances—adultery, abuse, and abandonment—God does not command divorce. He merely permits it. And divorce is always a trauma. In this age of no-fault divorce, Christians ought to do everything possible to protect their marriages."[12]

Studies have found that married couples who stay together through their problems usually end up having happier marriages. Researchers led by University of Chicago sociology professor Dr. Linda Waite found from a survey of 5,232 married adults that "two-thirds of unhappily married spouses who stayed married reported that their marriages were happy five years later. In addition, the most unhappy marriages reported the most dramatic turnarounds: among those who rated their marriages as very unhappy, almost eight out of ten who avoided divorce were happily married five years later."[13] Dr. James Dobson, referring to the same survey, noted that the results reveal how a seemingly irreparable marriage can indeed bounce back.[14]

The study also found that "divorce frequently fails to make people happy because, while it might provide a respite from the pain associated with a bad marriage, it also introduces a host of complex new emotional and psychological difficulties over which the parties involved have little control. They include child-custody battles, emotionally scarred children, economic hardships, loneliness, future romantic disappointments, and so on."[15]

Dealing with guilt is common for divorced people. Divorced women have much higher incidences of depression than married women,[16] and the incidences of loneliness are almost five times greater.[17]

And what happens to the children of divorce? Numerous studies show that children of divorced parents have a higher rate of depression, greater behavioral problems, more often become young offenders, and have poorer grades and greater social problems. Once they are older, they have more children out of wedlock, a higher rate of unemployment, lower economic levels, more marital problems, and a higher rate of divorce.[18]

Guard Your Marriage!

None of us is immune to the temptation of finding ourselves attracted to someone outside of our marriage. Fearing our own propensity toward sin is a good thing. God tells us, *"How blessed is the man who fears always, but he who hardens his heart will fall into calamity"* (Proverbs 28:14). Recognizing how easily we can fall into sin should drive us to the Lord and make us set up guards to protect our marriages.

But as long as we as Christian women believe that this will never happen to us, we will remain unprepared for the temptations that will come. We will continue to pile up statistics of affairs and divorce, and we will never be the models of light that Christ intended for us to be in the world.

I never believed infidelity was a possibility for me. I was happily married, in full-time Christian work, and faithfully serving the Lord. So how on earth did it happen?

4

How Could This Happen?

W e've got a date and place for our wedding!" I excitedly announced over the phone to my mother. "It's going to be outside on a lawn, January twenty-second!" There was a momentary pause on the other end of the line. "Honey," came my mother's restrained response, "outside in January?"

I knew my mom. What she *really* meant was, "An outdoor wedding in January? *Are you crazy?*"

Having grown up in Oklahoma, an outdoor January wedding did seem a bit insane. But in Southern California, anything is possible. And when January twenty-second finally arrived, the sky shone a brilliant blue as wispy clouds drifted overhead, carried by a warm ocean breeze. We felt as if God had stamped His approval on Stottler's and my union by blessing us with a picture-perfect, 78-degree day.

It had all started out ideally. Most marriages do. So what happens? Why does the picture begin to yellow and curl as if held too long beside a flame? What erodes the rock-solid foundation that every blissful couple believes will last "until death do us part"?

Five months before the Caribbean project began, Stottler and I endured a draining ministry trip to India, where we helped with translation work. The living conditions were a breeding ground for food contamination. Almost everyone on our team found himself doubled over at one time or another. The locals we worked with couldn't agree on anything; the equipment failed several times; and just about everything that could have gone wrong did.

God saw us through, and we were finally able to complete the work. But the battles had taken their toll. I was physically, emotionally, and spiritually drained. In ministry, that's not unusual, and it's all right if you deal with the exhaustion properly. I, however, decided that I was invincible and chose to continue working nine- to ten-hour days in preparation for the upcoming Caribbean project.

One of the ways I "maximized" my time was by skipping daily quiet times with God. Little by little, I became insensitive to that small voice inside that guides my conscience and actions. Sometimes, I would skip five consecutive days without reading Scriptures or praying and would think, *Wow, I haven't had time with the Lord for five days, and I'm really not doing so badly!* The fact that I *thought* I was doing well revealed the insensitivity of my hardening heart!

In August, the Caribbean Boat Project was finally set to sail. Stottler and I flew to the island of Grenada where we met the captain and crew. I was exhausted but excited about this opportunity to show a movie on the life of Christ throughout the islands. I also found myself intoxicated by the entire setting of sun, sand, and sailing. The ocean had always captivated me. It brought out of me what I described as my "wild side."

At the initial meeting with our captain, Eric, I sensed a camaraderie with him. Stottler and I moved onboard the catamaran along with the captain and our film/sailing crew of three crazy guys from Trinidad. We immediately discovered that although personal space is fairly limited aboard a boat, the six of us worked well together as a team. The project began, and our film showings were well received by the islanders. Although we worked long, hard hours, life was just plain fun.

The Trouble Begins

I began to spend many hours with Eric. Daily, he and I worked together on planning the sailing itinerary, overseeing the crew, organizing the film showings, and having long talks about everything. We even found time to squeeze in some scuba dives among the pristine reefs. It seemed we had so much in common!

At the same time, my husband seemed so misplaced in the tropics. Stottler didn't revel in the heat, the slow pace of Caribbean life, or the cramped quarters on the boat. He was hot and tired, though he never complained. I couldn't help but notice the contrast between him and the tanned sailor whose company I was enjoying so much.

It didn't take long for me to realize that I was allowing my heart to feel something toward Eric. I knew this wasn't wise, yet I didn't want it to end. I rationalized everything. I hadn't done anything wrong—Eric and I had only talked. No harm in that, right? Didn't I have a happy marriage? And certainly Eric wasn't interested in me, was he?

You've seen pictures of a tiny figure in the distance perched on the lip of a precipice 1,000 feet high. That's me. I have always liked to live life on the edge. I've always been the one who "hangs over the cliff." I love the thrill of the adrenaline rush. In fact, the mystery of this relationship was enormously exciting, like being an undercover spy with a deadly secret to guard.

"Some people thrive on the game," writes Dr. Shirley Glass in *Psychology Today*. "For them, part of the passion and excitement of an affair is the lying and getting away with something forbidden."[1] But what I was doing was a dangerous and foolish game with disastrous consequences. God warns us in Proverbs 10:23, *"Doing wickedness is like sport to a fool."* My adrenaline rush was actually a fool rushing toward spiritual suicide! My choices were just plain sin!

Sin is like a snowball rolling down a mountain. Once it begins moving, it picks up momentum and size until it is almost impossible to stop. *"'Woe to the obstinate children,' declares the LORD, 'to those who carry out plans that are not mine... heaping sin upon sin'"* (Isaiah 30:1, NIV). With every poor choice, I was heaping sin upon sin, gaining frightening momentum with every bad decision.

> *With every poor choice, I was heaping sin upon sin, gaining frightening momentum with every bad decision.*

After four weeks on the boat, my unsuspecting husband returned to California to finalize some work, and I was on my own in this land of sand, sun, and sin. For integrity's sake, I slept ashore, yet the captain and I continued many hours of secluded conversation during the day. Little time was necessary for my galloping emotions to move from thinking that nothing would ever come of this to believing that anything was possible—even desirable. Before long, I had "fallen in love."

After silently nurturing this passion for several days, I unwisely revealed my feelings to Eric, and he returned my interest—but only if I was "unattached." So I began to ponder, "What if the Lord were to take Stottler 'home'? Then I'd be free to marry the captain."

You can see how far spiritually I had fallen!

I had become insensitive to the Lord and didn't even realize it. I was far more concerned with Eric's feelings than my husband's. I felt intoxicated by the intensity of the feelings. Here we were, sailing together in the Caribbean islands. This wasn't simple temptation; this was a Molotov cocktail! I began to seriously contemplate never returning home.

How Women Get Into Problems

What could cause a perfectly sane Christian woman to become embroiled in an affair of the heart? I was blessed with a loving husband who encouraged and supported me. But exhaustion and spiritual dullness, coupled with romantic islands and a fascinating seaman, created a mix of excitement and allure that I refused to resist.

You may say, "If I had a loving, supportive husband, I would *never* be tempted!" Don't believe it. Remember, *none* of us is immune to temptation. Satan knows just the right ingredients to mix together to create a temptation uniquely designed for your weaknesses.

Women get involved in extramarital relationships for many different reasons. Psychologist Shirley Glass states, "Surveys show that for women, the highest justification [for an affair] is for love; emotional intimacy is next. Sex is last on their list of justifications."[2] Dr. Scott Haltzman, a psychiatrist specializing in marriage counseling, adds, "For an overwhelming majority of spouses who cheat—80 percent—the reason is not sexual. Most simply seek validation, warmth, understanding, or love."[3]

A recurring element is the desire for attention. As women, we have a built-in need to feel loved and cherished. Any marriage, however, will experience times when a wife doesn't feel loved or adored.

For example, you may be in a marriage where silent disrespect has taken root over the years. You may feel that your husband no longer views you as important. Or you may simply desire that your husband value your opinion or give you at least an ounce of encouragement.

If you find yourself in a marriage where life is painful, you may desperately desire some relief from the black depression into which you are sinking. Or you may be overwhelmed with children and have little time alone with your spouse. Consequently, your lives seem like two pieces of driftwood heading toward opposite shores.

Or you may be exhausted from long hours at work and simply long to have tender arms of understanding wrapped around you. Perhaps you, like me, may gravitate toward the exciting and the forbidden.

You may also have unconsciously embraced the myth of the Hollywood romance. My mother loved the old movies where boy meets girl, love blossoms under a starry sky (accompanied, of course, by a lush string serenade), and they live enthralled with each other ever after. My mother knew in her head that those movies portrayed an unrealistic picture of real-life marriage and lasting love, but in her heart the images continued to taint her contentment with her own marriage.

A lack of commitment to the marriage is also a factor. Countless "irreconcilable differences" may exist between you and your husband, but if you are committed to working through whatever comes your way, you will recognize many of those problems as a cover-up for your lack of commitment.

"Most people don't choose to have an affair," Dr. Haltzman writes. "Some may even be morally opposed to affairs. Frequently, it starts with a conversation. Then, it moves to a conversation about intimate issues and experiences in each person's own relationship...The distance between meeting someone and a first kiss is much longer than the distance between a first kiss and ending up in bed. It's a slippery slope, and you make choices all along the way...There is no such thing as an accidental affair."[4]

Opportunities Everywhere

Affairs mostly have to do with opportunity. And opportunity is everywhere. One warm evening, your husband's close business associate drops by the house to discuss some work. You have met several times before. Although not particularly handsome, his manner exudes genuine warmth and caring. Graciously you offer coffee, and as you and your husband casually chat with him, your eyes suddenly lock onto his for an instant. He gives you a quick wink. In that split second, your heart bursts out of the starting gate and begins racing down the track.

Infidelity occurs most often with someone you know and regularly see, such as a coworker or a friend. Statistics show that almost 50 percent of the women in an adulterous affair met their partner at work.[5] And as more women enter the workplace, this percentage continues to rise.

In all the reasons and rationales for infidelity, one common factor exists among them all: disobedience to God. We have seen what God says about keeping the marriage bed undefiled and His attitude toward adultery. Proverbs 7 and 9 describe a woman pursuing adultery as a person of folly who is crafty, boisterous, defiant, brazen, and deceitful.[6] How clever we women are at catching a man's attention. In God's eyes, how utterly foolish.

The process of becoming hardened to the things of God is simple. Each wrong choice is like laying a brick between you and God. How quickly that wall can be built! Suddenly, you find yourself caught behind the prison walls of an affair. And once you're in that trap, it is incredibly difficult to get out. The powerful emotion of romantic love becomes so intoxicating that you respond like an alcoholic. Whatever it takes to be with that person, you're willing to do. A normally rational, sane woman will become an irrational creature ready to sacrifice her family, her faith, her security, her friends, her job, and her reputation for the sake of this love.

How well I know! All I could think about was staying with this intriguing man, sailing around the world under the equatorial sun, lost in the delusion of this dream. It wasn't long before I found out that the fruit of my choices was bitter.

5

Stay or Leave?

I sat alone in my dingy island hotel room, despair sweeping over me like an ocean. Eric had remained in Guadeloupe with the boat and team, while I had gone ahead to prepare for our time in St. Martin. I had just poured out my soul to him over the phone for two hours. Now I desperately yearned to be with him —but I was also torn in two.

I had reached a crucial decision point—either to stay with the captain, or to return home. I knew I couldn't have both. So I made another phone call that turned out to be as valuable as gold.

Years before, I had established some deep, trusting relationships with a few Christian women older than I am. They had upheld me with strength and wisdom, as well as held me accountable many times in the past. Something in me (no doubt God's grace!) made me dial the phone to reach one of them now.

Making a Choice

Like a stab victim in critical need of triage, I emptied my heart to Holly. In response, she delivered a much-needed transfusion of reality. Her straightforward counsel struck fear in my soul: Repentance is a gift, and there can come a time in your life when you will no longer receive the ability to repent or change your course of action. *"Do you show contempt for the riches of his kindness, tolerance and patience, not realizing that God's kindness leads you toward repentance?"* (Romans 2:4, NIV).

In His Word, God gives us examples of individuals who became so hardened by continual choices of disobedience that He *"gave them over in the lusts of their hearts to impurity"* (Romans 1:24). In other words, God finally said, "Enough!" Then He removed His gracious protection and let them experience the full degradation of their sins.

> *I suddenly realized that it could be possible for me to refuse to heed my conscience one too many times until I was no longer able to turn back.*

Up to this point, God had been tolerant and patient with me. But I suddenly realized that it could be possible for me to turn too many corners, make too many wrong decisions, refuse to heed my conscience one too many times until I had hardened my heart to the point where I was no longer able to turn back.[1]

When I first became interested in Eric, I thought I was still in control, able to make whatever decision I wanted whenever I needed to. I believed I could always turn away from this intensifying love for him whenever I chose. But my friend advised me differently. Was I close to being one decision too late? That frightened me. I could lose so much.

I thought about the basis of my relationship with Eric. Suppose we did marry at some future date. On what grounds had our relationship been established? The roots of this relationship sank into the putrid soil of deception, disobedience, emotional infidelity, and selfishness. God could never bless that kind of marriage. How could I enter into a union that didn't have the blessing of my precious Savior and Lord?

And what about my ministry? During college I had become involved in a relationship that I knew was outside of God's will. His grace had dragged me from the jaws of that relationship and had given me strength to walk faithfully. So I was well aware that my ministry of teaching believers and leading others to Christ was purely a gift of His grace. If I continued down this current track, I could lose that blessing too.

Holly's unrelenting dose of truth also brought to my mind the picture of who stood behind this temptation. Understanding Satan's character helps me to see the motivation behind his temptations. Jesus described our adversary: *"He was a murderer from the beginning, and does not stand in the truth because there is no truth in him. Whenever he speaks a lie, he speaks from his own nature, for he is a liar and the father of lies"* (John 8:44).

There isn't one tiny shred of truth in anything Satan whispers in my ear. He was attempting to seduce me with the lie that life with Eric would be bliss. He wanted me to believe that it would be ludicrous to refuse such an opportunity. But in truth, it is ludicrous to gullibly believe a liar! Although *"Satan disguises himself as an angel of light"* (2 Corinthians 11:14), we can't afford to believe *one single word* he tells us! The results will only be misery for everyone involved, regardless of how enticing it all looks and feels at the moment.

Contrary to cartoons and movies, Satan is *not* some weak, funny, ghostly being who plays jokes, tickles my ribs, and brings mere inconveniences into my life. Our enemy is *far* stronger than we are. In fact, we cannot begin to imagine the depths of his hatred and treachery and deceitfulness bent on causing the destruction of our marriages and the ruin of our lives. When a wife gives in to Satan's temptations and leaves her husband for another man,

Satan rejoices. When the husband turns to drinking in his despair and becomes emotionally distant from his confused children, Satan cheers. And when the children become bitter and insolent and choose to leave the church, joining a crowd of partygoers experimenting with sex and drugs, our adversary exults over the complete destruction of one more family.

Satan *never* desires anything that is good for us. Not one plan he has for us will *ever* be a blessing or *ever* bring joy or peace to our lives. Never.

God, on the other hand, loves us with an everlasting love that will never change no matter what we do (Jeremiah 31:3). He will *never* do something malicious toward us nor desire to hurt us. He *continually* pours out that which is for our good (Romans 8:28), that which builds us up and gives us joy and grace and peace. His plans for us are *always* for our welfare (Jeremiah 29:11). Always.

Why would I ever make a choice that gives Satan pleasure, knowing that his motivation behind the temptation is to destroy my life?

The contrast between Jesus Christ and Satan is the difference between life and death. Christ tells us: *"The thief comes only to steal and kill and destroy; I came that they may have life, and have it abundantly. I am the good shepherd; the good shepherd lays down His life for the sheep"* (John 10:10,11). What a world of difference! The enemy comes to steal and destroy whatever is good in our lives, then eventually kill us. Christ comes to give us life overflowing with His joy and peace. Christ even lays down His life for us. Satan wants us to lay down our lives for him!

Knowing that Satan is the author of all sin—including my desire to desert my precious husband—and God is the author of all that is good, why would I *ever* choose to follow one who hates and despises me? Why would I *ever* make a choice that gives Satan pleasure, knowing that his motivation behind the temptation is to destroy my life?

But Holly saved the most convicting blow until last. She reminded me of my promise to God and to Stottler on our wedding day. On that perfect Southern California day in January five years earlier, I had made a vow. That promise was not just to my husband, but also to God. I knew that God takes vows *very* seriously. He tells us His perspective on vows and the consequences of breaking them:

> *When you make a vow to God, do not delay in fulfilling it. He has no pleasure in fools; fulfill your vow. It is better not to vow than to make a vow and not fulfill it. Do not let your mouth lead you into sin. And do not protest to the temple messenger, "My vow was a mistake." Why should God be angry at what you say and destroy the work of your hands?* (Ecclesiastes 5:4–6, NIV)

Being reminded of my wedding vows struck me like a sledgehammer. Promises are extremely serious to me. Long ago I realized that if my word couldn't be trusted, *I* couldn't be trusted. Consequently, I have determined to always be consistent in fulfilling any promises I make to the best of my ability.

My most important promise was my vow before God to love and cherish my husband till death do us part. And what pleases Him immensely is a person who *"keeps his oath even when it hurts"* (Psalm 15:4, NIV). Well, the decision to keep this promise would definitely hurt! But I had no other choice. The decision had been made on January twenty-second years earlier; I had just temporarily forgotten.

So despite gut-wrenching anguish and a river of tears, I begrudgingly made my way to the airport to fly home. My heart physically ached as if a knife had gashed it into pieces. A thousand-pound burden weighed down on my shoulders, and my stomach had turned to lead. In my head I knew this was the right choice, but my heart writhed in anguish.

What's in a Vow?

Right now, you may be thinking that your situation is quite different from mine. Your vows may have been made under less than ideal conditions. Maybe your parents disapproved of your marriage, and your wedding vows were taken privately before a civil judge instead of at a church. Does God consider civil wedding vows as binding?

Or perhaps before marrying you lived together. When you discovered you were pregnant, you felt pushed into taking marriage vows. Under such circumstances, does God consider those vows as permanent?

Maybe you've been married for twenty years and have watched your Don Juan turn into Dull John, someone who frequently treats you as house help rather than as a wife to be loved and cherished. Are your vows before God still relevant?

What if you have already experienced the trauma of one or more affairs? Although your husband doesn't know you have broken your vows, does God still consider your original marriage vow to be valid?

God tells us that once we make a vow, we need to fulfill it regardless of the difficulties we may encounter:

> *"When you make a vow to the Lord, be prompt in doing whatever it is you promised him, for the Lord demands that you promptly fulfill your vows; it is a sin if you don't...Once you make the vow, you must be careful to do as you have said, for it was your own choice, and you have vowed to the Lord your God."* (Deuteronomy 23:21,23, TLB)

And again, Moses writes:

> *"If a man makes a vow to the LORD, or takes an oath to bind himself with a binding obligation, he shall not violate his word; he shall do according to all that proceeds out of his mouth."* (Numbers 30:2)[2]

Fortunately, we have a loving God who gives us grace and help in our struggles and failures. Marriages are never perfect, but thankfully God is in the repair business. He is always ready to pick us up, heal our hearts, and give us strength to fulfill what we have promised. He tells us, *"I want your promises fulfilled. I want you to trust me in your times of trouble, so I can rescue you, and you can give me glory"* (Psalm 50:14,15, TLB). He longs to rescue us in times of trouble and provide the strength we need to be faithful to our wedding promise.

> *God is in the repair business. He is always ready to pick us up, heal our hearts, and give us strength to fulfill what we have promised.*

Where Do I Go from Here?

How then can you begin now to honor your promise to God and to your husband? One excellent way is by renewing your vows.

When Holly reminded me of my vow to love and cherish my husband until death parted us, I made a commitment by my will before God to again fulfill what I had promised. Many couples choose to actually renew their vows together in some type of formal ceremony before a pastor or priest. Whether or not your husband is willing to take this step, *you* can still go before the Lord and recommit to remaining faithful to your marriage vow by His strength. In the following chapter, we will look at ways to begin restoring your marriage and reclaiming what you may have lost.

At that juncture in the Caribbean, my decision before God to remain faithful and return home came solely from my will because my heart ached to stay with Eric. As I moved through the motions of boarding the plane home, numbness overtook my senses. Nothing seemed real. Although previous trips had taken me to remote countries, this felt like the longest flight of my life. A black fog enveloped me as I curled up on the plane seat and hoped to disappear.

6

Rebuilding Our Marriage

T he plane finally touched down in California. The grace of God, along with the counsel and prayers of others, had brought me home. It was one of the hardest things I'd ever done. As if moving through a haze, I staggered down the ramp to meet my husband. The weight of despondency dragged at every step. I had phoned Stottler from St. Martin, revealing part of the story, and I told him I was coming home. Now it was time to face him. By God's grace there had been nothing physical between Eric and me, but emotional infidelity seemed equally as painful.

When we arrived at our house, Stottler and I sat tensely on the couch, my legs shaking with fear, anticipation, and exhaustion. Weary of the battle against God, I yearned for His fellowship again. I missed having a tender heart that could sense His leading. I also hurt over the anguish I had caused my sweet husband. But the healing of my relationships with God and Stottler was only possible if I began making right choices.

Proverbs 13:21 says, *"Adversity pursues sinners."* When we choose to sin, problems and sufferings will drag behind us like a ball and chain. The only way to break the chain is to deal with the root cause—confess the sin. So I told Stottler how I felt about Eric. I told him that I had seriously considered staying in the Caribbean. Then I asked for his forgiveness.

I am enormously blessed to have a godly husband. We cried together many times, and we began the process of rebuilding what I had so quickly torn down. Yet for a time, my emotions continued to bleed.

Addiction and Withdrawal

Much like a drug addict in isolation, I experienced withdrawal symptoms from Eric. In many ways, an affair is similar to an alcohol or drug addiction. The process of breaking free brings intense feelings of pain, anxiety, and depression. For several months I longed to be with Eric, and a continual dull throb lodged in my heart. Life often seemed bleak, and the future uninviting.

Through my disastrous choices, I learned a very important truth: Never underestimate the power of attraction!

Although I don't remember having thoughts of suicide, they are not uncommon for people mired in affairs. A woman can't imagine life without her lover, yet she also recognizes the grief she is causing her family. Suicide may seem the only way out. But time does heal wounds. As the days wore into months, my internal hemorrhaging slowed to a drip, then finally began to close.

It was a slow process back. I had constructed a brick wall between God, Stottler, and myself through one bad choice at a time. Now I needed to make good choices one at a time to tear down that wall. Although the process was painful, each day became a little easier—as long as I stayed away from Eric.

As I began to delve once again into God's Word, the Lord clearly showed me three steps I *should* have taken when faced with the temptation toward Eric. These steps also apply to any woman who chooses to rebuild her marriage after making poor choices.

Step 1: Be Honest with Yourself

Looking back on my entire scenario in the Caribbean, I wondered if the romance with Eric was unavoidable. I alone was responsible for the preparations and daily operations of the boat project. Therefore, each day I had to work closely with a charming captain while being surrounded by an enticing, seductive setting. Was all the heartache avoidable? The answer: Absolutely! I *could* have stopped myself before the infatuation ever began.

Through my disastrous choices, I learned a *very* important truth: *Never underestimate the power of attraction!* When attracted to a man, it's easy to convince ourselves that the feelings could never really grow, so we try to rationalize them away.

Yet we can so quickly begin daydreaming about this attraction. *I wonder where he is right now. I really enjoyed our conversation yesterday. When can we talk again? Of course, this friendship is harmless. I would never want anything to happen—I just enjoy his company.*

I had those thoughts. They are an open door to a room full of deadly cobras. The enemy wants you to believe those little lies so that he can slowly ease you into the room. And once you're in, you *will* be bitten. Playing with poison will ruin your life.

The danger of even peeking through a door marked "Infidelity" is that we want more. We want to take the next step. At first, just talking to some attractive guy (and I *don't* mean physically attractive) elevates your blood pressure. But as the excitement of talking becomes routine, you want more. Now you desire some physical contact, such as holding his hand. And once you've broken the barrier of touching, you wonder what a kiss would be like. And on and on it goes.

As we begin toying with an attraction, by necessity we hide our feelings and actions from our husband. The Lord says, *"Deceit is in the heart of those who devise evil"* (Proverbs 12:20). Deceit always leads to further deceit as sin takes us further and further into danger. It's so much easier to close the door and never step into the snake pit in the first place!

Step 2: Be Honest with God

I believe that what made me the *most* vulnerable for my involvement with Eric was my lack of daily time in God's presence. Nothing in my life has had the consistent power to transform me more than my daily times of reading the Bible and praying.

For several months previous to the Caribbean project, I had been ignoring God's daily call to come away with Him for a time of refreshment and renewal. By the time I arrived on the boat and met the captain, I had a wall of poor choices blocking my sensitivity to the Lord. Because I had allowed my heart to become spiritually insensitive, I refused to bring my feelings toward Eric to the Lord. I refused to acknowledge His conviction, seek His perspective, and rely on His strength to resist my wandering emotions. It was a recipe for disaster.

> *I am convinced that the most critical element in protecting your marriage is your personal time alone with God. It is irreplaceable.*

I am convinced that *the most critical element in protecting your marriage is your personal time alone with God.* It is irreplaceable. There are no substitutes—not listening to Christian music or Christian radio, not going to church or attending Bible studies. Only as we spend regular one-on-one time in prayer with the Father and time reading His Word will we keep our heart sensitive to obeying His voice in the face of temptation.

Step 3: Be Honest with Your Husband

Once Stottler and I were aboard the boat, it was only a matter of days before I knew a strong attraction existed between Eric and me. But I failed to use the protection that God had provided to help me lock the door on temptation—honesty with my husband.

As soon as I felt that excitement of attraction toward Eric, I should have told Stottler. Telling your husband is a marvelous way to dispel the mystery of a secret intrigue. As long as no one knows, you nurture that attraction, create romantic scenarios in your mind, and dream the fantasy. But as soon as you invite your husband into the fantasy bubble, it bursts. Its ugliness is exposed. And though revealing the temptation to your husband may feel uncomfortable at the time, doing so will save you both from incredible long-term heartache.

God gives our husbands to us as an umbrella of protection.[1] Their prayers for us are God-ordained coverings of shelter. If I had told Stottler immediately upon sensing my attraction to Eric, my thoughts would have been exposed and Stottler could have prayed for me. His prayers and wisdom could have strengthened me to remain sensitive to God's leading throughout my dealings with Eric. My accountability friends should have been told as well. Giving an account to others is a wonderful deterrent to disobedience.

I also should have determined never to be alone with Eric and sought Stottler's accountability on this as well. When the need arose to work with Eric, my husband or one of the team members should have been included. But that would have been awkward or inconvenient, right? What if no one else was available? What if the team had to leave without me? We can always make excuses. But we can also find ways to maintain integrity *if* we really want to. Just as I can be incredibly inventive in finding ways to sin, I could instead choose to use that creativity to remain pure and above reproach. It's all a matter of will.

You may not have a godly husband like mine, yet a commitment to honesty in any marriage is still essential for reconciliation as well as an ongoing healthy relationship. This commitment to honesty includes unveiling any past involvement, even those you committed before your marriage. Psychologist Dr. Willard Harley writes:

> It isn't easy to be honest. Honesty is an unpopular value these days, and most couples have not made this commitment to each other. Many marriage counselors and clergymen argue that honesty is not always the best policy. They believe that it's cruel to disclose past indiscretions and it's selfish to make such disclosures. While it makes you feel better to get a mistake off your chest, it causes your partner to suffer. So, they argue, the truly caring thing to do is to lie about your mistakes or at least keep them tucked away.
>
> And if it's compassionate to lie about sins of the past, why isn't it also compassionate to lie about sins of the present— or future? Either honesty is always right, or you'll always have an excuse for being dishonest.[2]

The "No Secrets Policy"

Upon returning home to California, I developed a "No Secrets Policy" toward Stottler. What a relief it was to have the closet door opened and all the darkness exposed! My No Secrets Policy relates to any area of my marriage or my walk with God that will affect Stottler's and my relationship. For example, feelings of attraction to another man, past moral indiscretions, impure fantasies, and a stagnant fellowship with the Lord can all create a wedge in a marriage if not dealt with immediately.

Honesty, however, is not an excuse for a lack of restraint in our words. The No Secrets Policy does *not* give me the right to say anything to my husband that pops into my head, especially on those days when I feel like spitting nails. Spewing every negative thought I may have toward Stottler in a moment of anger or physical depression is a sure way to *drive* a wedge into our relationship. Those moments require self-control.

Honesty protects both our husbands and us. It helps our husbands know our predisposition toward certain temptations so that they can help us face those challenges. By revealing to Stottler any current temptation I may be facing, he can help me to avoid further disasters. And if I continue pursuing the temptation, I will have to tell him. What a wonderful deterrent that is! It's easier to just resist the temptation in the first place than to reveal my failure to my husband after the fact.

If establishing honesty in your marriage means exposing an affair from your past, proceed carefully. Make sure you have confessed your sin to the Lord and that your heart is broken over your wrongdoing. Then think through how to reveal this news, knowing that it will most likely elicit strong emotions.

When you reveal a previous or current indiscretion, your husband will very likely be upset. Therefore, you may want to talk with a pastor or a Christian counselor first to receive his wisdom on how to share a dark secret. If your husband has been known to be abusive, ask someone to accompany you. Although building a foundation of honesty may be frightening, keep in mind Dr. Harley's words: "As painful as it is to discover an affair, very few ever divorce because of it. In most cases, both spouses make adjustments that help avoid a repeat. But without the truth, there is little assurance that it will not happen again."[3]

Elements of Restoration

Is it truly possible to rebuild a marriage once infidelity has pierced its very core? Absolutely. As I sought the Lord and devoured His Word, He not only showed me the critical need for honesty with myself, honesty with Him, and honesty with my husband, but He also revealed three key elements needed to allow my relationship with Stottler to heal. These elements are essential in repairing what an affair tears apart and in helping build positive barriers against future infidelity.

Cut Off All Contact

The power of an affair truly is addictive; you'll do whatever it takes to be with that person. Therefore, extreme action may be necessary to cut off all contact—even if it means changing jobs or moving to another state.

The idea of such extreme measures may seem unreasonable. Without doubt, taking such action will be difficult and require certain sacrifices. Yet in the end, sacrificing a job or a house is certainly secondary to the importance of saving and caring for your family.

After our boat project in the Caribbean, Eric left for another sailing job in the middle of the Atlantic Ocean, so contact with him would have been difficult. Yet I could have found a way. For a person to resume communication, however, is to completely reverse the healing process that's begun and will start the cycle of withdrawal all over again. It will also greatly test the patience of a husband to continue working through the fiasco.

As the years go by and your marriage has been restored, you may once again be tempted to renew contact with that person. He was a pleasant part of your life at one time, so an internal curiosity remains to see him again. Your passionate emotions have healed and your marriage is now healthy, so you may reason that danger no longer exists if you were to restore contact. *At least just once,* you think, *to see what he's up to. That should be harmless.*

Don't do it! Besides being incredibly cruel to your husband, the original attraction may still be present, waiting to be stirred to life. It is *very* easy to reawaken those feelings. Picture your sleeping emotions as a grizzly bear in hibernation. If disturbed, he will respond with ferocious fury and tear you apart. Let sleeping bears lie!

Set Your Priorities

As I began to study God's perspective on marriage, I was immediately confronted with my skewed priorities. Christian writer Lawrence Crabb says:

> The essential foundation for a biblical marriage relationship is an unqualified commitment to the goal of ministry. Each partner must be willing to minister to the needs of the other regardless of the response. Although all of us will fail to implement that commitment perfectly, our responsibility is to remind ourselves continually that our highest purpose as husbands or wives is to be an instrument for promoting our partners' spiritual and personal welfare.[4]

As wives, our first priority must be our relationship with God, *then* with our husband, *then* our children—never the reverse order. Not running the carpool, not being the perfect Girl Scout leader, not even full-time ministry or any other job.

Since I had allowed work to consume my life, I needed to rearrange my schedule according to God's priorities. First, I had to replace my constant thoughts of Eric with what is true and honorable, right and pure (Philippians 4:8). So I began spending time in God's Word every day, rain or shine, convenient or not (and it is *seldom* convenient). What a dramatic difference daily time in His presence wrought in my life, and therefore in our marriage!

Second, after time with the Lord, my highest purpose needed to be promoting Stottler's spiritual and personal welfare. Ministering to and serving him had to once again take precedence over ministry and work.

A wealth of information has been written to guide couples into creating a more godly marriage, so I will not attempt to cover that here. I have listed some of these in the Resources at the back of the book, and they provide wonderful insight into God's design for our marriages. I have also listed resources to help a couple rebuild what infidelity has stolen.

Rebuild Trust

An affair is undoubtedly one of the most traumatic trials any marriage can face. Infidelity shatters trust. If the wife has been unfaithful, the husband is suddenly confronted with a very different person than the one he thought he had married. It would be like thinking he had been married to Betty Crocker all these years, only to suddenly discover that all along his wife had actually been cooking up biological weapons! What a shock! His entire perception of their marriage must now be rebuilt.

Our God loves to work miracles in a human heart that chooses to obey Him. Bill Gothard writes: "The world recommends divorce when our own resources of love and patience are exhausted. God delights in taking our exhausted resources and proving to a skeptical world the reality and power of His love."[5]

It *is* possible for that trust to be reestablished, but honesty and time are essential. Stottler needed to know that I wasn't hiding anything else from him. Each day I would tell him what I had been doing. I was open to answering any questions he had and volunteered pertinent information even before he asked.

But it's not an overnight healing. The longer the affair and the deception have gone on, the more time it takes to rebuild the trust. And most marriage therapists agree that counseling can play a crucial role in the process.

Rebuilding trust involves learning how to resolve conflicts. Conflict resolution stands out as a consistent predictor of the success or failure of any marriage. Couples who learn to face and resolve the problems that contaminate their marriage not only survive, but thrive.

Although the process of reclaiming a marriage takes time, it is *very* possible. Next to my relationship with the Father, my marriage to Stottler is now the joy of my life. I can confidently face trials because I know we can work through them. I also know Stottler is there to help me with my own weaknesses and that he loves me through them. It is wonderfully freeing to be transparent with nothing to hide. We now have far greater confidence and maturity in our relationship. And though not everyone may experience such a wonderful marriage, God rewards *our* faithfulness to obey Him regardless.

Whatever your current marital situation may be, the core issue comes down to your relationship with God.

Now that we have addressed some of the problems that marriages face concerning infidelity and lack of devotion, we can turn our attention to preventing further damage or to keeping infidelity from ever touching our marriage. Whatever your current marital situation may be, the core issue comes down to your relationship with God. A strong, fulfilling marriage grows out of the hearts of secure and loving individuals. As we turn now to examining our relationship and daily fellowship with God, we will see how that directly impacts our marriage. A marriage containing the three crucial elements of physical, emotional, and spiritual wholeness can be built only when God is at the center of the relationship. I can tell you from personal experience that knowing and loving God will not only change your marriage, but will also turn your entire life into an adventure! We'll look into that life-changing adventure in the next section.

Part Two

How Our Relationship With God Affects Our Marriage

"In all these things we overwhelmingly conquer
through Him who loved us."
Romans 8:37

7

Our Relationship with God

At this point, you may be thinking: *I've messed up my life so badly that my relationship with God will never be the same. After all, I've broken my marriage vow, I've hurt my family, and I've done things of which I'm greatly ashamed.* Or perhaps you have never committed the actual act of adultery but you have let many other things or people come between you and your husband. So many women feel estranged from those they love, and therefore feel distant from God.

God is in the healing business. All through the Bible we find true stories of people who messed up their lives and were either restored in their relationship to God or began all over. David committed adultery and murder, yet God called him a friend. Rahab was a prostitute who worshiped idols, but she became famous in Israel for her faith.

Recently, I read a story by Barbara Johnson that illustrates what God desires to do with a messed-up life:

> An English fisherman went into an inn at the end of a long, cold day and ordered a pot of tea. Bragging to friends about his big catch of fish, he stretched out his arm with a

sweeping motion. In an instant he knocked the teapot off the table and against the wall. A dark stain splashed across the wallpaper.

The fisherman was aghast at what he had done and apologized profusely to the innkeeper. He tried to wipe off the tea, but already it had made an ugly blotch. Shortly, a man seated at the next table came up and said, "Calm yourself, sir." The stranger took out a coal pencil and began to sketch around the shape of the stain. In moments he created a picture of a majestic stag that looked as if it had been designed for that wall. Soon he was recognized as Sir Edmond Lancier, England's foremost painter of wildlife.

What Sir Edmond Lancier did with an unsightly tea stain in a fine English inn, our God is doing every day. He is working in the lives of people who wonder how they'll ever recover from the ugly things that have happened to them. He is making masterpieces of our lives that stand as testimonies to His love and power.[1]

That's what God wants to do with our lives. He loves us so much that He wants to live through us so that we can experience His joy and fulfillment.

God's Amazing Love

No matter how great our sin, God is able to remold our lives into a beautiful picture. In spite of our bad choices, He offers to pour out His love and forgiveness if we come to Him. King David writes, *"O Lord, you are so good and kind, so ready to forgive; so full of mercy for all who ask your aid"* (Psalm 86:5, TLB).

God wants only that which is for our good. Remember the difference between Satan and Christ that we looked at earlier? Satan comes to *take* from us whatever is good so that he can steal and destroy our lives. But Christ comes to *give* all that is good for us. He desires to transform our lives so we can experience His love, peace, comfort, and contentment. He promises, *"I will give you a new heart and put a new spirit within you; and I will remove the heart of stone from your flesh and give you a heart of flesh"* (Ezekiel 36:26).

What God offers us is amazing! He holds out to us forgiveness, lovingkindness, and the exchange of our old sinful desires for a new heart and spirit!

As women, we hunger to be cherished, yet too often we are "lookin' for love in all the wrong places," as the country song goes.[2] My friend Twila grew up without a father. As a young lady, she married and divorced within two years and is now hopping under lots of sheets, desperately seeking a love that will fulfill her heart's cry. Yet how many men will it take for her to feel loved? Just one. The *only* One who can meet her deep longings for security, peace, and love—Jesus Christ.

> *Satan comes to take from us whatever is good so that he can steal and destroy our lives. But Christ comes to give what is good for us.*

But we can't experience God's fulfilling love if we remain apart from Him. Our sin —anything that puts our will above God's —has made a separation between us and our holy, loving God. His Word says, *"All have sinned and fall short of the glory of God"* (Romans 3:23). Many of us don't require convincing that *"the heart is more deceitful than all else and is desperately sick"* (Jeremiah 17:9). We *know* how quickly our hearts can lead us into sin! And the penalty for that sin is spiritual separation from our wonderful Lord (Romans 6:23). Sin keeps us from receiving that new heart and spirit that only God can give. And at death, our separation from Him will last forever!

What Is Sin?

Sin is anything that displeases God. It is like a cancer inside me that when left unconfessed eventually infects every part of my life. Sin's tentacles also reach out and affect the lives of others around us. What I *think* affects how I *respond*. How I respond affects every person who comes in contact with me.

And it's not just our responses and actions that can be disobedient. We can sin in our heart without lifting a finger or saying a word. God tells us that *"the devising of folly is sin"* (Proverbs 24:9). To even *think* about disobeying the Lord is sin in His eyes.

"But I haven't done anything!" someone will cry. Jesus gave us God's viewpoint when He said, *"Everyone who looks at a woman with lust for her has already committed adultery with her in his heart"* (Matthew 5:28). To *consider* adultery is to have committed it in your heart.

When I sat on the boat and envisioned spending time with Eric, though we hadn't "done anything," my thoughts were displeasing to God and were therefore sin. When I considered remaining in the Caribbean and not returning to my husband, in God's eyes I had committed infidelity in my heart.

And what lies in our heart spills over into our lives. For example, few men can "multitask" like we women can. It comes as second nature for us to be able to read a book while listening to a speaker, or to change a diaper while doing laundry and instructing our children.

But for most men, each task has its own separate "drawer," and they function best by opening only one drawer at a time. Stottler can barely talk and drive at the same time. And when I interrupt him at work, he tells me that in order to talk to me, he needs to totally switch his brain to a different program. He must close the mental drawer marked "work" so that he can open the drawer labeled "listen to wife."

Typically, women don't have separate drawers. We have one long, huge drawer containing everything all jumbled together in an inseparable mixture. It's like opening a "delicates" bag full of nylons after a wash cycle—you need an engineering degree to get them untangled! In the same way, when we sin in our thoughts, that affects how we think and act in *every other area*. If I am angry with Stottler, or if I am thinking about some other man, it affects my relationship with God and with Stottler, as well as how I respond to everyone else. Our sin is not "worse" than our husband's—it's just that we can't hide it as easily. And that's actually a blessing because it forces us to confront our sinful nature.

Sin always snowballs. Jeremiah 9:3 says, *"They proceed from evil to evil."* Sin starts by allowing one little thought, then another, then another. The farther the ball rolls down the hill, the faster it goes, and the harder it is to stop.

We never gain anything by choosing to sin. Sin never ultimately satisfies because it brings only spiritual death and alienation from God. That's why sin in our lives leads to frustration, confusion, and depression. And why not—we weren't designed to live cut off from God! Of course sin is going to cause frustration—I'm fighting against the Lord! Of course it will cause confusion—I can't hear God because I've turned away from Him. Of course sin is going to cause depression—I'm out of God's plan for which I was created and designed! It's like trying to force a ballet dancer to be an accountant; she's going to be utterly miserable!

The Root of Sin: Pride

Sin always boils down to one root—pride. I want my will over God's will. Pride is at the heart of every issue of selfishness, anger, lust, adultery, divorce, pornography, and on and on.

God hates pride. He tells us, *"Pride and arrogance and the evil way and the perverted mouth, I hate"* (Proverbs 8:13). God warns us that *"pride goes before destruction, and a haughty spirit before stumbling"* (Proverbs 16:18). When we become proud, we will fall. The Lord humorously illustrated this principle one day through my mother.

My mom loved to fly. In her day, it was unusual for a woman in her fifties to earn a pilot's license in rural Oklahoma—but to have a twin-engine rating was just plain extraordinary! She especially enjoyed flying her twin-engine plane to meet other pilots at small airports around the state.

Mom had the reputation of being a conscientious and careful pilot. She diligently followed all she had been taught. Flying overhead in preparation for landing at some new airport, she was required by law to announce over the cockpit radio her intentions to land. Her female voice flowing over the airwaves would usually cause quite a stir in the small rural airports. "That was a woman! Will you look at that—she's flying a big ol' twin engine!"

One perfectly cloudless day, Mom was flying into yet another small Oklahoma town. When she announced her landing, she heard the typical surprise in the voice of the fixed base operator when he acknowledged her landing call. As had happened so many times in the past, she knew that a sea of male faces would be plastered across the window of the tiny airport watching this lady pilot land the "big ol' twin-engine" plane. So Mom wanted to show off a bit and bring in a really smooth landing.

As she approached the runway, she timed the last-minute flair of her plane precisely, executing a picture-perfect landing. Rolling past the tiny airport building, she saw a row of faces watching her from the large pane window. Slowing to the end of the runway, then turning to taxi back to the building, she was feeling pretty cocky. She had greased in a perfect landing; she was all dressed up in a classy suit; and life was lookin' good.

Mom rolled to a stop directly in front of the window, turned off the engines, and gathered her flight bag. Opening the cockpit door, she proudly stepped onto the wing, then descended to the next little stepping bar. As she took the final step to the ground, suddenly the heel of her shoe caught and sent her flailing face down, spread-eagle on the pavement before all those men! Mom wasn't hurt, but her pride took quite a beating!

Actually, our pride accomplishes the exact opposite of what we are seeking. God's kingdom is upside down from man's. The very thing pride desires—attention, honor, recognition, control —are not what it will accomplish. *"A man's pride will bring him low, but a humble spirit will obtain honor"* (Proverbs 29:23). God says that those who are humble will be the ones to receive honor.

Pride is also the root of our belief that we are strong enough to withstand moral temptations. I would rather pray each day, *"Let not the foot of pride come upon me"* (Psalm 36:11) than to blindly believe I am above some temptation. None of us is above falling to any temptation known to man.

God warns us that *"pride ends in destruction"* (Proverbs 18:12, TLB). He does so because He knows that pride in our lives leads only to death, destruction, and separation from Him. Those are severe consequences to face.

Christ's Gift

Is there a way to bridge this separation between us and God? Is there any hope for this prideful, diseased heart that leads us into trouble at every turn?

Picture God as being in Hawaii, and we are standing on the California coast. We realize how desperately we need Him, so we try to swim to Hawaii to reach our precious Creator. Of course, we can't make it; we'll drown before we reach Catalina Island twenty-two miles offshore! We can't cross that expanse on our own effort.

Knowing our dilemma, God provided a way for us to reach Him. This way is through His Son, Jesus Christ. Jesus tells us, *"I am the way, and the truth, and the life; no one comes to the Father but through Me"* (John 14:6). Only Christ can bridge the separation. God says, *"There is salvation in no one else; for there is no other name under heaven that has been given among men by which we must be saved"* (Acts 4:12).

When we die, we must pay the penalty for all of our own sins, which eternally separate us from our holy God. But because Christ lived a perfectly sinless life on earth, He could offer His life as a substitute payment for our sins since He had none of His own. He offers this as a free gift to each of us.

> *Until you personally accept the gift of Christ's sacrifice to pay for all of your sins, you are "dead in your trespasses and sins."*

I once saw a painting of a cross laid flat like a bridge spanning a bottomless pit. On one side of the chasm lived frantic, unfulfilled people. On the opposite side dwelt God's peaceful presence. The only way from the frenetic life to the peaceful life was by walking across the cross. Only Christ offers us this incredible blessing of passing from a life of frustration and discontent to one of fulfillment and peace in His presence. When Christ allowed His life to be taken, the gift of His sacrifice paid the ultimate price for every sin I have ever committed and will ever commit. Now my only job is to accept His gift!

One of my favorite songs tells about coming to the cross of Christ and seeking His forgiveness:

> I come to the cross seeking mercy and grace,
> I come to the cross where You died in my place.

Out of my weakness and into Your strength,
Humbly, I come to the cross.
Your arms are open, You call me by name.
You welcome this child that was lost.
You paid the price for my guilt and my shame.
Jesus, I come, Jesus, I come,
Jesus, I come to the cross.[3]

If you have never given your life to the Savior, then you will never experience His forgiveness and power to bring permanent change in your life. Until you personally accept the gift of Christ's sacrifice to pay for all of your sins, you are *"dead in your trespasses and sins"* (Ephesians 2:1).

But you don't have to stay that way! You can receive Christ's payment for your sins right now. God promises, *"As many as received [Jesus], to them He gave the right to become children of God, even to those who believe in His name"* (John 1:12). All you have to do is receive His gift! It's like someone offering to give you a billion dollars with no strings attached. It would be crazy to turn away an offer like that!

When I was thirteen years old, I asked Christ to pay for my sins. I remember experiencing a sensation of floating through the junior high school corridors for about a week. Others have accepted Christ's payment for their sins and have had no change of feelings whatsoever—and either way is fine. Our feelings don't determine the truth. The important thing is trusting Christ to do what He promised. And His promise is: *"Behold, I stand at the door [of your life] and knock; if anyone hears My voice and opens the door, I will come in to him"* (Revelation 3:20).

When Christ makes a promise, you can stake your life on it! He is God, and His promises never change or fail (2 Corinthians 1:20). Christ promises to pay for your sins if you simply ask Him. And asking Him is an act of faith. The easiest way to express that faith is in prayer, which is simply talking with Him. This is a prayer you could pray:

> Jesus, I need *You* to pay the penalty for all of my sins. I need Your peace and joy and presence in my life. I give You my life. Mold me to be who You designed me to be. Amen.

I would encourage you not to read any further until you have settled this issue with God. It is impossible to live out the principles we are talking about without the power of the Lord. You can try harder; you can promise to be a loving wife; but your self-efforts will all lead to frustration. You are like a computer that hasn't been plugged into the socket; you simply don't have the power to function in the way you were designed. But through Christ, you can experience forgiveness, peace, and His transforming power!

Be Sure of Your New Life

Ready to read on? Here's some incredible news: When you receive Christ's payment, His Holy Spirit comes to live in your life (Galatians 4:6)![4] You are a new person and will never be the same again (2 Corinthians 5:17)! If the Spirit truly lives in you, He *will* bring about changes in your thoughts and desires. You will want to please Him. The Bible says, *"By this we may be sure that we know him, if we keep his commandments"* (1 John 2:3, RSV). This desire to keep His commandments is the evidence that you have truly received His forgiveness and have His new life within you.

Another bit of wonderful news is that if we have honestly asked Christ into our life, we can be absolutely sure that all of our sins—past, present, and future—are paid for. As a new believer in Christ, I didn't understand that my sins were paid for once and for all, so I worried: Have I been "good enough" for the

Lord today? If I die in my sleep, will I go to heaven? Do I need to ask Christ into my life again? That was a very disquieting way to live each day. Then I read the promise that God gave to us:

> *The testimony is this, that God has given us eternal life, and this life is in His Son. He who has the Son has the life; he who does not have the Son of God does not have the life. These things I have written to you who believe in the name of the Son of God, so that you may know that you have eternal life. (1 John 5:11–13, emphasis added)*

We don't have to worry if we've been good enough that day, or any day, because He's already paid our way. It's not by *our* merit that our sins are forgiven—it's by Christ's merit alone. Therefore, I don't have to perform a certain way or worry that I have lost my salvation. What a relief and sense of peace that brings!

Someone may say, "If I trust in Christ's payment for my sins and don't have to be good to earn an entrance into heaven, then I can do whatever I want, right?" The simple answer is that if living in continual sin doesn't make you miserable, you don't really have salvation in the first place. When Christ's Spirit enters our life, He changes our desires so that we *want* to obey Him.

You may have asked Christ to be your Savior earlier in your life, yet are still struggling with guilt and frustration. This happens when we fail to maintain our closeness with the Lord. But we don't have to stay that way! We can restore our fellowship with God and experience again His blessed peace. In the next chapter we will tackle this problem of maintaining our closeness to God. But for right now, simply thank the Lord for all He has done for you. If you have accepted Christ's payment for your sins, thank Him for His wondrous forgiveness, and that He will never leave you (Hebrews 13:5). That's cause for rejoicing!

8

Transparent Repentance

ere is a question that you may be asking at this point:
How does a person who has received Christ and has
witnessed change in her life maintain that ongoing closeness with Him that brings such blessed peace? The answer: By
keeping short sin accounts with God. In wifely terms, don't let
sin pile up like a stack of dirty laundry!

God wants us to experience His continual peace and direction. Therefore, He gave us a built-in alarm system to flash a
warning light on any disobedient area in our life. The Holy Spirit,
who now lives within us came to *"convict the world concerning sin
and righteousness and judgment"* (John 16:8). He convicts us of
anything that disrupts our relationship with God. This conviction
is the guilt we sense caused by our disobedience to God.

God's alarm system is such a blessing! To continue in sin *always* leads to more sin, multiplied deceit, a hardened conscience,
problems, adversity, and broken relationships. In fact, unconfessed
sin can lead to physical problems. King David described the
effects of his adultery: *"When I kept silent about my sin, my body
wasted away through my groaning all day long...My vitality was*

drained away as with the fever heat of summer" (Psalm 32:3,4). The disobedient Israelites were even more graphic: *"Surely our transgressions and our sins are upon us, and we are rotting away in them"* (Ezekiel 33:10).

When I returned home from the Caribbean, my sin felt like rottenness in my soul, eating away every ounce of peace. To begin the journey back to holiness, I had to confess those sins to God. Yes, my sins were forgiven when I accepted Christ's payment for them, but when I harbor them, they keep me from experiencing the joy of God's inner peace. It's like winning a million dollars, then burying it in the ground. You own it, yet you never experience any of its benefits.

Satan's Goal

Satan's goal is to entice us to choose sin—to steal God's goodness from us, to destroy our lives, and to ultimately kill us (John 10:10). God gives us a graphic picture in nature.

Temptations are wrapped in such beautiful packages that we refuse to acknowledge the skull and crossbones waiting inside the box!

Have you ever flipped through the TV channels and run across a nature program showing a lion silently stalking its prey through the tall African grasses? A herd of innocent zebras contentedly munch on the grass, oblivious to the fact that one of them will soon become lunch. The big cat quietly observes them, skillfully maneuvering to a position where it can suddenly leap upon a weak, unsuspecting member of the herd.

Then like a giant spring unleashed, the huge cat launches through the air toward its prey. The herd scatters in terror, and a panicked baby zebra attempts to flee. Stride upon giant stride, the cat swallows the ground between them.

Then in one enormous leap, it springs with fangs extended to land on the haunches of the young animal, ripping its flesh as it pulls it mercilessly to the ground.

That vivid image pictures Satan and his methods. He silently stalks us, waiting for our weak moments, then springs upon us with a temptation that ultimately rips our flesh and pulls us down. If we give in to temptation with another man, Satan accomplishes his goal as our marriage is ripped apart, lives are destroyed, and Christian testimonies are ruined.

God's Word clearly instructs us to not give in to the flesh, *"for the flesh sets its desire against the Spirit, and the Spirit against the flesh; for these are in opposition to one another, so that you may not do the things that you please"* (Galatians 5:17). God gives us these warnings because He desires *only* our good and His glory. Obedience to His Word protects and covers our lives like a storm shelter shielding us from a deadly tornado.

When I disobey God, I am choosing the very thing that will hurt me. It's like deliberately cutting off my finger or severing my own arm! Temptations are wrapped in such beautiful packages that we refuse to acknowledge the skull and crossbones waiting *inside* the box! Sin is *designed* to hurt you. *"He who sins against me [God's wisdom] injures himself; all those who hate me love death"* (Proverbs 8:36).

Oh, if we could just learn that to disobey God's commands only injures ourselves! God loves us so much! He alone knows what is absolutely the best for each of us. When I choose to follow my own fleshly desires, I cannot see what God sees. When I rationalize my disobedience as being harmless, God sees the total picture. Although a temptation may seem to lead me into a beautiful field of flowers, from God's vantage point, He sees me walking into the middle of a firing range!

We should be scared to death to even dabble a toe in the waters of temptation. Knowing God's attitude toward sin, knowing the effect it has on our lives, and knowing who is behind all sin should make us run at the first sight of it.

But we often think it's fun to toy with temptation and sin. How much can I flirt with that guy before causing problems? How far can I pursue infidelity without being caught? What degree of sensuality can I watch on TV before it starts to affect my imagination? Instead of wondering how much we can "get away with," we should see how far away from temptation and sin we can run! *"A prudent man sees evil and hides himself, the naive proceed and pay the penalty"* (Proverbs 27:12).

If a believer refuses to leave the path of continual disobedience, the Lord may choose to bring about her physical death as well. We are given several examples in the Scriptures. In one passage, Paul chastises the Corinthian church for allowing an immoral believer to remain in their fellowship. Concerning the unrepentant believer, Paul writes, *"I have decided to deliver such a one to Satan for the destruction of his flesh, so that his spirit may be saved in the day of the Lord Jesus"* (1 Corinthians 5:5). Later, he tells the Corinthian believers that because of sin *"many among you are weak and sick, and a number sleep"* (1 Corinthians 11:30). "Sleep" doesn't mean they're taking a nap—it means death![1]

The Importance of Transparent Repentance

God gives us a way to experience His love, forgiveness, and peace again. It's through the practice of *transparent repentance*—honestly, humbly agreeing with God that what we did was sin, and it displeased Him. This should be a common part of every Christian's life. The great reformer Martin Luther said that "the whole life of believers should be repentance."[2]

Yet so often we don't want to admit we are wrong. We foolishly choose to smother under the oppression of guilt and its consequences rather than admit our sin and experience the refreshing cleansing of God's forgiveness again. Many people will hide "secret sins" for years, wallowing under the burden of guilt rather than releasing it to a loving, restoring Father. God tells us the result: *"He who conceals his transgressions will not prosper, but he who confesses and forsakes them will find compassion"* (Proverbs 28:13).

Why would we cling to our pet sins when they only infect our lives like a rabid skunk? It seems rather silly, doesn't it? Remember who is behind sin. Satan will whisper to you that it is far too humiliating to confess those sins. He will tell you that it is better to hide them deep inside. And his motivation? To destroy your life! He leaves out the part about unconfessed sin eating away at your soul like a fast-growing cancer.

Our daily, hourly choices *do* matter. Each choice builds or destroys our "life house": *"The wise woman builds her house, but the foolish tears it down with her own hands"* (Proverbs 14:1). We think little choices won't really matter in the long run, but every house is built one board and one nail at a time. If one beam is missing, the roof collapses. If one piece of siding is left off, a gaping hole allows the rain to enter. One missing nail could bring down the gutter that in turn floods the foundation and collapses the entire house!

God desires to bless us and to make our lives a blessing to Him and to others. Transparent repentance means that we must be willing to meet with Him in prayer, honestly confessing all sin, holding nothing back. It's like being a glass door—totally transparent before the Lord, hiding nothing inside.

To remain transparent before God, no act of disobedience is too small to confess. The *moment* we sense that we have displeased God by exerting our will over His, we must heed God's conviction. When the red light glares on the dashboard—*stop!* Otherwise, sin quickly builds up and we find ourselves hardened to the Lord faster than we believed possible. How well I know!

An easy way to practice transparent repentance is by using a concept Dr. Bill Bright teaches called "spiritual breathing."[3] When we breathe, we exhale the impure air and inhale the pure. When I am convicted of sin, I *exhale* the sin by agreeing with God that I was disobedient. Then I *inhale* by asking Him to fill my heart and to control my life again. Only then am I free to once again experience His love and power.

True repentance will *always* result in a change of action. If my actions do not change, the repentance was not genuine. No fruit equals no repentance (Matthew 3:8).

Incomplete repentance occurs when we are concerned about having been caught or how the consequences of our sin will affect us, rather than having sorrow over the sin itself. For example, if a woman is caught in an affair, and she cries and begs for forgiveness yet turns around and continues the affair, her repentance was incomplete. She was far more brokenhearted over having been caught than over her disobedience and selfish behavior.

God's Unlimited Grace

God is so gracious and compassionate. When we turn from our selfish pride and the sin that resulted from it, He will lift us up again and again. After King David was confronted with his sins, he opened his heart and transparently confessed them before the Lord. Only then did he experience release from the oppression of his guilt:

> *I acknowledged my sin to you and did not cover up my iniquity. I said, "I will confess my transgressions to the LORD"—and you forgave the guilt of my sin.* (Psalm 32:5, NIV)

How blessed is he whose transgression is forgiven, whose sin is covered! (Psalm 32:1)

My life is a testimony to God's unending grace. I laughingly say that I've used up my allotment of grace and about four other people's as well. (Sorry if you're one of the four!) But of course there is no limit to His grace for each of us when we come humbly to Him, *"for of His fullness we have all received, and grace upon grace"* (John 1:16).

When I left the Caribbean and returned home, I went before the Lord in prayer to confess all that I had done. My heart felt raw and bruised, and my emotions still yearned to be with Eric. Yet I knew leaving was the right decision because it demonstrated obedience to God. So even though my heart was still in the islands at that point, I confessed that I had refused to listen to the Lord's conviction and had hurt many people in the process—especially my husband. I had been living a lie while trying to do ministry. I once again wanted to be a transparent glass door toward the Lord.

Transparent repentance involves making changes so we don't repeat the sin. For me, it meant leaving the Caribbean and choosing to sever all contact with Eric. Was it easy? Not on your life! But it was right, and obeying God results in good for everyone, whether it feels like it at the time or not.

Restoring Relationships with Others

Because our sins affect other people, we also need to make things right with them. Jesus tells us to *"first be reconciled to your brother, and then come and present your offering"* to the Lord (Matthew 5:24). If others know of what I've done or have been offended by me, then as a fruit of true repentance I need to make things right with them as far as I am able.

Paul says, *"I also do my best to maintain always a blameless conscience both before God and before men"* (Acts 24:16). Yet how easy it is for us to bury "small" acts of disobedience in a dark, forgotten corner.

Lately, I've been sifting through each room of our home to find lost treasures for a rummage sale. It's not a large house, so one would think there should be few places in which items could hide. But oh, the surprises I have found tucked away in dusty corners! A "yak yak" T-shirt from Nepal, a slinky nightgown, a Cary Grant audiocassette—all covered with dust and forgotten in corners of closets.

How easy it is for the rooms of our lives to contain hidden secrets as well. That angry word spoken to a coworker was so long ago that we've long since adjusted our relationship to be distant and cool rather than deal with the root problem. Or what about those times of anger when we were too impatient to help our children who have now become emotionally cold and distant teenagers?

We think those dusty corners won't affect us if they remain undisturbed. Yet eventually my allergies will react and remind me that things aren't as clean in my house as they may appear. We can try to ignore cancer cells and believe they won't harm us, but left untreated, the results are catastrophic for our lives.

No sin is insignificant to God, no matter how small or large, no matter how long ago we committed it. We need to be willing to do whatever is required to maintain a clear conscience before others. To borrow a definition from Life Action Ministries, a spiritual revival ministry, "Having a clear conscience means that there is no one alive that I have ever wronged, offended, or hurt in any way that I have not gone back to and sought to make it right with both God and the individual."[4]

When I first heard this definition of a clear conscience, my initial response was, "You've got to be kidding!" I knew my list of offended individuals would be long. Yet after several days of the

Holy Spirit's conviction, I realized that I would rather have a clear conscience before the Lord than to try to protect my pride. So I wrote out a three-page list of people to call or see.

It wasn't easy, but asking forgiveness of each individual on that list was worth every ounce of humiliation I may have felt. The sense of relief at being transparent before both God and others was enormous! Having no skeletons to hide brings such freedom! *"How blessed is the man . . . in whose spirit there is no deceit!"* (Psalm 32:2).

Someone may reason at this point, "If I have unconfessed sin in my life that affects how I think and act toward others, then to have a clear conscience do I need to ask forgiveness of everyone I've been around?" If that were the case, I would have needed to round up a good portion of the Caribbean island population and asked their forgiveness!

Asking forgiveness applies to those individuals who have been directly affected, hurt, or offended by our sin. For instance, my infidelity hurt Stottler and affected Eric. So when I returned home from the Caribbean, one of the first things I had to do was to ask Stottler's forgiveness for all the deceit, lies, and hurt I had caused him. I asked his forgiveness for my emotional unfaithfulness. As God reminded me of other ways I had hurt him, I also asked forgiveness for those. And though I had broken off communication with Eric, I did e-mail him to ask for his forgiveness as well. I had been a terrible witness for Christ; I had defrauded him; and I had put him in a compromising situation. I severed all contact after that.

Since the team members were unaware of my thoughts and actions toward Eric, I didn't sense the Lord directing me to ask their forgiveness, even though my sin certainly diminished the effectiveness of the project. The same holds true for the children of a woman involved in an affair. Unless they were aware of the infidelity, or the Lord convicted the mother to tell them, it's probably not necessary to involve them. But the Lord is always the final word, so seek His leading above all else.

Once I had confessed my unfaithfulness to God, Stottler, and Eric, little by little His peace began to return. God is *always* faithful to forgive us. He promises: *"If we confess our sins, He is faithful and righteous to forgive us our sins and to cleanse us from all un-righteousness"* (1 John 1:9).

A great by-product of transparent repentance is its deterrence to further sin. I am committed to keeping short sin accounts with God and with others. And though confession is always right, it's also hard because humility hurts! Therefore, it's just easier not to sin in the first place.

Conviction vs. Condemnation

At first, the practice of transparent repentance may seem over-whelming. But there is *always* hope in Christ. The apostle Paul had zealously persecuted Christians before turning to Christ. He could have been haunted by his past, yet through God's grace and for-giveness he wrote, *"One thing I do: forgetting what lies behind and reaching forward to what lies ahead, I press on toward the goal for the prize of the upward call of God in Christ Jesus"* (Philippians 3:13,14). Paul knew he had been forgiven and could therefore fo-cus on becoming more like Christ and serving Him wholeheart-edly. What an encouragement to those of us who have failed!

Don't let past failures rob you of your future. Yes, there are al-ways consequences to any sin. I grieve that I hurt Stottler. I grieve that I was such a poor witness to Eric, to our team, and to others we met in the islands. I will always have to guard my thoughts carefully. But once I had transparently confessed to the Lord, I knew I was forgiven.

One of Satan's little tricks is to divert us from experiencing God's forgiveness. He does this by constantly reminding us of sins already confessed so we will feel guilty all over again. There is a vast difference between God's conviction and Satan's condemnation.

When I first heard this truth, I found it difficult to grasp. I was so used to beating myself up concerning my sins that this seemed too good to be true. So I determined to review these truths every single day for two weeks until they sank into my heart. (That kind of review, by the way, works well for any truth that is difficult to grasp.) The following chart can help you differentiate between God's conviction and Satan's condemnation.

Conviction	Condemnation
Comes from God	Comes from Satan
Conviction is specific	Condemnation is general
Focuses on a specific attitude or action: "My impatience with my child was sin before God."	Focuses on my character/who I am: "I'm such a failure. I'm a terrible mother."
Leads to confession, resulting in a change of actions and a godly self-image	Leads to further guilt, resulting in depression, defeat, and a poor self-image
Action: When convicted, confess the specific sin to God (and others, if applicable), then claim His forgiveness.	**Action:** When condemned, make sure you have confessed the specific sin to God (and others, if applicable), then claim His forgiveness and the righteousness you have in Christ.
"If we confess our sins, He is faithful and righteous to forgive us our sins and to cleanse us from all unrighteousness" (1 John 1:9).	*"For by that one offering he made forever perfect in the sight of God all those whom he is making holy"* (Hebrews 10:14, TLB).

God always convicts us of *specific* attitudes or acts of disobedience. Satan, on the other hand, likes to condemn our character in *general* terms. For example, God recently convicted me of some impatient words spoken to a friend. Satan wanted to take that conviction and turn it into condemnation: "Judy, you sure are a rotten friend. You'll never learn to hold your tongue. You are a terrible Christian." My response? I confessed to the Lord that my words had been unkind. Then I also asked my friend's forgiveness.

I want His light of conviction to expose any sin lurking in the dark corners of my life. Never again do I want to allow sin to build up.

Having confessed my sin to God and having asked my friend's forgiveness, my conscience was clear and I was free to experience God's love and forgiveness. If I still *felt* guilty, that meant I was choosing to listen to the enemy's little voice of condemnation telling me that I was a rotten friend and a terrible Christian. When that happened, I would claim God's forgiveness and refuse to listen to Satan's accusations or to live by my emotions. I like to remind the enemy that I have been washed white as snow by Christ's blood and repeat Hebrews 10:14.

My failure in the Caribbean highlighted the critical need to constantly maintain an unhindered, transparent relationship with the Lord. I *want* His light of conviction to expose any sin lurking in the dark corners of my life. Never again do I want to allow sin to build up and snowball into a disaster.

Five years ago, Stottler had an angiogram that showed a clear picture of his heart. To our great surprise, the image revealed that all was not well. Several blockages that had been previously hidden were now suddenly exposed. Though it came as an initial shock, it was good to have the truth revealed so it could be dealt with.

In the same way, we should do a spiritual angiogram each day to expose the true condition of our heart. Am I hiding any bitterness or jealousy toward anyone in my heart? Is there any sin in my life that needs to be confessed? Am I fantasizing about another man and I have yet to confess it before the Lord and tell my husband? Is there *any* area of disobedience lurking in my life?

The Lord has given us a wonderful prayer to help us remain transparent before Him every day:

> *Search me, O God, and know my heart;*
> *Try me and know my anxious thoughts;*
> *And see if there be any hurtful way in me,*
> *And lead me in the everlasting way.* (Psalm 139:23,24)

Will you begin to practice transparent confession so that you can continue to experience the joy and peace of Christ's forgiveness? Once His Spirit lives within us, He can use our tarnished, flawed lives—even our failures—for His good purposes. But to be usable, we must maintain a transparent relationship with Him by coming before Him with a humble, broken heart. Only He can turn a stained life into a beautiful picture reflecting His grace and love.

9

The Spirit-Controlled Life

Before entering full-time Christian ministry, I worked as a professional musician. If you've been around musicians much, you'll know that most of us possess what's been termed a "melancholy temperament." Translation: "moody."

I call it the "musician's temperament": major highs, major lows, and no ground in-between. I had lived that way for as long as I could remember. I knew the joy of flying above the mountaintops (unaided by any substance, I might add), and I also knew the blackness of depression. My combination of a sensitive, artistic side coupled with a no-holds-barred, adventurous side resulted in some wildly vacillating emotions. The problem was that I either flew or flopped. Level ground didn't exist.

Sometime during high school, I decided that actually living a consistent Christian life was impossible for anyone with a temperament like mine. It felt like God had played some cruel, sadistic joke on me. When I became a Christian, He had given me the desire to live according to His Word, but the package deal didn't seem to include the ability! I truly wanted to live by what I knew was right, but that remained an unattainable goal.

The older I got, the higher my mountain peaks rose and the lower my valleys descended. Life resembled one constant roller coaster ride, and I was definitely experiencing motion sickness.

As this struggle continued during college, a faithful friend persuaded me to attend her local church. There I became friends with the pastor and his wife, only to observe with great consternation that this pastor also possessed a melancholy temperament, yet *he* maintained an even-tempered, consistent walk with God. How did he do that? Had God forgotten to give me some "holiness gene" when I had received Christ?

I so desperately wanted to use all my creative energy for serving the Lord rather than for devising inventive ways to sneak around doing the very things I really *didn't* want to do. But how does a zebra change its stripes?

Shortly after college, I reluctantly attended a special evening service at church. Suddenly, I heard words that pierced my mind! It was as if a giant light bulb had turned on inside my head, and all the angels above me had broken into the "Hallelujah Chorus." For the first time, I finally understood that as a believer, the power of sin had been broken in my life, and I never had to choose sin again! But how is that possible?

God's Incredible News for Christians

These two circles help illustrate our life before and after we receive Christ's forgiveness for our sins:

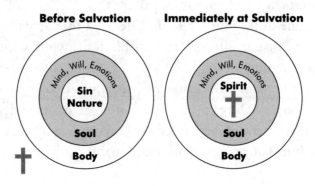

Before a woman receives Christ, her spirit is controlled by a corrupted sin nature. In this condition, a person is a slave to sin and has no choice but to sin (John 8:34).

As non-Christians, our sin nature ruled our lives. Even the "good" things we did were an abomination to the Lord because they came out of our selfish nature (Isaiah 64:6). We might appear to suppress sin in one area, but it would just reappear in some other part of our life. It's like trying to block a gopher hole —the gopher will just pop up somewhere else in your yard. And we couldn't escape from this condition on our own.

But praise God that although *we* can never change our sin nature, *Christ* can! The moment we receive Christ's payment for our sins, our sin nature is completely killed, thereby ending its reigning authority and power to make us sin! The Holy Spirit comes to live inside each person who receives Christ, replacing the old sin nature and giving us the power to conquer sin. We become new people who will never be the same (2 Corinthians 5:17). This is the greatest news ever given to Christians, because in practical terms it means that the old nature that made us sin is now dead and *we don't have to choose to sin anymore!*

We are free from the power that made us sin! *"For we know that our old self was crucified with him so that the body of sin might be done away with, that we should no longer be slaves to sin"* (Romans 6:6, NIV). We now have freedom of choice—to sin or not to sin.

This new life is similar to the difference between living inside or outside a prison. Being a non-Christian is like living in prison; you have no freedom of choice. But once you receive Christ, the prison doors are opened. Now you have the freedom to leave prison and to make right choices. You also have the freedom to go back into prison. It's your choice. We can live by Christ's power and stay outside the prison walls, or we can choose to live by our own corrupt flesh again and march right back into the prison cell of sin.

The greatest power sin has in a believer's life is making her think that she is bound to fail and can never be free from sin. I certainly thought that was true. But when I understood that my old sin nature was *completely* dead and that Christ's resurrection power within me could give me victory over every temptation, I was ecstatic! At the end of that church service, I leaped from my seat and sprinted up to the speaker, yelling, "I finally understand! I've got it! I really don't have to sin anymore!" It was as if I had been released from a life sentence. I hadn't known that the prison door had stood open all along. After struggling with defeat for so long, I finally understood how victory was possible!

But change didn't happen overnight. Little by little, my emotions began to even out. Small glimpses of level ground began to appear, then develop into miles of level plains. Now my mountaintops still remain, but below them the devastating sinkholes have been transformed into mere depressions.

Living Inside Out

If our old sin nature is truly dead, then why do we still sin? Simply because we choose to! Although we now have the Holy Spirit to give us the *power* to conquer sin, a part of us is not automatically changed. We are still *able* to sin because the "flesh" (mind, will, emotions) retains its old patterns and habits. Our work now comes in retraining the flesh.

Every time I sin, I choose to place my will over God's and refuse (or forget) to call upon the Spirit within me for His wisdom and strength. I fail to let the inside dominate the outside.

Galatians 5:16 reminds us to *"walk by the **Spirit**, and you will not carry out the desire of the flesh"* (emphasis added). So how do we "walk by the Spirit"? In daily life, whenever my mind, will, or emotions start to rebel against God, I must call upon the strength of my new nature. *I* certainly don't have the power to resist temptation. It's only by depending on the new nature inside me—the power of Christ—that I can have victory. And that power is *always* available.

To be *"filled with the Spirit"* (Ephesians 5:18) means that His Spirit should control every part of us—our mind, our will, our emotions, and our body. Our lives are like an empty glove. Unless a hand fills the glove, it remains flimsy and useless. In the same way, we are lifeless and useless for the Lord unless we are filled and controlled by the power of His Spirit. And when His Holy Spirit is in control, the results profoundly affect every part of our lives.

God promises that no temptation will be too strong to resist, therefore I have no excuse for caving in to sin.

When tempted, I immediately call on the inside (the Holy Spirit) to dominate the outside (my corrupted flesh) by shooting up a "bullet prayer" and asking the Lord for His strength. Then knowing that I have the power of the Holy Spirit, I choose to act according to His will. No longer can I blame the devil or circumstances or other people or even my own nature for my sin, because as a new creation in Christ nothing can *make* me sin. God promises that no temptation will be too strong to resist (1 Corinthians 10:13), therefore I have no excuse for caving in to sin. If I do, it's simply because I choose to.

When I don't feel like being loving to my husband, I pray for Christ's strength, then choose to demonstrate love. When I don't feel like going to work (which is a frequent feeling), I pray for Christ's strength, then choose to go. When I don't feel like holding my tongue from responding in anger, I pray for Christ's strength, then choose to keep my mouth shut (well, most of the time). God has given me the power to do His will regardless of how I feel (Philippians 2:13). Therefore, I have no excuse not to obey.

Patty knew about struggling against the flesh. She, her husband, and their children had just moved into the home of their dreams. And as an added bonus, the neighbors seemed sincerely warm and loving. Especially Jack next door.

Because Jack worked out of his home, he had been available to pry the stuffed dinosaur out of the kid's toilet and fix the broken sprinkler that sent a geyser shooting across the yard. As Patty sat with him on the sidewalk after the sprinkler incident, she suddenly felt her emotions pulled toward this kind neighbor. And the more she thought about him, the more she "fed" her fleshly desires. Like giving food to a ravenous animal, the more she fed her growing fantasies about Jack, the stronger they became.

Our flesh and our Spirit are in a constant battle (Galatians 5:17). When we "feed" the flesh by giving in to its lusts and desires, we will reap a life of frustration, defeat, strife, and quarrels. But if we starve the flesh by continually turning to the Spirit and His power, our old habits and patterns will be retrained, resulting in a life of joy and peace.

When I first felt drawn to Eric, I foolishly chose to feed those fleshly emotions by looking for opportunities to talk and be together. And the more I fed those desires, the stronger they became. But had I instantly chosen to starve those sinful desires by calling on Christ's strength, then refusing to dwell on the feelings as well as revealing them to my husband, those emotions would have withered and faded away. It all depends on what we feed.

On the Altar

For the inner Spirit to fully dominate the outer flesh, we must give the Holy Spirit complete control over every part of us. Romans 6:13 tells us to yield everything to His control: *"Do not go on presenting the members of your body to sin as instruments of unrighteousness; but present yourselves to God as those alive from the dead, and your members as instruments of righteousness to God."* Paul urges us *"to present your bodies a living and holy sacrifice, acceptable to God, which is your spiritual service of worship"* (Romans 12:1). In other words, we need to daily surrender our mind, will, emotions, and body to the Lord so that He is given complete control.

I do this each morning (and more often, if necessary) by using a mental picture. Each day as I begin to pray, I picture a white marble altar, rather like a flat table, about four feet high. I place myself stretched out on that altar, vulnerable before the Lord, and then give myself completely to Him to do with as He knows is best. Because He loves us perfectly, I know that He desires only that which is for my good and His glory. He is completely trustworthy. As I lay on that altar, I pray a simple prayer of complete surrender that I learned from Stottler:

> Rich or poor, sick or well, dead or alive, I am completely
> Yours, Lord, to do with whatever You choose.

To give my life without reservation to the Lord means I choose to trust Him. And that wasn't always easy for me to do! It was frightening to be so vulnerable! At first, I practiced surrendering my life solely as an act of faith. Then as I continued practicing this act of sacrificing myself on the altar, my heart slowly came to believe that He *is* completely trustworthy.

Our heavenly Father's love toward us is so great! He doesn't desire to kill our joy and spoil our fun. Joy is found *in* Him! As we understand and know God's perfect love for us, we can trust Him. His Word assures us, *"There is no fear in love, but perfect love casts out fear"* (1 John 4:18). Because of His love, He has graciously set up His commandments to protect us and save us from our own foolish choices. We don't ever need to fear following His will because it is always the best thing for our lives.

Brother Yun, a Christian leader in China who suffered many years of torture in prison, said, "We must submit ourselves to God and embrace whatever he allows to happen. Sometimes there are times of peace, other times struggle and persecution. But both are from the Lord, to mold us into vessels he wants us to be."[1]

Giving God control of every part of your life is the only life that brings glory to Him. It's as if each of us within the body of Christ is a piece of a large puzzle. None of us has the picture box to know what the puzzle is to look like, or where our individual piece fits. But God knows. *Only* as I lay my life on the altar and let Him pick up my piece of the puzzle will I ever fit in the space for which I was designed. And because I can trust His perfect will for my life, I now feel safer in God's care than anywhere else in the world!

Earlier we looked at the need to confess our sins in order to maintain unbroken fellowship with God. Because our old fleshly habits are so ingrained, we often find ourselves crawling off the altar. The moment we do, we must practice exhaling by confessing the sin and inhaling by surrendering control to Christ, once again yielding our will to Him and placing ourselves back on the altar.

How do we *stay* on the altar? By making sure that we live from the inside out, calling on the Spirit's strength to respond and to act according to God's will in all things. When tempted, I call on His strength, then choose to resist. When another man suddenly catches my eye, I call on His power to take those thoughts captive and to see marriage and infidelity through His eyes.

When I yield to God, my strong emotions give me the love, drive, and fire to serve Him. When not yielded to Him, those same emotions drive me straight *into* the fire! So as many times a day as necessary, I climb back up on the altar and give my life back to His control.

Some women bear deep scars and unhealed wounds in their lives. Only as they practice complete surrender to the Lord will these battered and broken areas receive healing. Many Christians attend endless counseling sessions, yet they never deal with the root of the problem by yielding everything in their lives to His total control and then choosing by His power to act in obedience. Christian counseling is wonderful as long as we learn to bring *everything* before Him, give *everything* to Him—our bodies, our sexuality, our dreams, our hurts, our broken hearts. We need to lay it all on the altar before Him. And though it may be frightening at first to trust the Lord like this, it is the beginning of a life transformed by His awesome power. He *is* faithful and loving, and His desire is to heal us and make us whole.

The Process May Be Slow

Someone may ask, "Does living the Spirit-controlled life mean my marriage will suddenly be easier?" Maybe, and maybe not. Choosing the Spirit-controlled life will certainly make a difference in *your* life. You will be making right choices before the Lord, maintaining a clear conscience, and pleasing Him. *You* will create fewer problems in your marriage, and the change of attitude in your life will certainly have an effect on your entire family.

Of course, your sacrificial demonstrations of Christ's Spirit won't necessarily mean that your husband automatically reciprocates. But God gives us encouragement to keep responding by His Spirit even in difficult circumstances:

> *This finds favor, if for the sake of conscience toward God a person bears up under sorrows when suffering unjustly... But if when you do what is right and suffer for it you patiently endure it, this finds favor with God. For you have been called for this purpose, since Christ also suffered for you, leaving you an example for you to follow in His steps.* (1 Peter 2:19–21)

My friend Sharon lives in the midst of a difficult marriage filled with verbal abuse. She told me that without depending on the Spirit's strength moment by moment, she would have left. But Sharon discovered that as she consistently chose to depend on the Lord, she was then far more able to respond rightly in her marriage through the power of the Spirit-controlled life. Faithfulness to God translates into faithfulness to our spouse.

For me, the process of learning to consistently live the Spirit-controlled life was a slow, moment-by-moment battle at first. Yet to know that I didn't *have* to give in to sin and that I already *had* the strength from the Lord to choose righteousness made all the difference in the world.

To help retrain my mind, I wrote Bible verses on little cards and carried them everywhere. Whenever I faced a temptation, I would pull those verses out, read them, and claim God's power over sin. Then I would draw on the strength of the Lord and choose by my will not to give in to sin. Were my *feelings* excited about this venture into holy living? Not on your life! Sometimes I would fail. But little by little, the choices got easier, and the temptations grew further apart. And my feelings, like the caboose on a train, would always catch up. Not instantaneously, but they would eventually always follow along.

Thank goodness feelings aren't sin! Jesus felt everything, but He trusted God in the midst of His feelings and chose to do the right thing. We shouldn't try to ignore our feelings or act like they don't exist. Instead, we can use them as beacons to remind us how to respond in obedience.

Always remember that *God's Word is truer than anything you feel.* His Word must be the basis for *all* our decisions. Then we can rely on His Spirit to give us strength to obey His Word. I, "The Emotional Rollercoaster Queen," am living proof that it *is* possible to be an emotional woman and still live a consistent Christian life.

You are establishing now what you want to be true of your future. Each choice you make today—whether to live by Christ's power and resist sin, or to live by your flesh and choose sin—establishes spiritual habits in your life. Just as a wise man diligently plants his crops with a view toward reaping food to eat (Proverbs 28:19), we need to make daily wise choices now that establish the spiritual habits we want for the rest of our lives.

Our Response

If you have never understood the freedom you have from the power of sin—that you don't have to choose sin anymore—why don't you stop now and thank the Lord for this incredible truth? Then take a moment and picture yourself on an altar before the Lord. By faith, give Him every part of you to do with as He knows is best. Christ loves you so much that He gave His life for your sins. You *can* trust His overflowing love and care for your life. Please take a moment and sincerely express this simple prayer of sacrifice to Him:

> Rich or poor, sick or well, dead or alive, I am completely Yours, Lord, to do with whatever You choose.

What a difference surrender to the Lord and trust in His power can make! Today, when I give testimony to my former lifestyle, people respond in amazement and tell me they have a hard time picturing me with volatile emotions. *That* is a testimony to God's transforming power! I call myself a work of grace from beginning to end because there is no doubt that *"by the grace of God I am what I am"* (1 Corinthians 15:10).

What happened to my accursed melancholy temperament? It has become a blessing! Now being able to have great breadth of feeling is such a joy! Whereas I once clenched my teeth to restrain tears of depression and frustration, I can now cry with overflowing gratefulness for my Father's kindness and mercy toward me. I often mentally picture my arms thrown around the feet of Christ in boundless love and gratitude for His transforming power.

I would urge you to begin each day by laying your life on the altar before Him. Then moment by moment choose to live from the inside out. Call upon the Holy Spirit's power, then choose to resist sin, knowing you don't have to sin anymore.

Sacrificing your life on the altar and living the Spirit-controlled life each moment are the foundation for your entire life with God. They also form the foundation from which all the following chapters in this book are built. Therefore, until you understand and begin implementing these critical aspects of the Christian life into your own daily life, I urge you to reread this chapter.

I stand as a testimony to what can so easily happen when we don't allow Christ's Spirit to control our lives *every day*. I know how easy it is to take little steps of disobedience that start the ball rolling into deeper and deeper sin. My initial baby steps of not living the Spirit-controlled life daily eventually snowballed into a hardened heart capable of leaving my precious husband! The depth of my disobedience impelled me to realize how susceptible I am to sin. That's why I cling to the Lord so desperately each day!

Yet I am also a testimony to the fact that when we do choose to give the Lord control, He pours out His blessings upon us. *"The LORD gives grace and glory; no good thing does He withhold from those who walk uprightly. O LORD of hosts, how blessed is the man who trusts in You!"* (Psalm 84:11,12).

As we face our own frailty and our need to continually draw on His strength to walk in obedience, we realize the importance of spending time with Him daily. Doing so is *key* to the Christian life. Over the years, the Lord has shown me a secret that has transformed my times in His presence. This is where it gets fun...

10

Our Desperate Need

L ike a sardine jammed tightly in a tin, I took a seat among the 18,000 college students packed into the enormous hall. This gathering shattered all records as the largest winter conference ever held for Christian college students in the United States. Excitement charged the air like an electric current as we anticipated Elisabeth Elliot's startling tale of her missionary husband's murder in Ecuador.

That night, Elisabeth Elliot challenged each of us to decide that we would be the one individual among all those thousands of students who would lay down his or her life before God to use however He chose. I desperately wanted to be that person. From that week on I earnestly began to pray, "Lord, use me to make a significant difference for the cause of Christ."

I had a long way to go! Through all the years and the mistakes, I have discovered that the *only* way I can be available for God's use is to stay in daily fellowship with Him. Consistency in my daily times with God had never been one of my strong suits. Yet this discipline is one of the *major keys* to the Christian life.

Why are these daily times in His presence and in His Word so critical? Let's look at a twofold purpose God has for our life, then the reason consistency with Him is so critical, and why we desperately need Him.

The Purpose for Our Lives

Not long after the huge Christian conference, another defining moment occurred in my life as I drove through the mountains of Colorado. I was listening to a cassette tape that dealt with the purpose of our lives. Although I had never thought about defining a purpose for my own life, I realized that having one would be a good plumb line by which to direct my future. So I prayed for God's wisdom to help me establish a purpose that would guide the rest of my life. And God directed me to claim a purpose that has stood as my lighthouse through the many years since: "To know God and to be what He wants me to be." Let's dissect that.

To Know God

One of my favorite quotes is from J. I. Packer's book *Knowing God:*

> What makes life worthwhile is having a big enough objective, something which catches our imagination and lays hold of our allegiance; and this the Christian has in a way that no other person has. For what higher, more exalted, and more compelling goal can there be than to know God?[1]

What a captivating challenge! The goal of truly knowing our immense, magnificent God makes life exciting! *"Oh, the depth of the riches both of the wisdom and knowledge of God! How unsearchable are His judgments and unfathomable His ways!"* (Romans 11:33). But does knowing God really make any difference in our daily life? All the difference in the world!

Dr. Bill Bright writes:

> Our view of God determines everything we do: our lifestyle, the friends we gather around us, the literature we read, the music we enjoy. Everything is determined by our view of God. So study, meditate on, and memorize the attributes of God. We must know and understand who God is—our Creator God and Savior, a God of love, a God of grace, a God of power, a God of wisdom and compassion.[2]

We must have a *biblical* view of God because if we believe God is so loving and compassionate that He will overlook sin, then we will be permissive toward sin and encourage others to join us. On the other extreme, if we believe God is just and righteous and ignore His grace and mercy, then we will falter toward legalism, executing judgment on others as well.

Of course, we can't truly know God without spending time with Him in His Word. It's like dating. Spending hours with that other person is how you get to know him. I know Stottler well because of all the time we've spent together. Often I find myself declaring, "I knew you were going to say that!" because I even know his thoughts. Similarly, we can know the mind of the Lord only by spending time in the Word of the Lord. And the joy of getting to know our awesome God is unending!

To Be What He Wants Me to Be

It is equally imperative *to be what God wants me to be*. Christ is not just part of my life—He *is* my life. Growing in the Lord is not just learning about Him, but it is becoming more like Him in all I think and say and do.

Remember the transformer toys? They start out looking like one thing, but when reshaped, they transform into something that looks and acts entirely different. We too can be transformed from the self-centered, proud women we are into women who radiate the attributes of God. Romans 12:2 gives us "the formula":

> *Do not be conformed to this world, but be transformed **by the renewing of your mind**, so that you may prove what the will of God is, that which is good and acceptable and perfect* (emphasis added).

If we renew our minds daily in the Word of God and in prayer, we will be transformed into women who radiate the Lord, who show love and respect to our husbands, and who live consistent godly lives before others.

But these qualities cannot happen if we don't renew our minds daily because God's ways are completely upside down from ours. He says, *"My thoughts are not your thoughts, nor are your ways My ways"* (Isaiah 55:8). For example, we may consider people with power and position more important, so we treat them with special deference. But God says that the lowly, the weak, and the servant are the exalted ones. The little forgotten widow who spends her days praying, not the self-indulgent movie star, will be the honored guest at Christ's banquet. We spend hours in the gym each week and hundreds of dollars on clothes each year to improve our outward appearance. God says that although bodily discipline is necessary, it is of little value compared to spiritual discipline.[3] God's work within us lasts through this life *and* the life to come.

In his commentary on the book of Romans, John Stott said that we can either look like the world or like Christ—those are the only two options. These two value systems are so incompatible with one another "that there is no possibility of compromise." Only a mind transformed by Christ can discern and "determine to obey God's will."[4]

How desperately we need His perspective on life! Day after day I'll enter into my time with Him tired and grumpy and come out with a new attitude of peace, joy, and motivation. It's like turning my eyes inside out! But it happens only when I spend time in His presence.

Getting alone with God each day is the only way for us to become the wives we are called to be. God tells us that *"a prudent wife is from the Lord"* (Proverbs 19:14). A prudent wife—one who exercises sound judgment, is not rash, knows how to control her tongue, and maintains pure thoughts—is definitely from the Lord because *only* God can bring about those qualities! That's why we need His transforming work within us each day.

> *If your relationship with God isn't right, then all of your other relationships will be out of sync— especially the one closest to you.*

When we spend daily time in God's presence, the difference is astronomical! Just ask Stottler. During my quiet time, God realigns my perspective with His, rearranges my priorities, gives me a God-centered love instead of my naturally selfish love, makes me teachable where I'm hurting or annoying my husband or others, fulfills my deepest longings for love and security in Christ, and gives me grace to deal with the hard times. Any husband would notice those changes, whether he says so or not!

Therefore, daily time with the Lord is the first step in solving any marital problems or in keeping a marriage strong. But if your relationship with God isn't right, then all of your other relationships will be out of sync—especially the one closest to you.

Spending daily time with God doesn't mean that all of your marital problems will be solved. But it does mean that as you draw on His strength to walk in obedience, *you* are pleasing to the Lord. And if you find yourself in a difficult marriage where your spouse refuses to seek the Lord or to change, you can know that

God will reward *your* obedience as you walk in daily fellowship with Him.

Consistent vs. Inconsistent

As a frazzled wife and mother, do you need joy and encouragement? Do you need the strength to persevere? For a busy mother competing for "Supermom of the World," everything can crowd out her few moments with the Lord—until suddenly she finds herself empty and needy. God tells us that in reading His Word we find the strength and hope we so desperately need.[5]

Do you need stability? Do you succumb to mood swings like the pendulum on a clock? Isaiah writes, *"He will be the stability of your times, a wealth of salvation, wisdom and knowledge"* (Isaiah 33:6). By spending consistent time with the Lord through Bible reading and prayer, we develop a stable foundation that carries us through even when our emotions rise and fall like an elevator in a skyscraper. The longer we practice walking daily with Him, the more consistent and stable our emotions become. I'm living proof of that!

Each time we stop allowing the Holy Spirit to renew and transform us, we remove ourselves from His protection. And make no mistake—the battle is more difficult than we can imagine. Paul writes, *"Our struggle is not against flesh and blood, but against the rulers, against the powers, against the world forces of this darkness, against the spiritual forces of wickedness in the heavenly places"* (Ephesians 6:12).

When we don't meet with the Lord each day, we become spiritually hardened and insensitive. Soon we've built a brick wall between God and us by one poor choice after another. Instead of renewing our minds with God's truth, we fill them with TV programs and conversations that dull our sensitivity to God. We've seen so many programs about women having affairs that adultery doesn't seem so bad anymore. Pretty soon we become insensitive to warning signs in our own marriage because we are numb toward God. Then one day, along comes a guy who is kind and genuinely caring. Before you know it, this man will own your heart and you're headed for an affair and a divorce.

Before I realized how desperately I needed the Lord each day, my times with Him were fairly inconsistent. Therefore, I was blindsided when I arrived in the Caribbean. My defenses were down; my heart was insensitive to the Spirit; and I was a sitting duck for destruction.

But since then, having experienced years of consistent daily time in His presence, I've found that His Word and intimate fellowship truly have done a transforming work in my life. Almost every day God changes my perspective, and I leave the room a different person.

We had a saying in music school that if you skipped practicing your instrument one day, you could tell the difference. If you skipped practicing two days, the other musicians could tell it. And if you skipped practicing three days in a row, *everyone* could tell the difference. When I miss spending time with the Lord for one day, I can tell that I'm just not as sensitive and quick to respond to the prompting of the Holy Spirit. When I skip two days, Stottler notices. And when I skip three days, I'm sure that everyone around me can tell the difference!

Every single time that I spend daily time with the Lord, I grow in leaps and bounds spiritually. The fruit of the Spirit automatically starts blooming (Galatians 5:22,23). And every single time I would stop spending consistent time with God, I would fall into some type of sin.

We need God every single day! To choose not to meet with the Lord is actually to say, "Today I think I'll do just fine on my own. I don't really need Christ's work in me to change my perspective, to remold my heart, to guard my lips, or to direct my thoughts."

In addition, we never know when God may call upon us to make a significant difference in others' lives. If we are out of close daily fellowship with Him, we can easily disqualify ourselves from the privilege of serving Him in some life-defining moment. Pastor Jack Graham, elaborating on the words of Winston Churchill, said, "To each, there comes in their lifetime a special moment when they are figuratively tapped on the shoulder and offered the chance to do a very special thing, unique to them and fitted to their talents. What a tragedy if that moment finds them unprepared and unqualified for that which could have been their finest hour."[6] I don't want to miss that special moment to be used by the Lord simply because I'm out of fellowship with Him!

We are the "instant" generation. However, there are absolutely no instant ways to mature in Christ. Spiritual growth has no shortcuts.

Eric Liddell, portrayed in the movie *Chariots of Fire*, suddenly faced a choice of whether or not to run in an Olympic race on a Sunday. His decision to remain true to his convictions and not to compromise, regardless of enormous pressure, made an impact in history that continues to this day. That was his moment.

Because of Stottler's close daily walk with the Lord, he felt the Spirit prompting him several times to visit a friend. In obedience, he dropped by his friend's home each time, only later to be told that at the moment of both his visits, his friend had been contemplating suicide. Those were Stottler's moments.

Anything worth having requires work. Knowing God and knowing how to live victoriously over sin and temptation are definitely worth the effort. But we are the "instant" generation. The microwave is too slow. The computer is too slow. God didn't answer my question when I prayed once, so God is too slow. However, there are absolutely no instant ways to mature in Christ. Spiritual growth has no shortcuts.

Meeting with God each day doesn't come naturally. How many mornings do we wake up and say, "My, my, I have nothing to do today; I think I'll just sit and read my Bible and pray for an hour"? Right. Even though I love the Bible topic I am currently studying, many mornings I feel tired or pushed for time, and frankly I'd rather skip my quiet time and get on with my business. But I know what happens to my life if I don't spend time in God's presence daily. It is the *most* important thing I do every day.

Our Desperate Need

Spending time with God daily *sounds* so simple—yet how difficult it is to actually do! We *want* to spend time with God; we *mean* to have a quiet time each day; we *plan* to meet with the Lord— but it just doesn't happen consistently.

After asking Christ into my life at age thirteen, I received some solid spiritual training. I learned the importance of daily times with the Lord and really wanted to consistently spend time with Him. But it just never quite seemed to happen on a regular basis.

I *would*, however, practice my oboe without fail three to five hours a day. Throughout high school and college I knew that my goal of being principal oboist of every ensemble required hours of practice in order to improve my performing abilities. I found time for oboe practice because I was highly motivated to see my performing skills transformed. But I had no such motivation to make time for the Lord because I didn't understand how desperately my *life* needed to be transformed by Him.

God had to let me get to the point of almost leaving my husband before I realized the true depth of my fallen nature. I knew in my head that I could commit any sin in the book, yet in my heart I didn't believe that *I* could be capable of marital infidelity.

No way! I'm in full-time Christian work! It was only when I confronted the depth to which I could so quickly fall that He showed me two truths in His Word that have formed my motivation for lifelong consistent times with Him ever since.

If you struggle with having consistent times with the Lord—which is true for the vast majority of Christians—then I would suggest that the following two essential elements are missing in your heart. I am convinced that unless we believe these principles, we will always struggle with spending consistent time with God.

No Good Besides You

David writes in Psalm 16:2, *"I said to the LORD, 'You are my Lord; apart from you I have **no good thing**'"* (NIV, emphasis added). Do you believe that about your life? Do you truly believe that apart from the Holy Spirit inside you and the grace of God at work in your life, there is *not one good thing* within your flesh (mind, will, emotions)? It's true! Although we now have Christ's Spirit living within us, our old corrupted flesh still desires to pull us down every moment.

With divorce as rampant among believers as unbelievers,[7] we see how easy it is for us to hinder Christ's transforming work within us. When we don't yield every aspect of our life to the Lord daily, our lives reap the fruit of anger, selfishness, conceit, a judgmental attitude, the desire to control, jealousy, and on and on.

Romans 3:10–18 clearly teaches us that apart from Christ, we have *no* righteousness. In fact, we don't even desire righteousness apart from Him! The godly apostle Paul looked at his own life and said, *"I know that nothing good dwells in me, that is, in my flesh"* (Romans 7:18). Apart from the Spirit of Christ, we have no good thing within us.

We can't take credit for one good thing in our lives (James 1:17). *God* chose us; *He* gave us the desire to know Him; *He* gave us the faith to trust Christ; *He* gave us new life; *He* transforms us as we yield to Him; and *He* even gives us the desire to yield in the first place. We can't do any of those things. *Nothing* good comes from our own nature.

I used to read Bible stories and say to myself, "I can't believe those people in Jerusalem turned against Christ and demanded His crucifixion." Or, "I can't believe that Ananias and Sapphira lied to the apostles." Or, "I can't believe David committed adultery with Bathsheba and even had her husband killed."[8]

However, when I read passages like that now, I say, "That's *me!* Without Christ transforming my heart each day, I would do the very same things!" That realization drives me to come daily into His presence to be transformed from the old patterns of my fallen flesh into the new patterns of Christ's life lived through me.

Our adversary, the devil, will go to great lengths to dupe us into feeling comfortable and complacent in our spiritual life. He *never* wants us to realize that our fallen flesh is *completely* fallen. Then we might become desperate and begin to yield our life daily to God for His strength! But as long as we don't realize our dire need for God, we will go day after day depending on ourselves, becoming hardened to His Spirit, primed and ready to slide into sin.

Apart from You I Can Do Nothing

The second truth about having consistent times with God is found in John 15:5. Jesus tells us, *"I am the vine, you are the branches; he who abides in Me and I in him, he bears much fruit, for **apart from Me you can do nothing**"* (emphasis added).

Perhaps you're thinking, "What do you mean I can do nothing? I can get up out of this chair, slam this book down, and stalk out of this room. Just watch me!"

Yes, that's true. You can do that, but unless you are yielded to Christ and obey Him by the power of the Holy Spirit, your actions will have no value to the Lord. Apart from Christ working through you, you can do nothing of eternal value for God.

If we cut ourselves off from the work of God's Spirit, then we lose the flow of His strength. It's like water running through a hose. The source of the water comes through the spigot. When the valve is opened, the water flows freely. But once the spigot is shut, the source is cut off and the water ceases to flow.

In the same way, if we choose to live by our own power, we cut off Christ's flow through us. Yes, we can still do "things," but they will have no spiritual power, and therefore count nothing for eternity. Only Christ's Spirit working through us can accomplish that which has eternal value.

God doesn't call us to "get our act together" and *then* come meet with Him. In fact, if you think you've got it all together, you *won't* come to Him because you don't see your need. He calls us in our frailty because it's only when we recognize our weaknesses (and are we ever weak!) that we depend on Him. Jesus says to us: *"My grace is sufficient for you, for my power is made perfect in weakness"* (2 Corinthians 12:9, NIV).

Joni Eareckson Tada became a paraplegic in a diving accident when she was only seventeen years old. At a recent conference, she spoke about what it feels like to wake up each morning paralyzed and helpless. She needs others to move her out of bed, to help her bathe and dress, and to enable her to accomplish even simple daily routines. Joni said that about 75 percent of the time she wakes up with her body hurting, her emotions low, and feeling completely dependent on the Lord for even a smile.

Joni is confronted every moment with her utter dependence on God. Yet she went on to say that maybe she's not really the handicapped one. Possibly it's the self-sufficient person who jumps out of bed when the alarm rings, downs a quick cup of coffee, takes a fast shower, gives God a ten minute nod, then rushes out the door to work. From God's perspective, which person is truly "handicapped"?[9]

Sometimes it isn't until we bury ourselves so deeply in problems and reach the end of ourselves that we will finally look up and realize how fallen we are apart from Him and how we can do nothing of eternal value apart from His Spirit. Hopefully, then we will understand how critical it is to stay humble and dependent on the Lord every day.

When I returned home from the Caribbean, for the first time in my life I clearly saw the depths to which my fallen flesh could quickly drag me. It made me fear what I was capable of doing and drove me to the Lord each day. And fearing what we can rapidly become when cut off from the transforming power of the Lord is a *good* thing. *"How blessed is the man who fears always, but he who hardens his heart will fall into calamity"* (Proverbs 28:14).

If I don't wake up each day and say, "There is no way I can be kind to my husband today, or be patient and loving with my children, or say the right things to anyone, or be motivated and disciplined without the power of Christ working through me," then I haven't come to realize my desperate need for Christ to work through me. God says, *"Blessed are the poor in spirit, for theirs is the kingdom of heaven"* (Matthew 5:3). Only when I realize my spiritual poverty and how needy I truly am for *His* power and grace will I daily, hourly cling to Him.

So first, I realize that I have no good in me apart from Christ (Psalm 16:2). Then I recognize that apart from Christ I can do nothing of eternal value (John 15:5). How, then, do I inscribe these truths on my heart so that they drive me to the Lord in utter dependence each day?

First, spend time praying over the following Scripture passages that address who we are apart from Christ. Ask God to make them real for *your* life.

Psalm 16:2; John 15:5; Romans 7:18; Jeremiah 17:5–9; Proverbs 28:26; Galatians 5:16,17; 6:8; Proverbs 3:5–8; Matthew 26:41; Galatians 3:3; Romans 13:14

Second, ask God to show you what you are like apart from His transforming work. You will be appalled at what spews forth from your life!

Since my experience in the Caribbean, no one has to remind me to come before the Lord each day. No one needs to remind me that apart from Christ I have nothing good within me and am incapable of doing anything of eternal value. I am very aware of how desperately I need Jesus—and that's a great place to be! I echo the verse from the hymn "Come, Thou Fount of Every Blessing":

O to grace how great a debtor daily I'm constrained to be!
Let Thy goodness, like a fetter, bind my wandering heart to Thee.
Prone to wander, Lord, I feel it, prone to leave the God I love;
Here's my heart, O take and seal it, seal it for Thy courts above.[10]

If these truths don't seem real in your life, ask God to implant them in your heart before you read further. I urge you to memorize Psalm 16:2 and John 15:5, as well as any of the verses above that speak to your heart. Your times with the Lord will remain a struggle if these truths are not etched on your heart. But once your heart has grasped them and you begin spending consistent time with the God of all creation, you will start to experience a depth of transformation in your life that you never even dreamed possible!

11

Our Time in God's Word

A s I sat in the Bangkok airport awaiting my next flight, I watched a 747 roll to a stop outside the plate glass windows. Passengers streamed from the enormous jet and began filing up a nearby escalator. As Americans, Europeans, Asians, and Africans paraded before me, I thought about each person's personal micro-world, laced with hundreds of interwoven lives and events. Just one individual's decisions can ripple across hundreds of other lives, affecting countless people in often unseen ways. And God is sovereign over every one of them.

Awe enveloped me as I considered how God knows each individual hair on every head passing in front of me. He knows every friend, every family member, every acquaintance in each one's life. He knows each event in every day they have lived and are yet to live. He knows what they dream for and what they fear. He knows the secrets that each one harbors. Yet at the same time, He holds every far-flung star and galaxy in its place.

What an amazing Being! *"You know when I sit down and when I rise up; You understand my thought from afar... Even before there is a word on my tongue, behold, O LORD, You know it all"*

(Psalm 139:2,4). *"Great is the LORD, and highly to be praised, and His greatness is unsearchable"* (Psalm 145:3). How unfathomably vast and yet how intimately involved He is!

That is the God I get to meet with every day! He is awesome in majesty and splendor, yet intimate in love and tenderness. He knows every microbe in my being, every thought and dream, every consequence of every action. And He loves to talk with me and guide me by His Spirit and His living Word. What a privilege to know Him!

As we set sail on the remarkable journey of getting to know Him each day, we will look at three aspects of our time with God. In these next several chapters we will explore in-depth how time in the Bible, time in prayer, and our response of obedience all work together in transforming our lives. In this chapter, we'll begin by looking at ideas that make us yearn to dig into His Word, the effects of the Word on our lives, and how we can find time to meet with the Lord daily.

God's Amazing Word

The Bible stands as a unique gift from God to us. Nothing comparable exists in all the world. It remains the most important book ever written. The Bible is a compilation of 66 books written over a period of approximately 1,500 years by more than 40 authors from diverse educational backgrounds. The authors wrote in a wide variety of locations and differing cultures, in three languages, covering an assortment of controversial subjects.

In his book about the Bible, Don Stewart writes: "One would expect that the result of such diversity would be a hodge-podge of contradictory literature, a chaotic text, full of contradictions and distortions. We see the wonder of the Bible in that it is completely consistent, coherent and trustworthy. None of the authors or books is either internally, of themselves, or externally contradictory. The Bible's remarkable unity, its continually unfolding story of redemption, is a true wonder."[1] Only *God* could do that!

In the Bible, we actually encounter God Himself! His words are not some dead novel or lifeless story. The Bible is an extension of God, alive and active (Hebrews 4:12), working in our hearts (1 Thessalonians 2:13), accomplishing His purposes (Isaiah 55:10, 11). His Word is written for us to know Him, to love Him, and to call on His strength and power for resisting every temptation.

As we've talked about, the goal of our lives as believers is twofold: to know God (Jeremiah 9:24) and to be transformed to be more like Christ (Romans 12:2). The Bible remains indispensable for both of these objectives. We can find no substitute for knowing God's amazing words. Christian author Andrew Murray says, "There can be only so much faith as there is of the Living Word dwelling in the soul."[2]

Yet author and speaker Henry Blackaby observes, "We don't take the Scriptures seriously. I think this generation knows less about Scripture than any generation in my lifetime. We're reading the books of men, but not the book of God."[3] A Barna survey recently revealed that while 85 percent of the Christians surveyed stated a belief that the Bible's teachings are "totally accurate," significant numbers of those same people held beliefs contrary to Scripture on specific issues.[4] We need to know the Word!

The Effect of God's Word in Our Lives

As we incorporate God's truth into our lives, we can stand on the fact that because His Word is an extension of Himself, the Bible will never, never, never lead us astray. *"There is no wisdom and no understanding and no counsel against the LORD"* (Proverbs 21:30). God is *always* right, and therefore, to follow His wisdom is *always* right. *"Many plans are in a man's heart, but the counsel of the*

LORD *will stand"* (Proverbs 19:21). The following are some practical steps that have helped me keep God's Word alive in my life.

Believe His Word

Because God is always right, it is therefore important that we not doubt or disbelieve His Word. The Bible says, *"Take care, brethren, that there not be in any one of you an evil, unbelieving heart that falls away from the living God"* (Hebrews 3:12). When we doubt God's Word, it can lead to a hard heart that causes us to snowball into ever-increasing sin.

When joining the ministry with which I work, I developed a close friendship with another woman also joining our staff. We attended Bible classes together, roomed together, prayed together, and played together. Then after several years with the ministry, she met a wonderful man, fell in love, married, and left our staff.

Because we can believe God's Word, that also means we can trust it when life's circumstances seem confusing.

I visited them several times, but after a few years I began to sense that something was wrong. In hindsight, I should have seen the signs. She began to argue that world events disproved God's love and kindness. She began doubting the Word because she saw things around her that didn't seem to fit. Within a few short years, she had divorced her husband and moved into a lesbian relationship.

Can we never question God's actions? God gave us minds with which to think, reason, and learn. However, we should always approach His Word as being the *final authority*, realizing we don't have full knowledge or understanding of eternity. We should analyze situations based on God's Word, rather than attempting to determine the truth of God's Word based on our limited perception.

Trust His Word

Because we can believe God's Word, that also means we can trust it when life's circumstances seem confusing. Remember the evening church service when I learned for the first time that as a believer the power of sin within me was broken? The speaker that night was Del Fehsenfeld, founder and director of a revival ministry called Life Action Ministries. God used Del and his organization to transform my spiritual life. I became friends with Del, and his teaching continues to impact my life to this day.

Sadly, not long after that meeting Del was stricken with a fast-growing brain tumor, and within about a year, he went home to be with the Lord. I was devastated. It didn't make sense. How could the Lord remove such a godly man who was making an enormous impact in churches throughout the United States? Del also left behind a wife and six young children. God's actions seemed unreasonable and cruel.

As I wept and prayed, God brought to mind Psalm 145:17: *"The LORD is righteous in all His ways and kind in all His deeds."* Well, *this* certainly didn't appear to be a righteous act, and it *definitely* didn't feel kind. A major dividing line confronted me. Either God's Word was completely true and I couldn't understand all His ways yet, or His Word was completely false and everything I believed was a lie. There could be no in-between, and I could not live the rest of my life without making a choice.

So although my emotions rebelled, I chose to believe by faith that even though I couldn't understand God's actions, somehow they were righteous and kind because His Word is always true. In my lifetime, I will never know all the reasons why God chose to take Del home. But I *can* know that His Word is always true, and therefore whatever He chooses to do in our lives is kind and right. My choice that day was not based on feelings or on circumstances, but on the trustworthiness of God and His Word. As

Isaiah says, *"The grass withers, the flower fades, but the word of our God stands forever"* (40:8).

Let His Word Affect Every Issue in Your Life

God's amazing Word addresses *every issue* in our lives. His unsearchable wisdom that founded the universe and holds it all together is the same wisdom available to us in the Scriptures (Proverbs 3:19,20; 8:22–31). And just as His wisdom brought order to the entire universe, so it can bring order to our lives as well.

Does this mean that reading the Bible will solve all of your troubles? Absolutely not. However, it *does* mean that as you grow in understanding God, trusting Him, and living by the Master's design, you will create far fewer problems in your own life. My time in the Word affects my marriage every day. My time in the Word affects my relationships with others every day. My time in the Word affects my work every day. My time in the Word gives me godly wisdom for handling problems and temptations every day. Time in the Word affects *everything!*

The impure thoughts had simply disappeared! God's Word so filled my mind that no room remained for impurity.

The problem is that we have relegated God and the effects of His Word to a small slot in our lives. We need to put God's Word into our daily world as a part of absolutely *everything* we do. Do I choose what movies I will or will not see based on what God says about perversion, or do I watch whatever catches my interest? Do I take seriously what God says about responding in love even when my husband has said something hurtful, or do I justify my retaliation? Is God's Word the basis for *every* decision I make? If not, I have developed a worldview based on a god of convenience, not on the God of the Bible who calls me to be holy as He is holy (1 Peter 1:16).

Let His Word Transform Your Life

Chinese pastor Brother Yun says, "You can never really know the Scriptures until you're willing to be changed by them."[5] I have witnessed repeatedly the transforming work of God's Word in my life.

At one point after college I experienced a time of intense struggle against impure thoughts. Because my times with the Lord were still inconsistent, I determined to spend an hour with Him every day, rain or shine. Within a few months, without any conscious attempt at refocusing my thoughts, I discovered that the impure thoughts had simply disappeared! God's Word so filled my mind that no room remained for impurity.

As we read His Word, God exposes where our mind, will, and emotions have rebelled against the Spirit. Then we are able to confess and once again yield our lives to the Spirit's control. I pray that *nothing* in my life opposes God's Word. Anything outside of His will only hurts me. So as strange as it may sound, I love the convicting work of the Holy Spirit. Although it hurts for the moment as I crucify my pride, confess my sin, and again lay my life back on His altar, the results are for my benefit and His glory.

When we discipline a child, we know it is unpleasant for the moment. But we see beyond that moment and know the long-lasting benefits if the child chooses to learn the lesson. In the same way, we can't see the future, but *God* can. If we obey and follow His wisdom, it *always* benefits our lives. As Scripture explains, *"He disciplines us for our good, so that we may share His holiness. All discipline for the moment seems not to be joyful, but sorrowful; yet to those who have been trained by it, afterwards it yields the peaceful fruit of righteousness"* (Hebrews 12:10,11).

Value His Word Above All

What would you really love to have in life: a great house, ideal children, the perfect career, a kind and loving husband? God says to value the wisdom of His Word above all these things. *"How blessed is the man who finds wisdom and the man who gains understanding. For her profit is better than the profit of silver and her gain better than fine gold. She is more precious than jewels; and **nothing** you desire compares with her"* (Proverbs 3:13–15, emphasis added).

Why is His wisdom so valuable? Because just as our bodies start to wither and malfunction if not fed properly, so our souls wither and stray into sin without God's living Word. His wisdom is the food of our souls (Proverbs 24:13,14). Do you value His Word above all?

What to Study

We have seen the invaluable work His Word performs in our lives; therefore, we need to begin regularly studying the Bible. But because of past experiences or due to our fallen nature, many of us may think that Bible reading sounds almost as enjoyable as doing the laundry. However, since I changed the way I approach my time in the Word, my daily Bible study is actually *fun*.

Here are a few suggestions that have made such a difference in my daily times.

Study What Interests You

Through the years I've been exposed to various Bible study methods. One involves analyzing a passage of Scripture by asking questions such as: Where did the action happen? Who did it? When did it take place? That's a great Bible study; however, when I tried it, I drowned in all the details and became overwhelmed. When I couldn't find an answer to one of the questions, I'd get frustrated and lose sight of the big picture. Then I'd quit.

On the other hand, I discovered that when I study a topic that interests me—some area about which I'm already curious or a subject that addresses a current need—I'm far more likely to stick with it. What *does* the Bible say about marriage? What *is* God's attitude toward my anger? What *is* God's description of heaven?

Recently, my friend Lisa told me of a Scripture-reading method that her husband had learned at a men's retreat. Each morning he would spend an hour praying through an outline of various Scriptures. Lisa decided to try it as well. But because she hadn't attended the retreat or heard the speaker, that particular study didn't mean to her what it did to her husband. Soon she felt bogged down, and in a matter of days she began skipping her times with the Lord. When we met together, I urged her to do what *she* found interesting. That made all the difference.

Study the Attributes of God

Someone once asked Bill Bright what he would study in the Bible if he were limited to only one thing. Without hesitation, he replied that the most important thing anyone could study would be the attributes of God, because what we believe about God determines what we think and do in every other facet of our lives. A. W. Tozer said, "What comes into our minds when we think about God is the most important thing about us."[6]

When I first heard about the importance of studying God's attributes, it instantly caught my interest. I knew that my "picture" of God was flawed and inaccurate. Since the first part of my life's purpose was "to know God," I decided to make Him my lifelong study.

Numerous wonderful books deal with God's attributes, and several are listed in the Resources. Over the years I have read quite a few, looking up every Scripture reference and memorizing many verses. Changing my perception of who God is according to His Word has changed my entire life. The area of trust, which was previously a very weak area indeed, has now become a strength! I now eagerly trust Him with every aspect of my life—rich or poor, sick or well, dead or alive.

I strongly recommend studying God's attributes. Growing in my understanding of who God is has certainly affected my daily times with Him. If I had not laid the initial groundwork of knowing Him, my quiet times would have become routine and dull.

Study a Particular Book or Read Through the Bible

Early in my Christian walk, someone mentioned a story from the Old Testament that I hadn't heard of before. I didn't want that to happen again, so I began reading through the Bible several years in a row. Not only did I gain a more thorough knowledge of the Word, but this also gave me a clearer picture of God's eternal plan.

Sometimes I feel the need to better understand a certain book of the Bible. Hebrews and Revelation have been my two latest "victims." When studying a particular book, I like to use a commentary, reading it along with the Word and writing down my thoughts.

Study a Certain Topic

We constantly confront difficult issues, either in our own lives or in the lives of others close to us. Years ago when I first encountered a friend considering an abortion, my understanding of this issue from God's perspective was fuzzy. To be His faithful representative, I needed to know what *He* said about the beginning of life. Issues like this drive me to the Word so that I can understand how to respond in truth and love.

When I choose to study a particular topic, like abortion, I first look in an exhaustive concordance for key words (like "life" or "birth") and make a list of each verse reference. Then I look them up in the Bible and write out the verses that apply. I find that as I'm writing a verse by hand, it slows me down so that I ponder each word or thought. I'll also see if each verse has any cross-references listed in my Bible. And once I've completed the topical study, I file it so I can refer back to it at any time.

There are endless possibilities for studying the Bible. Other ideas might be:

- Joining a Bible study like Precept Bible Studies or Bible Study Fellowship

- Doing a word study on a particular attitude, such as forgiveness, lust, or love

- Studying the life of an individual in the Bible, such as David, Daniel, or Elizabeth

- Using a daily Bible devotional, like *My Utmost for His Highest* (but make sure you spend time reading the *Bible*)

Be creative! If studying the migratory pattern of the birds of the Bible gets you into the Word, go for it!

We must also remember the importance of being part of a local church body that believes and teaches the Bible. God reminds us to *"not give up meeting together, as some are in the habit of doing"* (Hebrews 10:25, NIV) so that we are not led astray in our understanding of God's Word.

How to Study

Different ways of approaching the Bible and various study tools have made a big difference in what I learn from my time in the Word. The following have helped me greatly.

Decide on a Place for Your Quiet Time

The place you meet with the Lord is very important. It's not called a "quiet time" because it's in the middle of a soccer game! To move into God's presence, we need to eliminate distractions around us so that we can enter into the spiritual realm and approach the throne of God.

There is a realm of being in the presence of God that I believe we cannot experience with our eyes open. It is a realm beyond the limits of this physical universe, and as long as our eyes are open, we are limited and distracted by what we see and sense. Praying on a treadmill or memorizing Scripture while on a walk are wonderful additions to our personal time with Him, but nothing replaces that depth of intimacy that comes from shutting out the world and entering into the presence of His glory, His love, and His majesty. I *need* His deep internal transforming work that comes only when I meet intimately with Him, listening for His conviction and His will.

Our houses are active, noisy places. Is it possible to find a place where your children and husband won't disturb you? Maybe the laundry room? A closet? I've used the bathroom in many hotels. I've worn earplugs at the office when I couldn't get away from the chatter around me. The goal is to have undistracted time in the Lord's presence.

Begin with Prayer

When I sit down to begin my time with the Lord, the first thing I do is to briefly ask the Holy Spirit to *"open my eyes, that I may behold wonderful things from Your law"* (Psalm 119:18). His ways are so different from my ways that I need His Spirit to give me understanding (Isaiah 55:8,9). Since I began praying Psalm 119:18 before reading the Bible, I have seen a marked difference in what I glean from God's Word.

Read the Bible

After reading Psalm 119:18, I open God's Word. I've found that just as worship music in a church service softens and readies my heart to hear from the Lord, my time reading the Word of God softens and prepares my heart to hear from Him in prayer (which we'll cover in the next chapter). Since I don't necessarily wake up singing and rejoicing every morning, I usually need all the "soul softener" I can get! So I start by letting His Word soften my spirit.

Use Bible Study Tools

Listed in the Resources are reference tools that might be of help as you delve into your study. I find an exhaustive concordance to be invaluable. And unless you are a trained theologian, I recommend reading from a study Bible. It is helpful to have comments about a puzzling Scripture on the same page as the verse you are reading.

Take Notes

Whatever Bible reading or studying I am doing, I keep a pad of paper beside me. When a verse speaks to my heart, I write down my thoughts. Writing helps me articulate what the Lord has shown me and also helps cement the verse's impact on my heart and mind.

For instance, when I read the story in Genesis 8 about Noah waiting to leave the ark, I wrote: "Here sat Noah, having been in the ark for ten and a half months. He looks out and sees that the earth is dry, yet he waits almost two months more for *God* to tell him to leave the ark. Noah didn't just rush out, even though from his perspective it looked fine. He waited for *God*." Since writing that, I have never forgotten this illustration of waiting on the Lord.

When distracting thoughts pop into my head while I'm reading the Bible, I quickly jot them down so that I can return to my study. If I simply try to remember them, they remain a constant distraction. But if I just write them down quickly, I can then re-focus on the Word. And if my mind continues to trot all over the globe, I'll briefly stop, pray, and ask the Lord to help me focus. He loves for us to depend on Him for everything.

Say the Verses in Your Own Words

I have discovered that another good practice when reading the Bible is to put into my own words what I've just read. This challenges me to see if I truly understand what I have read, and it also buries the Word more deeply into my life.

Memorize Verses

King David provided us with some important insight when he wrote, *"I have hidden your word in my heart that I might not sin against you"* (Psalm 119:11, NIV). God tells us to *"treasure my commandments within you...Write them on the tablet of your heart"* (Proverbs 7:1,3). When we keep the Word of God outside our lives, it often doesn't permeate our daily choices and actions. But as we memorize and internalize it, then His Word becomes part of us, ready to help us confront questions and temptations (Proverbs 22:17–21).

> *As we memorize and internalize it, His Word becomes part of us, ready to help us confront questions and temptations.*

I realize that the mere suggestion of memorizing anything can throw many people into an instant panic. "I can't even remember my children's names! How on earth can I memorize Scripture?"

Maybe it isn't quite as difficult as we try to make it. We all read whatever appears in front of us. For example, who doesn't read the bumper sticker on the car sitting at the stoplight in front of her? I have a bumper sticker on the back of my car that people constantly pull up close to read.[7]

Similarly, when I read a verse that impacts my life, I simply write it on the back of an old business card and tape it on our study desk. Then every time I sit down, my eyes automatically read it. We women typically spend a lot of time in front of the mirror each day. That's a good place to put your memory verse because you can't help seeing it. Then each day during my quiet time I pray the verse back to the Lord, thanking Him for how it is working in my life. Without any great effort, I have memorized that verse within a week or so. Of course, I need to review it periodically.

There are many memory techniques available at Christian bookstores. Use the one that works best for you. The important thing is to get the Word inside of you.

Apply the Scripture Lessons to Yourself

When reading the Scriptures, I can be tempted to apply them to others. "Wow, that verse is talking about my brother! *He* needs to read this!" Instead, I need to look at how it applies to *me*. The truth is, when I am quick to point out a problem in someone else, it almost always reveals that same problem area in my own life. My criticism of others actually opens a window to see into my own soul, *"for you who judge practice the same things"* (Romans 2:1). So when you find a verse that reminds you of someone else, first ask the Lord if it applies to you.

How Do I Find the Time?

All this may sound really good—to study something that interests you and then watch the Word convict you and mold your life. But how does a busy mom possibly find the time? With an infant crying at all hours, preschoolers needing to be dressed and fed, carpools to run, office work, housework, meals to prepare, and time with your husband—not to mention laundry, groceries, shopping, and the five hundred other tasks that fall under the job description of Wife and Mother—a daily quiet time seems impossible. But don't despair before you start! It *is* possible to spend daily time with God.

Consider this: One afternoon you receive a phone call informing you of a random drawing in which you have been selected to receive ten million dollars *if* you do one thing. To win the money, you must watch an uninterrupted hour of television, the program of your choice, every single day for a year.

God will make a way for us to be in His presence if we truly seek it. He yearns to meet with us more than we can imagine!

Do you think you would find time to watch TV? You'd better believe it! You would plan your entire day around that hour, jealously guarding that time. When you went on vacation, you'd make sure the portable TV came along too. If you flew overseas, you'd find a way to divide your flight so you could stop and watch television.

And don't you think your family would understand the importance of your uninterrupted hour in front of the television each day? Of course they would! In fact, they'd help you do it: "Everybody quiet! Mom's watching TV! Lock the front door! Don't answer the phone!"

Would your husband understand your need to watch TV? Absolutely! He would even volunteer to take care of the kids for that hour. "Mommy needs to watch TV now so we can afford your college education and can always have groceries and a nice house."

You and your family would make these enormous efforts because you would all see the value of receiving ten million dollars. We always find time for what we *really* want to do.

But God offers us something *vastly* more valuable than all the money in the world! He offers a changed life full of godliness, peace, contentment, and fruit that will last for eternity. His lasting fruit in our life benefits us and our family far more than all the gold in the world. But it's all a matter of priorities.

Holly, a home-schooling mother of eight, is also a pastor's wife who counsels three to four women each week, leads a Bible study, sings with the worship team at church, helps provide content for a Christian women's nationally broadcast radio program, and teaches at women's retreats all over the country. Every morning, she wakes up realizing the utter impossibility of meeting the demands on her life without first being renewed and strengthened by the Lord. Knowing her need, Holly *depends* on her consistent, daily time in the Lord's presence and in His Word.

My friend Erin has a newborn and another child under the age of two. Because she recognizes the value of maintaining her intimacy with the Lord, she creatively spends time in the Word while nursing and time in prayer after the children are tucked in bed. Many other people like to have their quiet times in the morning so that they can receive His motivation and perspective to make it through the day.

I would suggest that instead of having the attitude, "When can I fit in time with the Lord?" we ask, "How can I schedule these other things around my time with the Lord?" And once you pick a time, *guard it*, knowing this will remain a daily battle.

How long should a quiet time be? I love spending an hour because it allows me to have quality time reading the Bible and praying. But if an hour sounds overwhelming, spend whatever time you can. For a mom with little children, or an Alzheimer's caregiver, free time can be scarce. Yet God will make a way for us to be in His presence if we truly seek it. He yearns to meet with us more than we can imagine!

Often when Stottler and I travel, our schedule simply won't allow extensive time in Bible reading and prayer. However, the critical thing for me each day is to *make sure* I have placed my life on His altar and yielded full control to Him. I can always find a few moments to read the Word, or at least to meditate on verses I have memorized, because I know my desperate need for His work in and through me!

One thing is absolutely 100 percent guaranteed—time with the Lord won't "just happen." If you wait until you are motivated and it seems easy to spend time with Him, you'll find yourself one day standing before His throne without ever having gotten to know Him!

So before you read on, please stop here and decide what sounds interesting to study in God's Word, where you will meet with Him, and when you will make time to do so. Remember, Psalm 16:2 and John 15:5 tell us that apart from Christ we have no good and can do nothing of eternal, lasting value. Therefore, we *desperately* need His Word and His presence in our lives daily.

12

Our Time in Prayer

The area of prayer challenges almost every Christian. I've heard it said, "If you don't want to embarrass someone, don't ask her about her prayer life." Revealing research shows that the average prayer time is under five minutes.[1] But why should prayer—that which ushers us into the throne room of God—be so difficult?

It all comes down to pride. Truly meeting with our Creator requires us to humble ourselves, admit our need, and demonstrate our dependence on Him. But because our pride *hates* to be humbled, prayer becomes a challenge. Consequently, we miss Christ's transforming work in our lives.

If we read the Word but spend little time in prayer, we miss the depth of transformation and the joy of intimacy that occurs only in God's presence. If we spend time in prayer but little time in the Word, we miss the training in righteousness that our lives so desperately require. Therefore, our daily times should include both Bible study and prayer.

Because the basis of prayer is a relationship, God eagerly awaits time with us. He loves our fellowship (Zephaniah 3:17). We will never catch the Lord sleeping or distracted (Psalm 121:3). I *great-ly* rejoice that my prayers will never be greeted by heavenly voice mail that throws me into an endless loop of recorded options!

God wants us to talk with Him about everything, whether we find ourselves joyful, brokenhearted, discouraged, or just plain mad (Philippians 4:6). Praise God that He cannot be shocked! He knows what we'll say even before a word is on our lips, yet we still need to communicate because verbalizing our thoughts brings them out in the open.

The psalms provide wonderful illustrations of men pouring out their hearts before the Lord in a vast array of emotions. When they exposed their hearts, God reminded them of the truth, then remolded their thoughts and attitudes. Over and over we read psalms that begin with an attitude of fear or anger and end with a declaration of faith and trust in God's sovereignty and goodness.[2]

After my daily Bible reading, I pray. Charles Spurgeon writes, "True prayer is neither a mere mental exercise nor a vocal performance. It is far deeper than that—it is spiritual transaction with the Creator of heaven and earth."[3] As I begin to pray, I close my eyes and take a moment to focus on His presence—just as if I were speaking to someone in the room.[4] And for me, praying aloud helps my mind stay focused.

Included in my prayer time are four aspects: laying myself on the altar, praising God, confessing sin, and putting on His armor. In other words: Dying, Adoring, Confessing, and Arming.

Dying

Each morning my soul strains to get on with the day in my *own* strength. That pride persists as a daily reminder of my fallen flesh —that I have no good apart from Christ and can do nothing of eternal value apart from Him. Therefore, that wall of pride must be broken down every morning.

Each day I must once again humble myself and crucify my pride on the altar. As I pray, "Rich or poor, sick or well, dead or alive, I am completely Yours, Lord, to do with whatever You choose," a remarkable change occurs. I suddenly see life through *His* eyes, and my entire perspective is transformed.

God isn't seeking great women He can use in His service. *"God has chosen the foolish things of the world to shame the wise, and God has chosen the weak things of the world to shame the things which are strong"* (1 Corinthians 1:27). God chose an over-the-hill Sarah, a teenage Mary, a despised tax collector Matthew, and a murderous Saul to be His faithful servants. Their main job requirement: to crucify self and allow *Him* to work.

God's "wanted" ad seeks women who will consistently empty themselves of pride and depend on Him. Then He alone receives the glory.

Adoration

Praising God is the only time when we fully focus on God alone. All other aspects of our prayer time have an element of "me" in them: when I see *my* need, when I confess *my* sins, when I pray for things on *my* heart. But praising God transfers our focus off ourselves to concentrate solely on His awesome magnificence.[5]

We are to *"continually offer up a sacrifice of praise to God, that is, the fruit of lips that give thanks to His name"* (Hebrews 13:15). The "sacrifice" occurs because we don't always *feel* like praising Him. Thankfully, we don't have to live based on our feelings!

Studying God's attributes greatly enhances our time of praise and adoration. When stagnancy or repetition overtakes my praise time, that staleness reminds me to return again to a study of His character. The more I know Him, the more I marvel at His inexhaustible vastness. And as I focus on God, I can also more readily recognize sin in my life.

Confession

God's awesome greatness, contrasted with our weak and humble state, leads us to confession. *"Search me, O God, and know my heart; try me and know my anxious thoughts; and see if there be any hurtful way in me, and lead me in the everlasting way"* (Psalm 139:23,24).

Years ago I briefly lived with a young family of five. One warm afternoon we prepared to drive their SUV into town. As we opened the car doors, a foul odor poured out. Overturned milk had soured as the car sat soaking up the warm California sun. We bravely drove on anyway, not taking time to clean up the problem.

The following day as we again prepared to pile into the vehicle, the foul odor had degenerated into a cloud of repulsive stench. The putrefying effect was now so horrific that survival depended on driving with our heads craned out the windows while tears streamed from our stinging eyes. After that, no one was willing to ride in the SUV (Smells Unbearably Vile) until the problem had been resolved.

Just like that car, sin allowed to remain in our lives putrefies and becomes a vile stench. It would be far better to simply clean out the sin before it ferments. And if areas of sin have already begun a decaying process in your life, those rotting areas will never go away until you willingly expose them to the Lord's gracious, cleansing touch. Only those who dig deep and allow His purifying process to reach those sinful areas will truly come to know God and be available for His service.

Whenever God exposes sin during our time reading His Word, we must act upon it. *"He who conceals his transgressions will not prosper, but he who confesses and forsakes them will find compassion"* (Proverbs 28:13).[6] When convicted, I need to go back through the exercise of confessing sin and restoring a clear conscience. *"Create in me a clean heart, O God, and renew a steadfast spirit within me"*

(Psalm 51:10). Oh, the blessed freedom found in maintaining a clean heart before the Lord!

Dying, Adoring, and Confessing lead us to Arming.

The Armor of God

I understood little about spiritual warfare before I began ministering in parts of Asia. However, after working in an area of the world where our enemy's forces run rampant, I gained a heightened awareness of Satan's tactics in our lives here as well. Therefore, I know that we must daily arm ourselves with God's strength, because what we cannot see is far more powerful than what we can see.

God reminds us of where our real battles lie: *"Our struggle is not against flesh and blood, but against the rulers, against the powers, against the world forces of this darkness, against the spiritual forces of wickedness in the heavenly places"* (Ephesians 6:12). Bible commentator Charles Ryrie writes: "The believer's enemies are the demonic hosts of Satan, always assembled for mortal combat."[7]

Satan's power far exceeds ours—but his power is *nothing* compared to God's! God never tells us to fight the enemy on our own, but instead commands us to use *His* armor and *His* strength. The armor of God passage begins by warning us to *"be strong in the Lord, and in the strength of His might"* (Ephesians 6:10, emphasis added). Our own efforts to battle the enemy will constantly fail. Therefore, I come to the Lord each day knowing that on my own, my fallen flesh will never withstand the enemy's assaults. I must take up God's armor *before* a temptation arrives so that I will not be moved or swayed when the world forces of darkness strike with their well-contrived schemes.

God says, *"Put on the full armor of God, so that you will be able to stand firm against the schemes of the devil"* (Ephesians 6:11). We need His *full* armor, not a haphazard partial covering. God's armor protects *every single area* of my life: my purity, my perspective, my dependence on Christ; what I see, hear, think; and what I resist.

But God's armor won't help us if we aren't trained in *how* to use it. During the Battle for Iraq, our troops executed their mission effectively and swiftly because they were so well trained in the use of their equipment. But if a soldier went into battle fully equipped with the latest technology yet completely unschooled in its use, all that gear would be worthless once the bullets started to fly.

Each piece of God's armor carries a specific purpose and protects a specific area of my life throughout the day so that I am not caught unprepared for the enemy's attacks. *"Therefore, take up the full armor of God, so that you may be able to resist in the evil day, and having done everything, to stand firm"* (Ephesians 6:13).

As I began the practice of donning God's armor, my prayer time was revolutionized from a routine duty to a wondrously intimate time in God's presence. The daily application of God's armor not only revitalized my quiet times, but it also affects my walk with Christ throughout each entire day. I *love* this part of my quiet time!

Let's look at the six pieces of spiritual armor God has provided for us in Ephesians 6.

*1. "Stand firm therefore, having **girded your loins with truth**" (v. 14).*

How do we "gird our loins" with God's truth? Simply by weaving it all around and through us so that it completely penetrates our lives. I picture a weaving machine with horizontal fabric strands being woven in and out of the vertical strands. Hundreds of separate fibers are woven into the other fibers. Once the piece of cloth is completed, those separate strands no longer remain discernable. You cannot tell where one begins and another ends.

In the same way, I picture weaving the words and truths of the Bible into my life so that they become part of the fabric of who I am, completely interwoven into every part of my life. Daily I pray, "Lord, I gird my loins with Your truth. Please make Your Word a part of the fabric of my being."

Then I begin praying through whatever God has shown me during my Bible reading. For example, when I read about Noah waiting on God's timing to leave the ark, I prayed, "Thank You, Lord, for this example of waiting on You. Remind me to seek Your guidance, Your will, and Your perfect timing. Teach me to not rush ahead and attempt to accomplish things on my own."

As I pray through things He has shown me in His Word that day, He often reveals even deeper insights into those passages. That motivates me to continue praying over His Word!

While "girding my loins," I also repeat any Scripture verse I am memorizing. Treasuring God's Word in our hearts remains one of our strongest defenses against any temptation.

2. *"Put on the breastplate of righteousness"* (v. 14).

First Corinthians 1:30 describes Christ as our righteousness, so to *"put on the breastplate of righteousness"* is to "put on" Christ. Righteousness is found only in Him. We certainly have none on our own!

As I picture putting on Christ, I ask Him to work in and through every part of me, pouring *His* righteousness through my life. I first pray, "Lord Jesus, I put You on as my breastplate of righteousness because I have no good besides You." Then I pray John 15:5, "Lord, apart from You I can do nothing."

As I'm "putting on" Christ, I picture Him coming to live inside of me. (Using my imagination helps a bit.) I ask Him to speak through my lips, so I say only *His* words. I ask Him to think with my mind, so I have *His* thoughts. I ask Him to see through my eyes, so I have *His* perspective.

Seeing things from Christ's perspective is like going to a 3-D movie. If you sit in the theater and watch the movie without putting on the 3-D glasses, you will completely miss the extra dimension and the entire purpose of the filmmaker. Only as we "put on Christ," our 3-D glasses, can we see life through *His* eyes so that we can grasp God's purposes and perspective.

After putting on Christ, I then think through the upcoming events of that day and pray specifically for Christ to work through me in each matter. For example, if I am leading a Bible study that day, I will pray, "Lord Jesus, please direct my thoughts and speak Your words through me." Knowing I will be spending time with my husband, I often pray, "Lord, demonstrate Your love toward Stottler through me." What a difference depending on Him makes throughout every part of the day!

3. *"Shod your feet with the preparation of the gospel of peace"* *(v. 15).*

My daily application of this verse reminds me to watch the path of my feet. Like a ball on a hill, our feet either carry us toward God or away—we never stand still. God says, *"Watch the path of your feet and all your ways will be established. Do not turn to the right nor to the left; turn your foot from evil"* (Proverbs 4:26,27).

"Shodding" (preparing) my feet is actually a twofold process. I flee *from* temptation, and I run *to* God's peace. I picture putting on shoes in preparation to flee *from* Satan's lures *into* God's peace and protection.

The Bible instructs us over and over to flee from evil. *"A prudent man sees evil and hides himself, the naive proceed and pay the penalty"* (Proverbs 27:12). So each morning I pray, "Lord, I shod my feet with the preparation of the gospel of peace to flee evil and to run to You for Your strength and protection."

As I mentally shod my feet each morning, fleeing from evil stays on the forefront of my mind throughout the day. If I sit down to watch television and some objectionable image or language fills the screen, I flee by switching to a different program (if I can find a clean one!) or by turning off the TV. If a conversation turns to gossip, I remember to flee by either changing the subject or leaving. God clearly instructs us to *"flee immorality"* (1 Corinthians 6:18), which means we must do whatever it takes to stay as far away from moral temptations as possible.

The more I practice fleeing evil, the easier it becomes. I love the picture in Proverbs 16:17: *"The highway of the upright is to depart from evil."* I want my path away from temptation to resemble an eight-lane freeway!

When I recall my time in the Caribbean, I immediately remember the roiling turmoil and internal upheaval that my choices created. The peace I *now* possess comes from being transparent and right with God, Stottler, and others. That peace is very, very precious to me. Therefore, whenever I sense any loss of His peace in my life, or when I sense something hindering our fellowship, I quickly run to God so that He can expose the problem and I can have restored peace in Christ.

> *This verse reminds me to watch the path of my feet. Like a ball on a hill, our feet either carry us toward God or away—we never stand still.*

Fleeing sin, however, does not mean fleeing responsibility. If we become involved in a conflict, we need to seek resolution. The Word tells us, *"So far as it depends on you, be at peace with all men"* (Romans 12:18). If Stottler and I have a conflict, I need to do all that is within my power to seek resolution. That often means humbling myself and asking for forgiveness. The faster we run to resolve issues, the sooner we will restore God's peace.

We also run to God for His peace to endure trials and afflictions. He may allow trials in our lives to teach us dependence on Him. We know that because He loves us perfectly, He allows into our lives only that which is for our good and His glory. We can also know that even though times may be very painful and difficult, He promises to provide the strength we need to endure *if* we run to Him (2 Corinthians 12:9).

4. *"In addition to all, **taking up the shield of faith** with which you will be able to extinguish all the flaming arrows of the evil one" (v. 16).*

Satan loves to hurl flaming arrows at our weakest points. So how do we "take up" the shield of faith to extinguish them? By choosing to trust Christ with every situation in our lives. Living by faith means laying all our cares, concerns, and burdens in His hands for *Him* to carry. That demonstration of faith in His strength acts as a shield against Satan's attacks.

Each day as I pray, "Lord, I take up the shield of faith," I am demonstrating dependence on Him. Therefore, *He* is my shield. *"You are a shield around me, O LORD"* (Psalm 3:3, NIV).

Then, I demonstrate my faith in Him by praying for all the things on my heart—people I care about, nonbelievers, worries, illnesses, situations I don't know how to handle, and personal requests. I start each prayer with the words "by faith," trusting the Lord alone to bring about the answers according to His will.

For example, I say: "By faith, Lord, I pray that You will draw Gina to know You. By faith I pray that You will heal Jonathan from his surgery. By faith I ask You to give Jackie Your grace and wisdom in her very difficult marriage." Only *God* can draw someone to know Him, only *He* can heal a body, only *He* can minister grace to a hurting heart. If He doesn't do it, it can't happen. So I recognize my total dependence on His work, then rest the results in His hands.

I also know that He may choose to answer my prayers differently than I expect. But when I pray everything "by faith," depending on God to work, *God* is responsible for the outcome. I can choose not to worry because the responsibility rests on the Lord instead of on me. His shield of faith protects me against worry and fear. And when I pray, I must also stay sensitive to see if He desires to use *me* as part of the answer. If I'm praying by faith that He will draw someone to know Him personally, He may choose to use me to share with her.

Praying by faith also means waiting for the Lord to answer. Whether through His Word or through His Spirit, God will give us specific answers to specific questions if we'll just stop to listen. But it's so hard for us to listen and to wait![8]

> *Only God can draw someone to know Him, only He can heal a body, only He can minister grace to a hurting heart.*

Demonstrating our complete dependence on the Lord brings wonderful results. God tells us, *"This is the victory that has overcome the world—even our faith"* (1 John 5:4). That's worth taking up the shield!

5. *"Take the helmet of salvation"* (v. 17).

Next, as I pray, "Lord, I put on the helmet of salvation," I picture a helmet covering my eyes, my ears, and my thoughts. God's helmet provides a filter through which I process everything I see, hear, and think.

Like the visors on helmets worn by medieval knights, the visor on my helmet shields my eyes from attack. My visor is made of a fine mesh of Scripture through which I filter everything that enters my eyes. The visor reminds me to look away from anything that is worthless, crude, immoral, or impure (Psalm 101:3). What does Christ consider worthless? The more you get to know Him, the more sensitive you will become to His heart. A good rule of thumb to use is: *When in doubt, don't.* If you question whether you should look at something, don't. You will be amazed at how this practice "tenderizes" your spirit.

My helmet also covers my ears to filter what I hear. God says, *"Nor should there be obscenity, foolish talk or course joking, which are out of place, but rather thanksgiving"* (Ephesians 5:4, NIV). This includes listening to conversations, music, and programs that are not honoring to the Lord. God also speaks in the harshest terms about listening to gossip, often listing it among a host of terrible sins (Proverbs 20:19).

My helmet also covers my entire head, daily guarding and protecting what I think. We should be *"taking every thought captive to the obedience of Christ"* (2 Corinthians 10:5). If we wouldn't want Christ to see the thoughts in our mind, then we'd better get rid of them! This definitely includes lustful or improper romantic thoughts involving someone outside our marriage.

Guarding what I think also includes negative thoughts that I repeat in my head. Remember the old vinyl records? When we repeat negative thoughts, we become like a stuck record needle wearing a deep groove in the vinyl as it repeats over and over and over. If you repeat something often enough, you begin to believe it and to live it out. For instance, if you allow yourself to repeat, "My husband really doesn't love me," or "My husband is so inconsiderate," or "This marriage will never work," you will begin to act on those thoughts.

Instead, we must minute by minute practice redirecting our thoughts. Paul tells us to let our minds dwell on *"whatever is true, whatever is honorable, whatever is right, whatever is pure, whatever is lovely, whatever is of good repute, if there is any excellence and if anything worthy of praise"* (Philippians 4:8). These qualities are found in God and His Word.

When I left Eric in the Caribbean and returned home, I found it difficult not to constantly dwell on thoughts of him. But I knew feeding the painful thoughts only reinforced them, so I continually poured Scripture into my mind and listened to Christian radio during every idle moment.

Now as I put on the helmet of salvation every morning to guard my eyes, my ears, and my thoughts, I remain conscious of maintaining God's purity throughout the day.

6. *"Take... the sword of the Spirit, which is the word of God" (v. 17).*

God's Word is more powerful than we can imagine. When the Lord tells us to *"resist the devil and he will flee from you"* (James 4:7), we do so by using the Word of God just as Christ did in the wilderness (Luke 4:1–13).

Yet how little we avail ourselves of this weapon! It's as if we are standing beside a table that holds a huge sword. By comparison, Satan threatens us with a little pocketknife, and to make him flee all we need to do is *pick up the sword!* But we don't. We usually try to fight him with our own pitiful will power, or we cave in without a fight.

How do we "pick up" the sword of the Spirit? Each morning I pray, "Lord, I take up the sword of the Spirit and ask that You will remind me to resist Satan according to Your Word throughout this day." Then when a temptation or condemnation comes to me during the day, I take James 4:7 literally and say, "Satan, I resist you in the name of the Lord Jesus Christ." I still marvel at how the temptation seems to disappear. Satan is persistent, however, so I might need to repeat this throughout the day.

As I resist Satan with the sword of the Spirit, I remember that the power of sin within me has been broken and that I don't have to sin anymore. I call on Christ's strength and I choose to continue living the Spirit-controlled life.

However, without taking up the sword daily, we can easily lapse back into attempting the battle with the enemy on our own. And though Satan has absolutely no power against God, he is *very* powerful against us. That's why we have God's armor and the authority of His Word to make Satan flee. As we practice this, consistent victory over sin becomes a reality. *We don't have to choose sin anymore!*

Choosing Wisely

Picture two women: one wise, one foolish. The wise woman stands erect, completely covered with the armor of God. Around her feet lie hundreds of smoldering arrows that have merely bounced off her armor, leaving her unscathed.

Beside her stands the foolish woman. Instead of fiery darts lying around her feet, God's armor lies uselessly strewn about the ground. Without protection, her body is pierced full of the enemy's flaming missiles, leaving her wounded and bleeding.

Which woman are you?

If the daily experience of Dying, Adoring, and Confessing is not part of your time with the Lord, I would urge you to observe the difference they make in your walk with God. And if you have never practiced putting on each piece of God's armor to prepare for the day's battles, please give it a try! As you daily practice arming yourself, God will begin to mold this to more personally fit your specific needs.

As I go through each of these elements in my daily quiet time, I find that I am far more prepared to flee from temptations throughout the remainder of the day. My life testifies to the dramatic change these practices can bring about, not only in the enjoyment of my daily prayer time, but also in walking victoriously by the power of Christ!

13

Our Response of Obedience

One day while spending time in God's presence, I sensed His convicting finger on an area that I had previously ignored. This particular issue to which He now pointed seemed so long ago that I momentarily wondered if I should bother. Yet for me, God's conviction is like a stomach bug—not debilitating, but impossible to ignore.

Because I fervently desire to remain transparent before the Lord, I knew I must either obey His promptings or be miserable. So compiling my stack of unpaid parking tickets, I trudged down to the police station, wondering how I could afford to pay this sizeable debt. In my haste during college, I had frequently broken the local parking laws, then "filed" the tickets in my glove compartment. Now God's Word hammered in my mind: *"Every person is to be in subjection to the governing authorities"* (Romans 13:1).

Waiting in line at the police station, I fidgeted nervously, wondering how foolish I looked coming forward these many years later. When my turn at the window finally came, I explained to the dour-looking cashier that the Lord had convicted me of my responsibility to pay for all these old parking tickets.

With a surprised expression, she took the pile (not an insignificant stack!) and browsed through the dates. Looking somewhat puzzled, she informed me that most of the tickets were so old, computer records of them no longer existed. Then she added, "I've never had anyone do this before. I guess the only thing to tell you is to just throw them away." I paid the few tickets remaining in their records, then left with an enormous sense of God's joy over my simple act of obedience.

Obedience forms the third element in the "Quiet Time Trio." We have talked about time in the Word and time in prayer. But in God's eyes, the best quiet time in the world counts for nothing unless it is followed by obedience.

Obedience to His Word is actually a mark of genuine salvation (1 John 2:4,5). We cannot possibly obey God's Word unless His Spirit lives within us (Romans 8:2). And when we have Christ's Spirit, we *desire* to obey God, *"for it is God who is at work in you, both to will and to work for His good pleasure"* (Philippians 2:13).

Elements of Obedience

I define obedience as *choosing to immediately obey all that God has shown me*. Let's look at the three elements of this definition, then talk about what motivates us to obey.

Obedience Is a Choice

As women, we allow our feelings to dictate so many of our choices. But obedience to God and His Word has absolutely nothing to do with feelings. In fact, we must often choose to obey by our will because His ways are so upside down from our natural ways (Isaiah 55:8,9).

Because God's ways are so different from ours, we desperately need His wisdom to know what choices to make. And He promises that His Word will *never, never, ever* lead us astray, but will guide us daily: *"Your word is a lamp to my feet and a light for my path"* (Psalm 119:105, NIV).

We must make God's Word the basis for all of our decisions, regardless of our feelings. Because we have the Holy Spirit living within us, we *always* have the power to choose obedience to His Word. To obey, we practice the Spirit-controlled life by drawing on His strength, then choosing by our will to obey whatever He shows us.

Just as the house of your dreams is built one brick and one board at a time, so your life patterns are established one decision at a time. As the boards eventually combine to make a house, so all of your choices combine to determine the shape of your life. The daily decisions you make today determine the patterns you establish for tomorrow (Proverbs 14:1).

Also, those patterns of obedience or disobedience we establish early in our lives become ingrained in our older years. And the older we get, the harder it becomes to change those patterns. In fact, at one point God told the Hebrews that their pattern of disobedience had become so ingrained, they were actually beyond change (Jeremiah 19:1,11)!

Obeying God's Word means constantly choosing to act on whatever He shows us. Isaiah 1:19 says, *"If you consent **and obey**, you will eat the best of the land"* (emphasis added). It's not enough to merely want to obey. James 1:25 reminds us that it is the one who *acts* in obedience who receives the blessings.

Some friends of ours have a daughter who recently graduated from high school and decided to move in with her boyfriend, much to her parents' dismay. When confronted with her choices, she replied, "But I'm having great quiet times." From God's perspective, that's not possible because He never separates hearing from doing. Jesus said, *"Why do you call Me, 'Lord, Lord,' and do not do what I say?"* (Luke 6:46). When we *hear* from Him, we are expected to *obey.*

As I prepare to meet with the Lord each day, I decide *beforehand* to act on every word He shows me. Whatever He reveals to me that day, I choose to obey. But I haven't always been that way.

I used to fight tooth and nail against God and His will for me. He would convict me of something I really wanted to hang on to (whether an attitude or action), and I would argue and resist and be furious at Him. I was a living example of Proverbs 19:3: *"The foolishness of man ruins his way, and his heart rages against the LORD."* I would choose sin, refuse to let go, and be livid with God over it. What I refused to see was that hanging onto my sin was like clinging to the blade of a sword with my bare hands. It was only hurting *me,* ripping me apart the whole time I refused to let go and obey Him.

Hanging onto my sin was like clinging to the blade of a sword with my bare hands. It was only hurting me, ripping me apart.

Then one day a light bulb went on inside my head and I realized that when I battled with God, I *never* won. (Duh!) God's Word tells us that *"whatever you devise against the LORD, He will make a complete end of it"* (Nahum 1:9). Fighting against the Lord only got me upset and often physically sick. Not only that, but the battle always ended up being a waste of time because I would eventually give in. If I had chosen to obey in the first place, it would have saved me (and those around me!) a lot of time and heartache.

Have you decided that every single Word of the Lord is right? Have you predetermined to obey whatever He shows you? Choosing obedience beforehand eliminates so much wasted time spent in futile battles against the Lord!

Obedience Is Immediate

Obedience must also be immediate. The psalmist says, *"I have considered my ways and have turned my steps to your statutes. I will hasten and not delay to obey your commands"* (Psalm 119:59,60, NIV).

God has a name for delayed obedience: *disobedience.* When He says to flee immorality, He doesn't mean to flee next week, or to flee when you see the net closing in. God's Word means *flee now!*

When God instructed Abraham to establish the covenant act of circumcision, Abraham instantly obeyed the Lord and circumcised every male in his household *"the very same day, as God had said to him"* (Genesis 17:23). But when Jesus called a certain man to follow Him, the man replied, *"Permit me first to go and bury my father"* (Luke 9:59). His reply really meant, "I will obey You once my father has passed away and all my obligations at home are completed, and it's convenient."

Delayed obedience leads to snowballing disobedience and an avalanche of consequences. During my Caribbean experience, I chose to ignore the Spirit's conviction, deciding that my feelings toward Eric would never amount to anything. Instead, I should have obeyed immediately and revealed my feelings to Stottler, as well as immediately decided to never spend time alone with Eric. My delayed obedience allowed wrong feelings to grow, resulting in pain and heartache for many.

How quickly our choices of disobedience can tear down all that we have built. I can echo Proverbs 5:14: *"I was almost in utter ruin in the midst of the assembly and congregation."* My disobedience required years to reestablish my faithfulness so that I could be found usable for the Lord's work again. Having witnessed firsthand the results of delayed obedience, I know the critical necessity of obeying immediately.

Have you decided to *immediately* obey whatever God shows you?

Obedience Is Complete

As we choose to obey immediately, we must also obey complete-ly. Incomplete obedience also equals disobedience.[1] God requires us to obey His *entire* Word, not just pick and choose only those parts we find easy to carry out.

I have a friend who loves to send spiritual messages on the Internet to all of her acquaintances. She frequently speaks with passion about various Christian causes. Yet recently when it came to a hard choice in her own life, she chose to leave her husband without scriptural grounds, then turned around and eloped. When confronted with God's truth concerning her divorce and remar-riage, she simply replied, "I'm still struggling with that one." (Ob-viously, not enough to make a difference in her decisions and ac-tions!) She also added, "But I know that God is forgiving." Many Christians adopt the unbiblical attitude that "it's easier to ask for-giveness than permission." That perspective is straight from the enemy because *no act of disobedience is insignificant!* There is no right way to do the wrong thing.

Every time we sin we will suffer consequences. Our disobedi-ent thoughts affect every response we make and every action we choose. My friend knew the counsel of God's Word, but when obedience became difficult, she chose to continue acting in her own stubborn self-will. She loves to wave the King's banner, but she won't follow Him into the battle.

Often Christians may be unsure of God's instructions con-cerning some issue, or they may question what choices they should make. I firmly believe in mentors. Paul frequently instructed be-lievers to imitate him and other mature believers.[2] If I hadn't had a strong mentor to call when I considered leaving Stottler, my life might have looked entirely different today.

Following the example of strong believers plays an important part in our spiritual growth. *"He who walks with wise men will be wise"* (Proverbs 13:20). God gave us teachers to help guide us. However, we must also make sure that all advice and instruction matches Scripture. God's Word always remains our *final* authority.

Have you decided to obey *all* that God instructs in His Word?

Motivations for Obedience

If you have children, you understand how important motivation is to obedience. Do your children understand why they should obey? Do they do so with a joyful attitude, understanding the benefits of obedience?

Like children before our heavenly Father, we also need to examine our motivation. We've seen three elements of obedience, but what does God say about our motivation to obey? Let's look at four things that motivate us.

Obedience Motivated by Trust

As I studied the attributes of God, I began to fathom the depth of His love for me. All of His decisions for my life spring from His love. *"The Lord is good to all, and His mercies are over all His works"* (Psalm 145:9). Because I know He loves me perfectly, I can know that everything He brings or allows into my life is for my good. Therefore, I can trust His will for me and choose to obey.

Stottler and I frequently travel with the ministry, and we are so grateful for the privilege of seeing God's creation. However, I did find one place on the other side of the world that I consider to be very unpleasant. I could live the rest of my life and be quite happy never to return there. Yet if God called us to move to that country, I would willingly go. Initially, my *emotions* wouldn't be excited, but I would know with complete certainty that His will for my life is the very best thing for me.

God's ways are often so different from the world's that at times His will may seem contrary to logic. Did it make sense for Moses to stretch a staff over the sea to split it apart, or to strike a rock to produce water (Exodus 14, 17)? Did it make sense for the little shepherd boy David to confront a giant over twice his size so the Israelites could win the war (1 Samuel 17)? Yet these acts of obedience produced astonishing results! We can trust God's will because His ways are *so* much higher than ours. That's why this walk of faith is so much fun!

Obedience Motivated by Protection

Obedience to God's Word is not only for our good, but also for our protection, saving us from sin and its consequences. When we disobey God's Word, we are actually choosing to hurt ourselves and others. God explained the consequences of obedience and disobedience to the Hebrews: *"I call heaven and earth to witness against you today, that I have set before you life and death, the blessing and the curse. So choose life in order that you may live, you and your descendants, by loving the LORD your God, by obeying His voice, and by holding fast to Him"* (Deuteronomy 30:19,20). God lays it out clearly: obedience brings blessings; disobedience brings problems. Why would anyone *choose* problems?

We possess such limited understanding of our actions' consequences. God sees all eternity and knows every consequence of every decision. Obedience to His Word *always* protects us from horrific results that we cannot see. For example, when God decided to judge the Egyptians for their hard hearts, the Hebrew people chose to obey His instructions by placing blood on the doorposts of their homes. That simple act of obedience saved the lives of their first-born children (Exodus 12).

When God tells us to flee immorality, it isn't because He desires to keep us from enjoying life. He knows the consequences of sex outside of marriage and sees the disasters that infidelity brings to us and our family. If I had heeded His warning calls when first attracted to Eric, all those involved would have been spared so much pain.

A few years after returning from the Caribbean, the Lord reminded me again how obedience protects us. Stottler flew to South America on a ministry trip, while I remained at home to finish a project. One evening, feeling very tired, I decided to watch a movie. When I selected the video, I sensed the Spirit's warning that my particular choice might encourage dreamy, romantic thoughts. But I watched the video anyway, rationalizing that I had seen this movie before so it probably wouldn't bother me.

The results of failing to obey God's internal warning reached beyond my imagination! At the end of the movie, I found myself transported to that surreal state of castle-in-the-sky imagination. Knowing I shouldn't remain in that condition, I wanted to call Stottler, but he sat on a plane thousands of feet over the Amazon. So I called Holly, my accountability friend. We talked and prayed, she stuck a pin in my dream bubble to bring me back to reality, and I confessed my disobedience to the Lord. However, throughout the following day I could tell that I had compromised my "edge" of spiritual sensitivity. A sense of oppression hung over me the entire day, as if I had cracked open the door to hell. All day long I battled against succumbing to my feelings.

As I lay down to sleep that night, before I even realized what was happening, my mind began to explore ways to reestablish contact with Eric! My heart pounded in my ears, and I cried out for the Lord's protection.

Realizing the foolishness of my "simple" act of disobedience, I spent time the following morning in tears before the Lord. He reminded me that I can never let my guard down for even an instant. Then He brought to mind the picture of war. In battle, a military commander will *never* say, "Men, we're doing well, so let's lose this part of the battle while we rest awhile." That would be utter foolishness! Similarly, in this life we each fight a continually raging spiritual battle. We cannot surrender an inch of territory for even a moment.

Being absolutely committed to transparency and honesty with Stottler, when he returned home, I admitted what I had done. He then covered me with his prayers. I also took that video out to the garage and smashed it to pieces so that it would never again be a temptation. These acts of obedience returned my life to normal, and God's intimacy immediately returned. What a reminder of how obedience to His will protects me and that *no act of disobedience is insignificant!*

Obedience Motivated by Blessings and Rewards

God loves to bless our obedience! He tells us, *"How blessed are those who observe His testimonies, who seek Him with all their heart"* (Psalm 119:2).[3] He encourages us with numerous examples all through Scripture. For instance, because Abraham was willing to offer Isaac as a sacrifice, God told him, *"Because you have done this thing and have not withheld your son, your only son, indeed I will greatly bless you, and I will greatly multiply your seed as the stars of the heavens and as the sand which is on the seashore...In your seed all the nations of the earth shall be blessed, because you have obeyed My voice"* (Genesis 22:16–18).

God yearns to reward us for obedience. Like a father stockpiling an entire warehouse with incredible gifts, He desires to pour blessings upon His children if they will only walk in obedience. Since I chose to leave the Caribbean and reestablish a faithful walk with the Lord, He has opened a ministry for me in faraway lands and has blessed me with opportunities beyond my wildest imagination. I feel as though I'm standing under a chute trying to catch an onslaught of packages from heaven! And He owns *storehouses* of good gifts He desires to give us, if we will only obey.

Of course, this does not mean that obedience will make all of our problems disappear. By obeying the Lord's wisdom, however, we do *create* fewer problems for ourselves. And even in the midst of the trials that remain, we find that our godly responses make an enormous difference in our perspective. David obeyed God in the midst of trials, and though his obedience did not eliminate all his problems, God blessed him with provisions, peace, and protection from his enemy, Saul. Then later God bestowed enormous blessings on him and his kingdom (Psalm 18:16–50).

Blessings and rewards may not come instantaneously. David obeyed the Lord, yet continued to flee from Saul's attacks for many years. Isaiah, Jeremiah, and Ezekiel did exactly as God told them to do, yet lived difficult, unappreciated lives. What happened to their blessings and rewards? *"Thus says the LORD, 'Restrain your voice from weeping and your eyes from tears; for your work will be rewarded,' declares the LORD"* (Jeremiah 31:16). God's promises never fail, though we may receive the reward in our eternal home. There we can enjoy them forever![4]

In this life we each fight a continually raging spiritual battle. We cannot surrender an inch of territory for even a moment.

But is it "spiritual" to choose obedience to receive a reward? In Hebrews, the Lord highlights Abraham and Moses as examples of believers motivated to obey *because* of rewards. Commentator Warren Wiersbe says that "the decisions we make today will determine the rewards tomorrow. More than this, our decisions should be *motivated* by the expectation of receiving rewards. Abraham obeyed God *because* 'he looked for a city' (Hebrews 11:10). Moses forsook the treasures and the pleasures of Egypt *because* 'he had respect unto the recompense of the reward' (Hebrews 11:26)."[5]

Our choices today effect our eternity. And though I don't know exactly what those rewards will look like, I do know that God blesses us beyond what we can even imagine. So I am motivated to obey so that I can enjoy His incredible rewards forever!

Obedience Motivated by Its Effect on Others

Our obedience effects those around us—none more profoundly than our own household. As wives, our decisions play an enormous part in setting the spiritual tenor of our homes.

I have observed many Christian couples where the wife's consistent walk with the Lord greatly influences her husband's spiritual growth. Even in my own marriage, when I realized my desperate need for God's daily work in my life, my consistent quiet times encouraged Stottler's consistency as well. On the other hand, I also know a couple where the wife doubts the Word and seldom spends time with the Lord. Although her husband knows God, his spiritual walk remains shallow and immature.

Proverbs 31 shows us a picture of a godly wife's impact on everyone around her. Her daily dependence on God affects her husband's prosperity, his reputation, their marriage, their children, the family's health, their employees, the community, the poor and needy, and her own reputation. That's influence!

On the other hand, we read in 1 Kings 21 about the Lord's indictment against King Ahab, *"who sold himself to do evil in the sight of the LORD, because Jezebel his wife incited him"* (v. 25). Oh, the powerful influence of a wife, for good or for ill!

We never live in isolation. *Every single decision* I make affects other people. Even those "private" decisions in my thoughts affect my intimacy with the Lord, and therefore everything else I think and do. Every Christian's sin drags the name of Christ and the whole body of believers into the mire, not to mention the doubt it creates in nonbelievers' eyes. Our actions can destroy our usefulness, reap disastrous consequences, and bring great sorrow to the Lord's heart and to those watching us.

I believe with all of my heart that the Spirit-controlled life and daily time with the Lord, followed by obedience, are *the most essential elements* found in any faithful believer's life. Having teetered on the brink of disaster, I pour my heart out to you now to make the Spirit-controlled life and daily time with God the foundation of your life. Without time in His Word and in prayer each day, you stand unprotected, completely vulnerable to the enemy's assaults. Without His Spirit directing your moment-by-moment choices, your heart will harden toward following His will. Unless these two essential elements form the foundation of your life, you *will* fall into some sort of sin. Guaranteed.

Please, please determine every day to yield to the Spirit's control, spend time in God's presence, and choose to walk in obedience. When we try to live on our own, we see how little we can do. But when we let God work, we get to see what *He* can do.

14

Our Lives of Integrity

One day while I chatted with a group of Christian women, I mentioned the name of a recent movie. The pre-release advertisements on TV had been saturated with sexual innuendoes and a recurring theme of women looking at men's crotches. Immediately, the women around me began saying, "I look at men's crotches. Don't you do that? Everyone does that. That actor is so cute. I'm looking forward to seeing that movie." A bit taken aback, I wondered what kind of example we are presenting to the watching world.

A recent poll by the Barna Research Group states that although faith in Christ changes people's lives, the impact seems "largely limited to those dimensions of thought and behavior that are obviously religious in nature." The survey results indicate that "people need more help in determining how their faith speaks to life issues beyond the obvious connection."[1] Henry Blackaby explains:

> The problem of America is not unbelievers; the problem of America is the people of God. There are just as many divorces and abortions in the churches as outside the churches. George Barna did a survey of 152 separate items comparing

the lost world and the churches, and he said there's virtually no difference between the two. Our gospel is canceled by the way we live.[2]

As a body of believers, we not only fail to influence our culture, but we continually adapt and adopt their ways. Nonbelievers observe us enjoying the same immoral movies they watch. They hear us whispering about others behind their backs just as they do. They see us laughing at the same crude jokes that they find humorous. However, it is impossible to compromise and still maintain holiness and integrity in our lives.

It's nothing new for us as Christians to be swayed into compromise because "everyone else is doing it." During Jeremiah's time, the Israelites had adopted and imitated the pagan cultures around them for so long that they felt completely comfortable worshipping Baal and even sacrificing their own children! They had become so blinded to their sin because "everyone else was doing it" that when Jeremiah exposed their offenses and God's anger toward them, they responded with amazement: *"For what reason has the LORD declared all this great calamity against us? And what is our iniquity, or what is our sin which we have committed against the LORD our God?"* (Jeremiah 16:10).

Why follow along with what is filthy and impure when we could lead in the way to righteousness and truth?

Sadly, our culture seems to be repeating history. For example, what used to be called *adultery* is now a desirable *affair*. What used to be *perversion* and *homosexuality* is now an acceptable *alternative lifestyle*. What used to be considered *murder* is now a sanitized *abortion*, and what used to be *pornography* has now become *works of art*. What we once called *indecency* is now labeled *fashion*, and what used to be called *lying* we now excuse as *exaggeration*.[3] But just because something is accepted doesn't mean that it's right!

God's Standard of Integrity

Does our faith in Christ really make any difference in the day-to-day "small" decisions and in the course of our lives? God says it should because He considers our personal integrity to be of paramount importance. So what is God's standard for our integrity?

The Lord tells each of us to *"be imitators of God, as beloved children"* (Ephesians 5:1) and calls us to be holy as He is holy (1 Peter 1:16). Yet we would rather compare ourselves against others and say, "Hey, I'm really not so bad!" God, however, challenges us to compare ourselves with *Him!* How are you doing compared with *Christ?*

If God calls us to be holy as He is holy, how on earth can we possibly meet that standard? Actually, we can't. It is *impossible* to maintain a life of integrity on our own. Holiness is only possible as we depend on the power of His Holy Spirit within us, constantly yielding ourselves to Him. Peter writes, *"His divine power has granted to us everything pertaining to life and godliness"* so that we can *"become partakers of the divine nature"* (2 Peter 1:3,4, emphasis added). Only as we yield to Him will we become like Him (Romans 6:13).

We cannot simply follow the majority. As a friend once said, "Sometimes a majority just means the fools are all on one side!" The important issue is what *God* says, and He calls us to be salt and light in the midst of our culture and to keep ourselves pure from the ungodly practices around us (Matthew 5:13–16; James 1:27). God wants each of us to be *"blameless and innocent, children of God above reproach in the midst of a crooked and perverse generation, among whom you appear as lights in the world"* (Philippians 2:15). As believers we are to be *leaders* in what is right and good and lovely and pure. Why follow along and adopt that which is filthy and impure when we could *lead* in the way to righteousness and truth?

Compromise with the world is the very issue that angered God toward the churches in Pergamum and Thyatira (Revelation 2:12–29). Like them, we befriend the world and adopt its practices by watching the same ungodly programs, dressing in the same suggestive clothing, and using the same unholy language—all the while declaring that we belong to a holy God! The Lord likens this compromise to adultery (Revelation 2:22; James 4:4). He proclaimed to the Pergamum church that unless they repented, He was coming to make war against them!

How Integrity Affects Our Lives

Should God's standard of integrity affect our everyday lives? Absolutely! Let's look at four areas where God's integrity should be transforming our lives and actions, then we'll see how our integrity also affects those around us.

1. Integrity Affects How We Live and Act at Home

Building holiness and integrity into our lives begins behind the closed doors of our homes. Charles Spurgeon says, "What we are at home, that we are indeed."[4] Cynthia Heald writes, "If I cannot be the woman God wants me to be within the confines of my home, then I have no valid message or ministry outside my home."[5] Our integrity is really measured by what we are when no one is watching and when no one will ever know.

Although I may attempt to act better outside the home than I do inside, the truth always comes out. Proverbs says, *"He who walks in integrity walks securely, but he who perverts his ways will be found out"* (Proverbs 10:9). We can claim to be living the Spirit-controlled life, but if we have not truly yielded everything to the Lord, our heart *will* be exposed.

For example, if I am a discontented, nagging wife, then when some stressful situation arises outside the home, that same internal anger will spew forth. If I pour lustful movies and novels into my mind while in the confines of my house, I can far more easily succumb to Satan's temptation of infidelity with some enticing neighbor or coworker when I walk out my front door. Our outward actions merely display our inward character.

Our children *especially* model what they see in us. Research shows that when parents live a lifestyle consistent with their faith, modeling the truths and values that Christ taught, their children are far more likely to accept that faith as well. The psalmist tells us of the far-reaching effect our decisions now will make on the generations yet to be born. God commanded parents *"that they should teach [His truths] to their children, that **the generation to come** might know, even **the children yet to be born**, that they may arise and tell them to their children, that they should put their confidence in God, and not forget the works of God, but keep His commandments"* (Psalm 78:5–7, emphasis added).

Our children desperately need to observe us modeling daily dependence on the Lord, living out His life of integrity in all of our decisions. Our faith must be central to *all* of our decisions and actions. Integrating our beliefs and convictions into every family decision remains far more valuable than mere words of instruction.

2. Integrity Affects What We Keep in Our Home

For God's standard of holiness to transform our lives, we also need to cleanse our homes of *anything* that dishonors the Lord or pulls us away from Him. When God convicted the people in Ephesus of their sin, they *"kept coming, confessing and disclosing their practices. And many of those who practiced magic brought their books to-*

gether and began burning them in the sight of everyone" (Acts 19:18,19). The Ephesians didn't just put their magic books in the garage or sell them at the next yard sale. They *burned* them so that no one could ever use them again. The Bible goes on to tell us that when the Ephesians had publicly acknowledged their sin and burned their magic books, *"the word of the Lord was growing mightily and prevailing"* (v. 20). Obedience makes a difference!

How many of our walls are decorated with pagan symbols of worship? We need to be aware that often objects called "art" may possess far greater spiritual force than we realize. No art that honors a false god can at the same time bring honor to Christ.

Years ago, my mother brought back a large Hawaiian *tiki* statue from a trip to the islands. For many years it sat prominently on a shelf. One day, I realized that the *tiki* symbolized a demonic god —and it was sitting in our home! Mom and I discussed this, and she decided to rid our home of anything that didn't honor the Lord, including that statue. We took Mr. Tiki out to a ditch behind our backyard and set him ablaze. As the statue burned, a horrid green smoke billowed to the sky! It was good to have that false god out of our house!

Many well-meaning Christians allow objects into their homes that glorify sinful attitudes and behaviors. How many movies in our cabinets glamorize sensuality and adultery? How many CDs do we own that sing about "my cheatin' heart"? How many books resting on our bookshelves glorify infidelity and sex? How many closets contain occultic items, such as Ouija boards, Dungeons and Dragons games, or horoscope predictions? How many violent video games have found their way into our children's rooms?

Many Christian women unknowingly harden their hearts by reading immoral romance novels and sensual love stories. And what about those movie magazines sitting on the coffee table that elevate actors to idols, glorifying their immoral, godless lifestyles?

Since we become like those we focus upon, it's a short step to imitating their lives instead of Christ's.

If CDs, movies, books, or magazines dishonoring the Lord's holiness sit comfortably in your home, I would strongly urge you to get rid of them. If anything in your house entices you toward sin, throw it out. If a letter, picture, or poem from someone rekindles thoughts of past sins, dispose of it. If certain "good" CDs or movies draw your mind toward fantasies, get them out of your house. For example, I love sentimental, romantic music, but those songs tempt my flesh away from the Lord. So now we keep only non-vocal jazz, classical, or Christian music in our home.

We defeat ourselves by retaining things in our homes that pull our hearts away from the Lord. Besides, God tells us that all these worldly things are going to end up burned anyway, so we might as well dispose of them now! *"The day of the Lord will come like a thief, in which the heavens will pass away with a roar and the elements will be destroyed with intense heat, and the earth and its works will be burned up. Since all these things are to be destroyed in this way, what sort of people ought you to be in holy conduct and godliness?"* (2 Peter 3:10,11). How much more satisfying to cleanse our homes and lives of these unholy things and fill them with beauty that glorifies God!

3. Integrity Affects What We Do Outside Our Home

Integrity touches *everything* we do, both inside the confines of our home and outside. God brought this point home sharply to me one day as I read His Word. Until a few years ago, the issue of speeding constantly remained an area in which I lacked integrity and obedience. Because I love to "hang over the edge," the California freeways served as a perfect racetrack to complement my adventurous lifestyle. The only problem was that my speeding failed to complement a *godly* lifestyle. So periodically I would sense the Lord's finger of conviction on this area of my life, and I would struggle to slow down, only to find myself once again participating in the Indy 500 a few days later.

Then one day in my quiet time I read, *"He who is faithful in a very little thing is faithful also in much; and he who is unrighteous in a very little thing is unrighteous also in much"* (Luke 16:10). I knew the first part of that verse about faithfulness, but suddenly the second part about unrighteousness pierced my heart! From God's perspective, my "small" act of unrighteousness in disobeying the speed limit actually meant I was *"unrighteous also in much"*!

At that moment of realization, God removed my desire to speed and replaced it with His perspective on holiness and integrity. Now I delight to do His will as I putter down the highway so that I may be found *"faithful in a very little thing"* in order to also be faithful in much.

I'm sure other areas remain to be exposed in my life, so I yearn for the Lord to reveal them so that *nothing* in my life opposes the Word of God. I am very concerned that I may be blinded to some sin because it has become commonplace in our world, and I desperately want to be pure from the inside out!

My husband constantly demonstrates personal integrity, even in the smallest matters. Several years ago, we parked in a lot that had no attendant or meters. Instead, the drivers were to place money in a box that prints a receipt to be put in the car window. We sat in the car awhile before getting out. When Stottler went to buy the receipt, he put several extra quarters in the machine. When I questioned why on earth he gave the machine extra money, he explained that we had already used the parking space for a while without paying for it. Then he told me about Proverbs 23:23: *"Buy truth, and do not sell it."*

We "buy" truth by choosing to live according to God's truths, whatever the cost may be. We "sell" truth and our integrity by disobeying His Word—whether that be adultery or cheating a parking meter. Stottler held onto his integrity and refused to sell it—especially for a few quarters!

As is typical for the Lord, He tested me on this shortly thereafter. On my way to the beach one day, I realized that I had forgotten to put on suntan lotion. We own multiple bottles of the expensive gooey stuff at home, so I definitely didn't want to purchase more. I stopped at a drug store to buy some water, and while looking at the suntan bottles to check their outrageous prices, I put the tiniest amount on my nose and face.

I bought the water and headed for my car—except the Lord was pounding on my conscience. Using the store's lotion amounted to stealing. I kept thinking of Stottler asking what it's worth to sell our integrity, and my integrity had just gone down the drain for a ten-dollar bottle of suntan lotion. I also knew that at some point guilt would consume me until I returned and asked the store manager's forgiveness. So I went back in the store and bought the bottle of lotion. Maintaining my integrity before God was *far* more important than the cost of that bottle. (Of course, the *best* scenario would have been not giving in to temptation and using the lotion in the first place!)

What is your integrity worth? A quarter? Ten dollars? Christ gave His *life* so that we could walk in integrity and be holy as He is holy. Maintaining holiness and integrity is worth everything!

4. Integrity Affects Everything

The key to a life of integrity comes in being willing to yield *whatever* the Lord tells us to. Paul writes that we should *"cleanse ourselves from **all** defilement of flesh and spirit, perfecting holiness in the fear of God"* (2 Corinthians 7:1, emphasis added). So if God pricks your conscience to leave a conversation laced with gossip, you must leave. If you know that looking at certain images gives you impure thoughts, you must look away. If God convicts you that items exist in your home that do not honor Him, then you need to get rid of them.

I previously mentioned a rule that I live by: *When in doubt, don't.* If I am unsure whether or not God would approve of something, I don't do it. This is especially essential in the area of sexual purity. Rather than attempting to see how much we can "get away with," we should see how far away from impurity we can keep our lives. By constantly applying this rule, God has given me a heart far more sensitive to His will. And I have *never* been less effective in ministry or in relating to others because I have not seen or done something questionable.

How Our Integrity Affects Those Around Us

Integrity impacts every area of our lives. And as God's holiness changes us, others will notice. Our integrity can have far-reaching effects!

Our Integrity Influences the Lives of Others

When we live holy lives of integrity, people notice. People are watching us. We actually have no idea how many people observe us to see if our walk matches our talk, so we must never underestimate the power of our life testimony, whether for good or ill.

Recently, a crusty ol' fellow confided to me that he repeatedly watched his boss walk out the door of a weekly Bible study to immediately swear at someone, or slander a person in the Bible study, or treat another employee like a dog. Shaking his head, the fellow repeated over and over, "I don't get it."

Nonbelievers may gravitate toward other religions because they don't see our walk with Christ making any difference in our lives. A friend told me that many people are finding Tibetan Buddhism attractive—a religion immersed in occultic and demonic practices—because they hunger for a "holistic" life. He went on to say that people look at Christians and observe that our lives look exactly like everyone around us, but those practicing Tibetan Buddhism seem affected in every aspect. This indictment pierced my heart!

As believers, our lifestyle can affect eternal destinies. While an adjunct teacher at a Christian university, Brad Kallenberg wrote:

> One of my freshman philosophy students . . . admitted to checking out Islam because she so admired the seriousness with which Muslims practice their religion. I was stupefied. What could I say to her? After all, she already knew the gospel. She was attending a Christian university, and had taken courses in Bible and theology.
>
> Although we spoke for a long time, I couldn't get rid of the nagging feeling that any defense of Christianity I could give would fall short of the mark. Why? Because my words could not give her what she really needed—hands-on contact with a robust community of believers who practiced Christianity with gusto.[6]

Byron Paulus, director of Life Action Ministries, agrees:

> The Muslim world vehemently opposes any lifestyle that dilutes its religion. Yet here in the West, even in our churches, we seem callused to those issues. We not only tolerate, but in some cases even endorse practices that are counter to the gospel we proclaim to believe—whether divorce, immoral movies, disrespect for authority, and even abortion.[7]

In God's plan, there are no "stealth Christians." Instead, we should illuminate the darkness with lives transformed by the power of Christ. If we allow the God of all creation to live through us, we *will* be changed! The believers in Thessalonica provide a wonderful example. Paul told them that because of their godly lifestyle, their *"faith in God has become known everywhere"* (1 Thessalonians 1:8, NIV). Can our non-Christian friends and family detect any difference our faith makes in our daily lives?

Our Integrity Influences Our Nation

God says that our integrity also affects an entire nation: *"Righteousness exalts a nation, but sin is a disgrace to any people"* (Proverbs 14:34). If we as the church live truly righteous lives of integrity as the Lord calls us to, this blesses our nation and induces change. But if we choose to sin and live no differently than everyone around us, we bring disgrace not only to ourselves, our family, and certainly the body of Christ, but to our entire nation as well.

As believers, we women could generate an *enormous* impact on our culture if we would just choose to live holy lives, refusing to participate in anything that is impure and ungodly. Women exert an incredible influence on their families. Think of the impact that could result from an entire nation of female believers actually living like Christ!

The Lord calls us to integrity in every facet of our lives. Our character and our integrity are built brick by brick through every choice of obedience we make. God says, *"Immorality or any impurity or greed must not even be named among you, as is proper among saints"* (Ephesians 5:3). He tells each of us to *"consider the members of your earthly body as dead to immorality, impurity, passion, evil desire, and greed"* (Colossians 3:5).

Walking into church won't cleanse our lives. Being in full-time Christian work won't cleanse our lives. Having daily quiet times won't cleanse our lives. Only a heart of brokenness before our holy God, yielding our lives to His will and choosing obedience moment by moment will create lives of integrity, pleasing and usable for His service. As Warren Wiersbe writes, "No amount of loving and sacrificial works can compensate for tolerance of evil."[8]

Instead, God tells us to *"cleanse ourselves from all defilement of flesh and spirit, perfecting holiness in the fear of God"* (2 Corinthians 7:1).

For a woman who struggles with the issue of sexual temptation, one area of integrity most likely presents the greatest challenge—the influence of the media in our society. Because of this pervasive problem, in our next chapter we will look more deeply into how we can live lives of integrity in our technology-saturated world.

But before we continue, take a moment and ask the Lord to search your heart for any practices that you may have accepted as normal, but which He desires to expose as sin. Put away *all* deception, *all* gossip, *all* coarse language and jokes, *all* impurity, *all* immorality, and *every* practice that dishonor our precious Lord. Then cry out, *"Oh that my ways may be established to keep Your statutes!"* (Psalm 119:5). Personal integrity matters!

15

Integrity and the Media

I f Christ were to knock on your door one Saturday night and join you in watching the television program you had previously been enjoying, would you suddenly feel uncomfortable? Would He be pleased with the pictures and language flowing through your living room? Joel Belz gives us an insightful perspective of what may be happening in our homes and lives:

It would have to be among the most startling of invitations you've ever received. You've lived next door to your neighbors for half a dozen years, and you thought you knew them fairly well. They are fine, upstanding folks in the community, active in school activities and little league. They're members of a different church from yours, but you know they're faithful there and that they take their Christian faith seriously. You've had some fun times with them, but also some serious backyard discussions about politics, kids' behavior, and music styles.

So you're not quite prepared for his invitation tonight. He drops by just before you sit down to dinner with your own family, pulls you aside, and calmly suggests: "Later tonight, my wife and I will be heading for bed—and my guess is we'll be—ah—well, you know, probably doing some of the things married people do. I thought maybe you and your wife would like to come by and watch."

You are aghast. The idea is so grotesque you can't imagine how to mention it to your wife—although when you do, it will certainly not be in the "shall we?" but more in the "how could he?" category of discussion. The images in your mind are repulsive.

Your neighbor is sensitive, and sees your uncomfortable surprise. "I'm not suggesting any hanky panky," he assures you. "Our marriage is terrific. I know yours is too. I'm just talking about watching." Then, sensing that your reluctance is real, he suggests an alternative: "Maybe this would be better. I have the phone number of a couple who would come over—a couple neither of us knows personally. That way, all four of us could just sit and watch them."[1]

Tonight, thousands of Christians will do just that—casually sit and watch some couple they do not know press their undressed bodies together in various sexual acts. Of course, they will be watching a video, DVD, or one of the many sexually oriented television shows aired nightly, rather than watching their neighbors or some other couple in person.

Oh, how tempting it is to rationalize our desires! But God gave us a guideline that I call "Integrity 101": *"I will walk within my house in the integrity of my heart. I will set no worthless thing before my eyes; I hate the work of those who fall away; it shall not fasten its grip on me. A perverse heart shall depart from me; I will know no evil"* (Psalm 101:2–4). When God tells us to set no worthless thing before our eyes and to not let any immorality, impurity, filthiness, or coarse jesting be among us (Ephesians 5:3,4), He never gives an exception clause to those instructions.

Someone may ask, "But don't we need to know what's out there in order to relate to nonbelievers?" For fifteen years, Stottler worked with children in the inner city, and he emphatically states that not once did his ministry with them suffer because he hadn't seen a movie containing immorality or sensuality. In fact, what those children desperately wanted to see was someone living a holy life, different from what they saw around them. They needed someone who was willing to love them and show them Christ's integrity. God yearns for us to love nonbelievers and *show them lives changed by Christ.* We can't very well do that if we act and talk exactly like them!

These days, it isn't necessary to attend an X-rated movie to see two naked people having sex under the sheets. We can simply flip to a major network or cable broadcast of the latest movie. And we don't even find the explicit sex shocking!

Satan loves the fact that many Christians believe such "harmless" entertainment will not affect their daily lives. But by allowing impure thoughts into our minds, the walls of protection around our marriage quickly weaken. As a woman's mind replays these explicit scenes of immorality, her sensitivity to the Lord grows cold, and her resolve for personal purity fades. The Bible tells us that what goes into our minds *does* come out of our lives: *"For as he thinks within himself, so he is"* (Proverbs 23:7).

From God's point of view, whenever we choose to watch or read anything that contains values that oppose His standards, we are choosing to be entertained by garbage. Every time we sit and absorb swearing, sexual images, innuendoes, violence, and perversion, it's like going to the city dump and finding entertainment in the stench and filth of decaying, putrefying refuse. As one fellow said, it's like "bathing in an open sewer ditch."[2] Is there a way to avoid this impurity and to build holiness back into our lives?

Integrity and the Movies

I love going to movies. During college I would attend every show that piqued my interest. And the movie industry knows *exactly* what appeals to women. Those movies aren't called "chick flicks" because they're designed to attract poultry!

I usually gravitated toward the romantic, sentimental movies, many of which portrayed infidelity as normal and desirable. I knew all too well what it was like to float out of a movie in a dreamy state, caught up in the mood of romance.

But as we absorb Hollywood's explicit portrayals of "love" (which are almost *always* at odds with God's definition of love), these impure mental pictures and ideas imprint themselves on our minds and subconsciously lower our standards and our guard against immorality. Often within hours of attending one of those movies, I would find myself struggling with impure thoughts. I wonder why!

Mental images have a powerful impact on our lives. What we allow to be imprinted upon our thoughts can cause far more damaging results than anything we may put into our bodies. Bad or fattening foods can be shed through exercise and diet. But a graphic sexual image imprinted upon our minds is like carving on a stone. Then when the right temptation comes along, those images can lower our standards and our defenses.

The power of visual images hit home with me recently when I reread the true story of the Von Trapp family's harrowing escape from the Nazi invasion of Austria. I have watched *The Sound of Music* probably four times and have read the story three times. And even though I recently reread Maria Von Trapp's wonderful autobiography, I simply *cannot* remember her actual story because the movie images are too deeply imprinted on my mind!

God's standard for holiness tells me to *"set no worthless thing before my eyes"* (Psalm 101:3). What does God consider worthless?

He tells us that *"among you there must not be even a hint of sexual immorality, or of any kind of impurity, or of greed, because these are improper for God's holy people. Nor should there be obscenity, foolish talk or coarse joking"* (Ephesians 5:3,4, NIV). Oops! That eliminates most of what we watch!

Yet compromise and conformity happen so often in the church today. Many "acceptable" movies touted by Christians do contain some biblical values—yet they also frequently include graphic sex scenes and coarse, filthy language. Even if the sex portrayed happens between a husband and his wife, we would never dream of going next door to watch our married neighbors enjoy tender moments together!

Our challenge as believers is to transfer Scripture into practical application. I heard of a ministry team who met for a week-long retreat and studied holiness one morning. Then for their afternoon break, many of them traipsed off to see an R-rated movie!

God commands us to *"abhor what is evil; cling to what is good"* (Romans 12:9). You don't sit and soak in things that you abhor. You don't pay money and give hours to something you detest. If we truly *abhorred* evil, we wouldn't give our time and money to sit in a movie theatre and soak it all in!

We are called instead to *"be wise in what is good and innocent in what is evil"* (Romans 16:19). Yet how can we stay innocent if we flood our minds with what God calls perverse and abhorrent? God says, *"The fear of the LORD is to hate evil; pride and arrogance and the evil way and the perverted mouth, I hate"* (Proverbs 8:13). But we don't hate evil; we pay money to enjoy it as entertainment!

So how can we resensitize our hardened spirits to the things God loves and hates? Is it possible for our spirit to become sensitive once again?

Taking the "R-rated Challenge"

Years ago, my accountability partner made an outrageous suggestion: commit myself to never attend an R-rated movie. At first,
such an idea seemed outlandish and incredibly narrow-minded.
But over the next couple of days, the Lord showed me that by
pouring immorality and impurity into my mind, I was making
choices that kept me constantly struggling with those very issues.
I was defeating myself.

Right then I decided to take the "R-rated Challenge" and avoid
watching movies containing that rating. And having maintained
that commitment these many years, I can attest to the resensitiz-
ing effect such a choice has made on my spirit. I can also tell you
that in making such a choice, I have never once missed out on
some important discussion, been considered less of a person, or
been less "in touch" with society.

"But what if there's just one little sex scene in an otherwise
pretty good movie?" someone will complain. What if I offered
you a piece of an enticing chocolate pecan pie and told you that
although a little horse manure had accidentally fallen into the
batter, the dessert was still excellent? Would you try a piece? No
way! A little "puckey" pollutes the whole pie! Likewise, God says
to set *no* worthless thing before your eyes. He didn't say, "Set no
worthless thing before your eyes unless the sex scene is only ten
seconds long."

"But what if it's rated R for something other than sex?" someone else will object. A movie bears an R rating for a reason—and
whether it's for sex, language, violence, or any other foul thing,
they *all* fall outside the parameter of holiness. God says that the
kind of person He will bless is the one who *"stops his ears from
hearing about bloodshed, and shuts his eyes from looking upon evil"*
(Isaiah 33:15). And unfortunately, what used to be considered R
content now routinely finds its way into PG-13 movies.

Moments still occasionally occur when I attend what I thought to be a clean movie, and a sensual scene pops on the screen. I *immediately* close my eyes. That way, at least I won't have any lasting visual images burned into my mind. (Don't worry, the music always tells me when to open my eyes again.)

Integrity and Television

Although survey after survey reveals that the overwhelming majority of people believe too much sex, foul language, and violence exists in the media, the average American injects more than four hours of television into his or her mind every day. Nightly, we invite strangers into our living rooms who curse our God, spout lewd jokes, and perform sexual acts in front of us.

Barna Research found that "born again adults spend an average of seven times more hours each week watching television than they do participating in spiritual pursuits such as Bible reading, prayer, and worship. They spend roughly twice as much money on entertainment as they donate to their church."[3]

Going Beyond the "R-rated Challenge"

Having taken the "R-rated Challenge" many years prior to my marriage, I still didn't realize how much garbage continued to infiltrate my mind just from watching TV. When I married Stottler, for the first two years I felt as if I had married my own personal censor board. He constantly got up from the sofa, leaving me alone to watch some evening television program. He didn't do so to condemn me; he just didn't want the garbage in his own mind.

Of course, *I* found his actions quite condemning! Stottler's choices revealed my own low standards. My initial reaction to having this spotlight on my hardened heart was (like most of us) to get angry. But once again, the Holy Spirit began to reveal my need to raise my standards, this time to the level of His Word.

Then as I began choosing to turn off the TV when anything impure came on (language, sex, violence, crude jokes, etc.), I suddenly noticed how those offensive things had previously fallen on insensitive, hardened ears.

When any thought or temptation toward sin comes upon us, we need to resist Satan and run to the Lord.

When I "shod my feet" during my quiet time (Ephesians 6:15), I often visualize fleeing from evil by changing the channel or getting up and turning off the television. I make these choices to guard my eyes and ears against anything that defies God's standard of holiness.

Now whenever a new television program catches my interest, yet I know its content displeases the Lord, I remember that He wants only that which is for my good and His glory. If God doesn't want me to put those images into my mind, then I don't want them there either because God knows that in some way they would harm me. And heaven knows, I don't need any more bad images in my mind! I have enough to last a lifetime!

Integrity and Print Media

For some women, romantic books or magazines present an enormous attraction. They revel in picking up some risqué reading material, curling up in a quiet corner, and fantasizing. Sometimes they may find it difficult to bring themselves back into the "real" world. Their work and family life may suffer because of their indulgences.

When any thought or temptation toward sin comes upon us, we need to resist Satan (James 4:7), run to the Lord, and replace those thoughts with *"whatever is true, whatever is honorable, whatever is right, whatever is pure, whatever is lovely, whatever is of good repute"* (Philippians 4:8). That surely applies to what we read. In fact, sometimes reading can produce more vivid mental images than movies or TV programs!

Resisting Lustful Reading Materials

It is often more difficult to avoid sexual reading material than impure movies and TV programs. To watch movies or TV, we have to station ourselves in front of a screen or television set. But printed material is everywhere—in the grocery store, at the drug store, even in your mailbox.

If buying sexual magazines or books is a temptation for you, travel different routes around town that avoid those stores. If magazine racks in checkout lanes lure you toward fantasizing about actors' lives or immorality of any sort, look the other way, or find a checkout lane without magazines.

Be proactive about combating temptations that come upon you suddenly by calling on God and His Word. Carry Scripture verses with you wherever you go. Memorize His Word, then stand on it in the midst of a temptation. Knowing His Word can make all the difference in whether we experience consistent victory or consistent defeat.

Integrity and the Internet

Shauna couldn't wait to get her children tucked into bed. As the last child's eyes finally drooped shut, she hurried into the study and flipped on the computer. Since her husband was out of town, she avoided all her normal precautions and immediately began pouring over pornographic pictures of nude males. Although her conscience continued to warn her that these actions were displeasing to God, she couldn't seem to stop her compulsion to view these pictures since stumbling onto them several months ago.

Ask almost any man, and he'll tell you that pornography is a male problem. Yet with more than half a billion people worldwide now accessing the Internet, the availability of obscenity at the touch of a finger has opened the door for *everyone* into the perverse world of pornography. It's not just "a man's thing" any longer.

Zogby International recently reported that almost one in five self-proclaimed Christian adults in America admits to visiting a sexually oriented website.[4] *Today's Christian Woman* magazine found in their survey that 34 percent of the female respondents admitted to intentionally visiting a pornography website.[5] And the Nielsen/NetRatings recently reported, "Nearly *one in three* visitors to adult Web sites is a *woman*"[6] (emphasis added)!

No longer does a tempted individual need to sneak over to the corner X-rated bookstore or strip club. With a few simple clicks of a mouse, lewd and perverse pictures come forth in the privacy of your home. In fact, *avoiding* pornography on the Internet has become difficult, as sexually explicit e-mails constantly appear in your in-box without your consent.

According to Ramona Richards in her article "Dirty Little Secret," "More than 25 million people visit porn sites every week and one out of every ten websites is dedicated to explicit sex... Seventy-four percent of all revenue collected online comes from porn sites, which amount to almost $1.2 billion annually."[7]

"Pornography is a bigger business than professional football, basketball and baseball put together," reports the *New York Times*. "People pay more money for pornography in America in a year than they do on movie tickets, more than they do on all the performing arts combined."[8]

But why would a woman be drawn to pornography? Marnie Ferree, a licensed marriage and family therapist, runs one of the few centers dedicated to helping women overcome sexual addiction. She says that the reasons range from childhood abuse to simply seeking companionship and relief from loneliness.[9] The forbidden-fruit aspect can also be quite tantalizing.

Many women—Christians included—develop their ideas of love from years of absorbing romantic movies, books, and television programs. Consequently, a woman may buy into the lie that her worth and appeal come from her sexuality. From there, it's an easy step into the Internet world of sexual images and pornography.

What may start as a curiosity can suddenly become an enslaving addiction. Pornography can captivate a person with a hold as insidious as heroin addiction. Ramona Richards says, "All forms of pornography can stimulate the user, releasing chemicals in the brain that act on the body in much the same way as cocaine does. It's an exhilarating but unfortunately short-lived euphoria. The loneliness returns, leaving the woman wanting more contact and more stimulation, thus creating the cycle of addiction."[10]

As one views pornographic images, the need for more exciting sexual stimulation escalates, quickly leading down the path toward adultery and perversion of every kind. The enslaving effects result in a believer acting no differently than a non-Christian. *"Having lost all sensitivity, they have given themselves over to sensuality so as to indulge in every kind of impurity, with a continual lust for more"* (Ephesians 4:19, NIV). To "toy" with pornography is like pouring gasoline all over your body, then playing with matches!

Often, the woman who begins secretly viewing pornographic images convinces herself that her actions really won't hurt anyone. But sin *always* affects others! Remember, Satan's perpetual goal is *"to steal and kill and destroy"* (John 10:10). What more effective way than through the destructive powers of pornography? While pornography lures a victim with the lie of meeting a need for sexual fulfillment and excitement, it actually steals her relationship with God, kills her sensitivity to His Spirit, and destroys her relationship with her husband and others.

As with sexual movie scenes, the residual effects of pornography can also last a lifetime. The perverse images are seared into one's thoughts like a branding iron on flesh. Those pictures can then replay in a woman's mind for the rest of her life. Even if a woman isn't addicted to pornography, the occasional look at a website or an explicit magazine still plants those pictures in her mind for decades, if not for a lifetime. It's not worth it!

As a woman delves into the underworld of porn, the need to cover up and hide the addiction leads to one lie after another, creating a gulf between the spouses. At the same time, viewing pornographic pictures and deviant sexual acts also causes greater dissatisfaction within the marriage. A Focus on the Family website reports: "Professors Dolf Zillman of Indiana University and Jennings Bryant of the University of Houston found that repeated exposure to pornography results in a decreased satisfaction with one's sexual partner, with the partner's sexuality, with the partner's sexual curiosity, a decrease in the valuation of faithfulness and a major increase in the importance of sex without attachment."[11]

Marriage therapist Marnie Ferree says, "More than 80 percent of women who have this addiction take it offline. Women, far more than men, are likely to act out their behaviors in real life, such as having multiple partners, casual sex, or affairs."[12]

God tells us that true sexual fulfillment can be found only in a committed, exclusive relationship with our spouse. Only when we become one flesh through marriage and live by God's standards of purity can we enjoy the height of sexual pleasure that He intended. Anything short of that rates second best. C. S. Lewis admonishes us that "you must not isolate [sexual] pleasure and try to get it by itself, any more than you ought to try to get the pleasure of taste without swallowing and digesting, by chewing things and spitting them out again."[13]

The Lord calls us to holiness and integrity in every area of our lives, repeatedly calling us to sexual purity. *"Beloved, I urge you as aliens and strangers to abstain from fleshly lusts which wage war against the soul"* (1 Peter 2:11).

With one in three visitors to sexually oriented websites being female, pornography has obviously bridged the gender gap. Yet few ministries acknowledge this growing problem among women. That being the case, any Christian woman caught in the engulfing quicksand of pornography feels ashamed and abnormal. Because pornography is usually seen as a "male-only" problem, she also feels isolated and alone. A woman trapped in such a position lives in terror that her oddity might be discovered.

Breaking Free of Addiction

Whether you have dabbled in pornography or find yourself immersed in addiction, the first step to breaking free is to admit that you need help. This sin will not dissipate by itself. Just as an alcoholic or a drug addict needs help, so do those addicted to pornography.

Help should start with your husband and your pastor. Your husband needs to know your weaknesses and tendencies in order to help you, pray for you, and hold you accountable. As frightening as this may sound, honesty *must* be the foundation of your marriage. Then trust can once again be built.

Also, no lasting healing can take place without confessing and baring your soul to God for His strength and transforming power. Charles Colson writes, "Nothing (and no one) can free the captives of addiction except God—something even the secular world has begun to recognize."[14] God is more than able to free us from every sin because *"if we walk in the Light as He Himself is in the Light, we have fellowship with one another, and the blood of Jesus His Son* **cleanses us from all sin***"* (1 John 1:7, emphasis added).

Also, seek professional help. "Women addicted to porn need professional therapy with a Christian counselor and a renewed sense of kinship with other women who understand," says Marnie Ferree. "They do need to be held accountable for their sins, but they also need help, support, and unconditional love."[15] The Resources in the back of this book list some places that provide help for any woman caught in this devastating addiction.

Because pornography can so easily destroy marriages and families, temptation in this area needs to be taken very seriously.

Steps also need to be taken to ensure that the person no longer has freedom to continue her destructive patterns in this area. God calls us to *avoid* sexual sin, not to place ourselves in positions where we must try to resist it—because we will fail.

So how can a woman avoid pornography? She may need to disconnect access to the Internet, or as one man called it, perform a "modemectomy." It is far more important to walk in holiness before the Lord than to be able to access all that the world offers through the Internet.

If nothing else, definitely place a "purity" filter on your Internet access, and place the computer in a well-traveled area of the house. If you must work on the Internet, find what you need and then disconnect quickly. Don't give in to browsing.

And don't connect to the Internet at night! When the sun goes down, it seems to take our will power and resistance with it. We all tend to give in to temptation *far* easier at night, so beware of evening computer use.

Place around your computer Scripture verses that call you to purity. And make your password a reminder of integrity. Taping a picture of your husband to the side of your computer screen is another good idea.

Because pornography can so easily destroy marriages and families—including missionaries, Christian workers, pastors, and their wives—temptation in this area needs to be taken very seriously. The lure of the Internet and all its opportunities for instant perversion mean that we need to pre-establish guards against this looming temptation so that our lives may radiate the purity of Christ.

How Are You Doing?

The battle for our marriages and our minds is so great that we cannot afford to take God's command for purity lightly. Romans 13:14 commands us to *"make no provision for the flesh in regard to its lusts."* What do you watch when no one else is at home? Do you soak in the lust, betrayal, and adultery of a daytime soap opera? If your husband travels, do you take that opportunity to rent romantic movies containing infidelity and sex? Do you sneak off to read a romance novel when you think no one is looking? Is your computer in a corner where you can hide what you're viewing?

I urge everyone to commit to the "R-rated Challenge" as a starting point. Then begin analyzing the content of everything you see and hear according to *God's* standards. Ask your husband and your accountability friend to hold you accountable for what you watch and read. If needed, drop your cable and satellite services. Or get rid of your TV and renew the lost art of reading good books and playing family games. If objectionable reading material hides in your home, feed it to the trash can.

Does that sound too fanatical or too hard? Does it seem like a lot to give up? I know Christian brothers and sisters who willingly suffer indescribable torture in Chinese prisons because they choose to proclaim Christ at the risk of their lives. And we whine over giving up our cable TV channels to walk in holiness!

Someone may complain, "This sounds too legalistic." It's not legalism—it's obedience and discipline! Only as we remain faithful in the "very little things" will God allow us to be used in greater ways (Luke 16:10).

We must stop thinking these "little areas" don't matter. They do! God tells us, *"Beloved, do not imitate what is evil, but what is good"* (3 John 11). These small decisions of integrity determine our ultimate character and whether or not the Lord can use us.

As we choose to live by the standards of purity that the Lord has given us, we cannot expect other believers to always understand or encourage us. But by faithfully choosing to walk in God's standard of holiness, what an example of integrity we can be! My prayer is that we will set a new standard that changes our lives, changes God's church, and ultimately changes our nation!

As children of God, we have the Spirit's power to live a life pleasing to Him, the discipline to meet daily with Him in His Word and prayer, and the wisdom to live obedient lives of integrity and holiness. This foundation gives us more confidence as we now turn our attention in the next section to building walls of protection around our marriage.

Part Three

How to Protect Your Marriage

16

Love and Your Marriage

Sailing across the translucent Caribbean Sea during our boat project, I had allowed my heart to cross into foreign waters. I had cast aside all wisdom and embraced the allure of our tanned, gentle captain. I really loved him—or so I thought. Yet shortly after making the painful decision to leave Eric and return home, one of my friends had made the audacious statement that what I felt wasn't really love. Was she crazy? Not real love? Hadn't I been willing to give up everything to be with this man? Hadn't I considered sacrificing my marriage and my ministry to dedicate myself to him? How could that not be love?

Make no mistake, romantic love is definitely a type of love. My feelings toward Eric were very real and incredibly powerful. And as I allowed the intensity of those feelings to grow, I lost all sense of judgment and reality.

Romantic emotions toward another man often disguise themselves as a once-in-a-lifetime opportunity to experience "true love." Yet these amorous feelings cannot provide the stable, maintainable foundation upon which to base a lasting relationship.

A couple enveloped in an affair usually enjoys a "fantasy" love —especially because they only present their "good" side. Shirley Glass wrote in *Psychology Today* that part of this unrealistic love comes from "the romantic projection: I like the way I look when I see myself in the other person's eyes. There is positive mirroring. An affair holds up a vanity mirror, the kind with all the little bulbs around it; it gives a rosy glow to the way you see yourself. By contrast, the marriage offers a makeup mirror; it magnifies every little flaw. When someone loves you despite seeing all your flaws, that is a reality-based love."[1]

Suddenly, this "ideal" relationship presents a whole new set of magnifying mirrors, once again revealing all the tiny blemishes and flaws.

A woman may naively believe that the fantasy love of an affair is her only opportunity to experience "true love." Seeking this ideal, she leaves her spouse—only to discover that the vanity mirror eventually shatters. Suddenly, this "ideal" relationship presents a whole new set of magnifying mirrors, once again revealing all the tiny blemishes and flaws.

Only about 10 percent of those who leave their spouse for a lover actually marry the affair partner. Once the reality of commitment sets in, the fantasy bubble bursts. And of those who do marry, few last. As one of Stottler's friends said after divorcing and marrying a second time, "If I had known marriage took so much work, I would have worked harder at it the first time!"

Because the intensity of amorous love always decays, basing a relationship on it is like building a house on top of a sand dune. Instead, God calls us to practice the kind of rock-solid, unconditional love demonstrated by Christ. This godly love must form the foundation of our marriage. It also forms the basis of our daily choices to protect our marriage from the onslaughts of the enemy. As we look at taking steps to protect our marriage, we must begin by laying the foundation of God's love.

Fantasy Love and God's Love

In the New Testament's original Greek language, different words were used to delineate various types of love. We find a romantic, infatuated type of love (which can include an erotic aspect), and a brotherly, affectionate type of love. But we also find a kind of love that God tells us to demonstrate in all relationships. Jesus says, *"A new command I give you: Love one another. As I have loved you, so you must love one another"* (John 13:34, NIV). An astounding passage in Philippians gives us a firsthand picture of this love in action:

> *[Christ], being in very nature God, did not consider equality with God something to be grasped, but made himself nothing, taking the very nature of a servant, being made in human likeness. And being found in appearance as a man, he humbled himself and became obedient to death—even death on a cross!* (Philippians 2:6–8, NIV)

I find it astonishing that the God who created you, me, and the entire world would willingly submit to torture by the very hands He created! Yet He offered His life *because* of love (Romans 5:8). Even though we disobeyed and despised Him, He willingly gave His life for us. *That* is love!

And *that* is the love He tells us to show toward one another. In 1 Corinthians 13, He spells out for us some very practical instructions on how to demonstrate this godly love. As we apply these precepts to our lives and marriages, they look something like this:

> *Love is patient* (even when my husband's repetitive whistling drives me crazy).

Love is kind (which means I choose by the Spirit's power to do something good for him even when he's done something unkind toward me).

Love is not jealous (though he seems to get all the accolades and I'm "just" a housewife).

Love does not brag (which means I seek God's approval above all else).

Love is not arrogant (because I remember Psalm 16:2, that "I have no good besides You").

Love does not act unbecomingly (though it's so tempting to correct my husband in front of his buddies).

Love does not seek its own (but seeks what helps and encourages my husband the most).

Love is not provoked (which can happen *only* by the Lord's strength).

Love does not take into account a wrong suffered (which means I choose to forgive instead of dredging up my favorite "Past Offenses" zinger).

Love does not rejoice in unrighteousness (so I seek to live a life that models Christ's holiness and integrity in our home).

Love rejoices with the truth (so I love that which pleases God).

Love bears all things (so I trust God to see my situation and handle it *His* way).

Love believes all things (so I trust God to work out for good even the difficult things in my marriage).

Love hopes all things (because I practice being a praying wife instead of a complaining wife).

Love endures all things (because by God's strength I never abandon my commitment to my husband).

Love never fails... But now abide faith, hope, love, these three; but the greatest of these is love" (1 Corinthians 13:4–8,13).

Love and Feelings

Do you know what stands out the most to me in all these demonstrations of love? *Not one of them has to do with feelings.* The passage never says, "Love is kind when I *feel* like being kind." It says that love acts kindly *regardless* of how I feel. Love acts patiently *regardless* of the desire to scream that I feel welling up inside me. *"Let us not love with word or with tongue, but in **deed** and truth"* (1 John 3:18, emphasis added). Love requires action, not emotion.

One of Satan's great deceptions has been to equate godly love with an emotion. Because the world inundates us with the idea that love springs purely from an emotional response, this concept of sacrificial, godly love becomes difficult for us to grasp.

Nearly every TV show and movie portrays passionate, emotional love as the basis for relationships. Programs showing a spouse sacrificing personal happiness to serve her partner and maintain a stable home have almost become a relic of the past. Because of this constant conditioning by the media, it's easy to believe that when you no longer *feel* love toward your husband, your marriage must be over. After all, "you've lost that lovin' feelin'."[2]

But godly love is a decision. Love is commitment. Love is sacrifice. I'm pretty sure that as the spikes bore through the hands and feet of Jesus, He wasn't experiencing any warm fuzzy feelings. But He chose to *demonstrate* love regardless.

Philippians 2:3 lays out the "gold standard" for demonstrating godly love: *"Do nothing from selfishness or empty conceit, but with humility of mind regard one another as more important than yourselves."* Godly love considers my husband's needs as more important than my own. Godly love sacrifices my rights to show kindness to him regardless of my feelings.

Stottler constantly demonstrates sacrificial love to me. For example, a recent project at work left him buried under details and deadlines. Yet in the midst of all this, he repeatedly asked if he could do anything to help *me!* When *I'm* buried with work, I definitely don't tend to seek ways to help others. Yet Stottler's demonstration of self-sacrificing love not only ministered to me, but provided a fantastic model as well.

As we constantly absorb Hollywood's portrayal of self-serving, emotional love, godly sacrificial love seems quite foreign. Yet our two greatest commands from the Lord address our need to demonstrate His love: *"'You shall love the Lord your God with all your heart, and with all your soul, and with all your mind.' This is the great and foremost commandment. The second is like it, 'You shall love your neighbor as yourself'"* (Matthew 22:37–39).

To love God and to love my neighbor—my husband being my *closest* neighbor—means making constant choices, empowered by the Spirit, carried out by the will. The Spirit-controlled life has little to do with feelings and everything to do with obedience. *"This is love: that we walk in obedience to his commands"* (2 John 6, NIV). We demonstrate love toward God and others by obeying His commands.

We are totally incapable of demonstrating this supernatural, sacrificial love apart from Christ loving through us. Therefore, we find yet another reason why we must run in desperation to yield our lives *every day* to His Spirit's control, putting on Christ's righteousness and being transformed through daily time in His Word and presence.

To help retrain my mind that godly love is not based on emotions, I practice something every day when I "put on" Christ. I not only ask Him to see with my eyes so that I have His perspective and to think with my mind so that I can know His will, but each day I ask Him to demonstrate His godly love through my hands, my lips, and my actions. This practice reinforces to me daily that godly love is *action*, not feelings. And little by little, it's working!

Living out this godly, sacrificial love can be like going to work. Some days I'm excited about my job, the goals that lie ahead, who I'll see, and what I'll accomplish. Other days, I must decide solely by my will to roll out of bed, get dressed, drive down the highway, and walk into that building. But I go to work regardless of my changing feelings. So it should be with love. Our *feelings* toward our husbands really are inconsequential in regard to our actions.

No two human beings will ever form a "perfect" match. Imperfection plus imperfection does not equal perfection! Therefore, if we try to trade in this current model for another later one that seems better suited at the moment, we will simply experience a different set of imperfections. God loves *us* unconditionally (despite all our faulty wiring), so by His strength we must obediently demonstrate His love to our imperfect husbands—for better or for worse. Christian author Arthur DeKruyter says:

> The Scriptures describe a giving love—a love that says, "Whatever I have, I want to share with you, and I want you to be what God meant you to be."…We can see immediately that this kind of love is not emotional. One does not fall into and then out of this kind of love. It is a love of the will. It is something addressed to our volition. We do it because we make ourselves do it. We order ourselves. Because of Christ, we are motivated to love. We do not wait for attraction or like interests.[3]

My love for Eric definitely sprang from my old, fleshly nature. Although my feelings certainly seemed like love, my actions proved otherwise. I failed to demonstrate godly love toward the Lord because I disobeyed His Word. I failed to demonstrate godly love toward Stottler because I acted selfishly, deceptively, and unfaithfully. I failed to demonstrate godly love toward Eric because

I defrauded a brother. My friend had been right—my self-serving "love" had no relationship to God's Spirit-controlled, selfless love.

An Amazing By-product

When we *do* choose by the power of the Spirit to respond with God's love toward our spouse despite contrary emotions, an amazing by-product frequently occurs. Often our emotions change and we begin to *feel* love again! As we practice living according to the design God created for us, the pieces fall into place—including our feelings.

But when we disobey God, everything gets out of kilter. When I sat on the boat overcome with "love" for Eric, I also felt emotionally lifeless toward my husband. I still cared about Stottler, yet my dead emotional feelings toward him seemed irreparable.

God, however, is in the resurrection business! Once I returned home and began to make right choices that demonstrated godly love, I discovered that inch by inch my *feelings* of love for Stottler also returned. When I chose to act in love by being honest, transparent, and broken, then the *feelings* of love seeped back in as well. Now I love my precious husband with Christ's godly love as well as with enamored, passionate love!

A friend from India commented about the American attitude toward love and marriage, "You marry the women you love; we love the women we marry." Therein lies a *profound* difference. In India, where the majority of marriages are still arranged by the parents, the divorce rate remains among the lowest in the world, at less than one percent! They start with commitment, and feelings *follow.*

Because this sacrificial love is so foreign to our old selfish nature, we must constantly practice dying on the altar and putting on Christ, asking Him to demonstrate His love through us. He's the only One who can!

Love and Protection

Demonstrating God's unconditional love is the best protection we have for our marriage. Therefore, let's look at four issues that make a huge impact on our ability to demonstrate His godly love. Then we'll look at why our marriage matters so much to God and to others.

Denying Selfishness

My mother delighted in seeing and experiencing new places. Every summer as I grew up, she would lead our family to some fascinating vacation destination, whether traversing the country by motor home or covering Europe by tour bus.

To make our trips carefree and fun, Mom spent months pouring over brochures and planning the tiniest details. So when it came time for the annual family outing, *nothing* hindered our trips—neither storm nor rain, broken bones nor stitches. I ventured out on quite a few of these family forays equipped with casts, stitches, and bandages of various degrees.

Coming from this background, Stottler's astonishing offer about seven months into our marriage made a profound impact on me. In our ministry, we travel quite a bit. In preparation for leading a team to Russia, Stottler had scheduled an initial trip there to lay the groundwork. Weeks had been spent working out all the details for this trip.

Four days before his departure, I became incredibly upset about something in our marriage. (I don't have a clue what it was about now, but I'm *sure* it must have been terribly important!) As we discussed this problem, Stottler made an astounding announcement: He would cancel the trip because I was far more important than his work.

My jaw dropped to the floor. Cancel a trip? No one *ever* cancels a trip! I could scarcely believe my ears. My husband would actually cancel a huge trip because he felt I was more important! That kind of sacrifice for our marriage and for me made a lasting impression!

But most of us don't display that kind of commitment. Instead, we nurture the black cloud of selfishness. Stemming from the root of pride, selfishness is a death coffin for any marriage. Why? Because selfishness *always* leads to strife and problems. "Selfishness" and "Strife" form one of the few permanently married couples. One pastor told me that selfishness resided at the heart of every single counseling session he had ever held.

In our culture, selfishness has been promoted so much that it almost sounds righteous. The radical feminist movement encourages us to "do what meets *your* needs." If you've been a wife and have sacrificed career and personal goals for your husband and children, surely there comes a day when it's time to think about *your* needs. And if *you're* more fulfilled by leaving your husband and children for someone else, then that's better for everyone. Right? Wrong!

Selfishness propelled my sinful choices in the Caribbean. The tingle of romance enticed my selfish nature, and I chose to nurture those feelings. I selfishly disregarded the feelings of my husband. In every case of infidelity, the married person focuses on feeding his or her own desires in utter disregard of the spouse's feelings.

Selfishness is a marriage-killer. But as we *"seek first His kingdom and His righteousness"* (Matthew 6:33), selfishness is crucified and we can give out of Christ's sacrificial love. Only as we choose to live the Spirit-controlled life can we then die to our selfishness and put our partner first. Remember the "gold standard" of Philippians 2:3, to consider others as more important? Stottler and I jokingly say that because we are both strong-willed individuals, we would have killed each other by now if we didn't practice dying to ourselves and yielding our lives to Christ each day.

So what does sacrificially putting my husband's needs above my own look like for me as a wife? It means not pressuring him to change. It means praying for him instead of nagging. It means refraining from dumping all my 40,000 stored up words on him when he comes home tired. It means seeking to encourage and minister to him even when I'm tired and weary. It means depending on Christ's strength to love him minute by minute.

Are you demonstrating sacrificial, selfless love?

Forgiving

My brother and his wife bake the most delicious bread in their bread maker. I still find that machine fascinating. The tedious process of kneading, rising, more punching and kneading, followed by more rising has now been reduced to simply mixing ingredients into the machine. Turn it on and out pops fantastic bread!

Just like a bread maker, God gives each of us a "peacemaker" called forgiveness. As we mix humility and forgiveness into a marriage, out pops peace! We all desire lives of peace, especially in our homes. And one of the main ingredients for producing peace is to ask for and to give forgiveness.

It sounds so simple, yet humbling our prideful natures can feel incredibly painful. After an argument with Stottler, the *last* thing I feel like doing is apologizing and asking for his forgiveness. The main reason we argued in the first place was because I knew *I* was right and he was *obviously* wrong.

Yet when I stop to think about it, *not* humbling myself and seeking forgiveness seems utterly silly! What harm can asking for his forgiveness do? My life always needs a dose of humility, and the only thing injured will be my pride, which *needs* injuring! On top of that, God *commands* us to forgive others: *"Be kind to one another, tender-hearted, forgiving each other, just as God in Christ also has forgiven you"* (Ephesians 4:32). Since God forgave *all* of my sins, is it too much for me to forgive *one* of my husband's sins?

The simple act of asking for and giving forgiveness helps restore peace and harmony in our marriage and in our home. Forgiveness protects our relationships from the downward spiral of bitterness, which can so easily lead to broken marriages and broken homes.

Are you quick to forgive and to ask your husband's forgiveness?

Taking Negative Thoughts Captive

Another important issue in our marriage, along with denying selfishness and demonstrating forgiveness, goes back to donning the helmet of salvation. When we put on the helmet of salvation daily, *"we are taking every thought captive to the obedience of Christ"* (2 Corinthians 10:5).

Yet we can so easily allow negative thoughts to build toward our husband. Whatever we repeat over and over in our minds, we begin to believe. And as we believe it, we act on it and make it come true. If I repeat to myself, "My husband is so thoughtless and inconsiderate," then I begin to believe that and act upon it. Just as a child will mirror what we expect of him, others will respond according to our treatment and attitude toward them.

Instead, I must replace negative thoughts toward my spouse with positive thoughts about the areas for which I'm thankful. The qualities I loved in Stottler when we first met—a cute sense of humor, being fascinating, godly, intelligent, sensitive, and fun —are qualities that last a lifetime. So when something negative pops into my mind, I purposefully thank the Lord for Stottler's many wonderful traits and choose to dwell on those instead.

Our "job description" as wives does *not* include fixing our husbands. God did not place us in the repair business—that belongs to Him. Yet within hours of taking our wedding vows, we have already set up the "Husband Design and Molding Shop" thinking we can create the perfect model.

However, the very best thing I can possibly do for my marriage is to concentrate on becoming the wife God desires *me* to be. And that means I *can't* concentrate on the negative things I think need fixing in my husband. Eleanor Doan writes, "Success in marriage consists not only in finding the right mate, but also in being the right mate."[4] Daily, I must take every negative thought captive, practice the Spirit-controlled life, and spend time in God's Word and presence so that He can transform *me* into a godly woman. That job alone will keep me busy the rest of my life!

Do you find yourself replaying negative thoughts about your husband? Are you constantly trying to "fix" him? Or are you quick to take negative thoughts captive and to thank the Lord for the positive aspects of your husband's character?

Giving Up My Rights

Another key issue toward maintaining a peaceful, Christ-centered marriage deals with giving up our "rights." Just as I lay my life on God's altar, giving Him full control, I have discovered that an important practice in marriage is to also lay my "rights" on His altar.

Our society tells us that we "deserve a break today." The media bombards us with the idea that for some reason, society and others owe us. Don't *I* deserve to be treated well? Don't *I* deserve to have a wonderful husband, a nice home, and a perfect family life?

Yet once again God's ways are upside down from ours. Christ's life teaches us to be living sacrifices, to serve, and to be last: *"Whoever wishes to become great among you shall be your servant; and whoever wishes to be first among you shall be slave of all. For even the Son of Man did not come to be served, but to serve, and to give His life a ransom for many"* (Mark 10:43–45).

For Christ to live His life through me, I must die to my selfish desires and expectations. For example, when I spend time cleaning and scraping off all the little spots and particles glued to our bathroom mirror, only to watch Stottler splash water on it moments later, the Frankenstein lurking within my flesh can suddenly come to life. To maintain peace, I need to give up my "rights" to having a clean mirror, as well as my "rights" to ownership of the bathroom. Nowhere in God's Word does He promise me a clean house.

To keep from becoming a raving housewife, I must identify the "right" of having a clean bathroom, then lay that on the altar before God. I also give up my ownership of the house, trusting that it belongs to God, and therefore He will decide how others treat it. As I choose to sacrifice my rights and ownership, I thank God for the outcome. Predetermining to thank the Lord for whatever happens proves that I have transferred that right and ownership back to Him and am trusting Him regardless of the outcome.

Yielding our rights occurs in all sorts of areas in our marriages. Stottler's lack of musical ability could be a major cause of tension in our marriage. Not only does he fail to whistle or sing on pitch, but he usually doesn't even know how the tune is supposed to go! And to make matters worse, he absolutely loves to sing and whistle certain melodies over and over and over and over and...you get the picture. Because of my background as a musician, his singing and whistling can make me want to run my fingernails down a chalkboard!

Everyone's marriage contains areas of annoyance like this. For me, I must constantly yield my rights to hearing well-performed music in our home. When Stottler begins his seventy-second chorus of "It's a Small World," I then remember to thank the Lord that He has blessed me with ears that are *able* to hear repetitive off-key music.

Yielding our rights, however, does *not* mean that we become doormats for our husbands to wipe their feet on. For example, periodically I can ask Stottler *in love* to stop for a while, or at least switch to a different melody. When a husband responds in a way that is harmful to the marriage relationship, that action should be addressed in love. Because we are all selfish creatures, we will invariably act in selfish ways. These actions need to be held accountable through loving confrontation within the marriage, forming what Dr. James Dobson calls "a workable system of checks and balances."[5]

And of course the Lord makes a distinction between rights and responsibilities. God gives us certain responsibilities that He expects us to carry out. Although I give my *rights* to a clean mirror over to the Lord, I maintain the *responsibility* to clean our house as needed. I cannot say, "Lord, I lay my rights to a clean house on Your altar, and therefore I will never need to clean it again." I wish! But it doesn't work that way. God gives us the responsibility of cleanliness, but we yield the rights of others keeping it that way.

We are also to yield the rights to our bodies. *"Do you not know that your body is a temple of the Holy Spirit who is in you, whom you have from God, and that you are not your own?"* (1 Corinthians 6:19). Not only does the Lord own my body, but He gives it to my mate. God says, *"The wife does not have authority over her own body, but the husband does; and likewise also the husband does not have authority over his own body, but the wife does"* (1 Corinthians 7:4).

Don Meredith writes in his book about marriage, "God steps boldly to the point...My body is not mine, but my mate's. I am here to please. Hereafter, to demand rights over my body is to disagree with God's instruction. God makes sex a sacrificial act that is redemptive, in that it gets my eyes off my needs and onto the needs of my mate."[6]

Irritation acts as a wonderful identifier of rights yet to be yielded. And as you practice giving these to God one by one, you will experience far greater harmony in your marriage.

Do you find yourself irritated over lots of little things? Will you lay each of those on the altar and thank the Lord for whatever He chooses to do?

A Testimony to Our Children

The divorce rate in the American church has sent a resonating message to our children that "Christian" marriages are no different from any other. And what we model at home is quickly imitated by our children and carried throughout the next generation.

We wives possess such power to set the atmosphere of either godliness or selfishness in our homes. As one bumper sticker says, "If Mama ain't happy, ain't nobody happy." If a wife resists the Spirit's control, and consequently responds toward her husband with little patience and love, a downcast tenor automatically results in the home. But as we allow the Spirit to produce His fruit of *"love, joy, peace, patience, kindness, goodness, faithfulness, gentleness, and self-control"* in our lives (Galatians 5:22,23, NIV), we then witness the change that results in our homes and in the generation following in our footsteps. Dr. Willard Harley writes:

> The greatest contribution that parents can make to their children's happiness and success is to love each other for life. If parents love their children, and want the best for their children, they must do everything possible to preserve their romantic relationship. That means caring for each other must be their highest priority—they must meet each other's intimate emotional needs. It's not a choice between caring for each other and caring for children. The reality is that if you want to truly care for your children, you must care for each other.[7]

Do your children feel secure in your sacrificial, loving commitment to your husband? Do they see you exchanging tenderness and love so they can outwardly say, "Yuck! Gag!" and inwardly rejoice and rest in the fact that mom and dad are totally committed to one another? The *most* important thing we can give our children is a stable, loving marriage relationship.

A Testimony to the World

Not only do our children watch us, but if we follow God's instructions on how to love, our marriage will become a testimony to the world as well. We have no idea how many people watch our lives to see if godly marriages really exist. Psychologist Dr. Neil Clark Warren writes:

> The truth is, many people have *never* seen a successful, thriving marriage, mainly because great marriages are becoming scarce. Several years ago, I conducted a survey in which I asked 500 individuals to tell me about the marriage they most admired. To my dismay, nearly half said they couldn't recommend even one healthy, exemplary marriage![8]

I can relate. Before turning 28 years old, I had no desire to marry. Up to that point, all the marriages I had witnessed consisted of stress and conflict. As a happy single, I reasoned, "Why trade in this carefree life for one full of arguments and strife?"

Then God graciously opened an opportunity to live with the six-member Lang family. Daily, I watched their marriage exemplify self-sacrifice, godly love, and commitment. Their home resounded with joy and laughter. Problems that inevitably arose from raising four young girls received biblical correction, grace, and forgiveness. Even when tragedy struck, I witnessed the way Bonnie faithfully stood by her husband and trusted God. What a testimony their marriage gave to my hungry soul!

One reason God is so concerned about how we present our marriage to the world is because our marriage represents Christ's love for His church, which is called the bride of Christ (Revelation 19:7). Jesus has demonstrated His faithfulness to His bride all through the centuries, despite our unfaithfulness shown in return. In "The Perfect Model for Marriage," Al Janssen writes:

> No matter what our circumstances, God desires that our earthly marriages be a reflection of Him and His love for us ...There is no problem that anyone has had in a marriage that God doesn't understand. Here is where we deal with the tough cases. Are we really expected to stay married when we are miserable? What if I give everything to my spouse and get nothing in return? By looking at God's example, I see that He has been in a one-sided marriage for centuries, and still He's remained faithful."[9]

What a privilege for us to be able to present Christ to the world through our sacrificial love for our spouse! What an opportunity we have to show others the love of Christ as demonstrated in our marriages. The world hungrily waits to see such marriages!

Whether loving unconditionally, forgiving, taking negative thoughts captive, or giving up my rights, a marriage relationship boils down to living the sacrificial life demonstrated by Christ. When Paul tells us in Philippians 2:3 to *do nothing from selfishness or empty conceit, but with humility of mind regard one another as more important than yourselves,* he hands us the *key* to marriage.

How are you doing? Are you daily demonstrating godly, self-sacrificing love? Are you asking for forgiveness, taking negative thoughts captive, and yielding your rights? Whatever the Lord may reveal, please begin to mend those areas now in order to protect your most precious earthly relationship. Establishing the foundation of God's unconditional love for your marriage is critical so that the walls of protection we are about to build can stand strong!

17

Caring for Your Marriage

I recently read about a conversation between football telecasters Frank Gifford and Dan Dierdorff. They were discussing Walter Payton of the Chicago Bears, an all-time leading rusher. Gifford said, "What a runner! Do you realize that all together, Walter Payton gained more than nine miles rushing in his career? Just imagine that—more than nine miles." To which Dierdorff added, "And to think that every 4.6 yards of the way, someone was knocking him down."[1]

Trying to live like Christ in the midst of a crooked and perverse generation can feel like being knocked down every time we try to stand. We must not forget that we are at war. With the divorce rate in the churches identical to those outside, and with 30 percent of all married women mired in some type of infidelity, an all-out battle rages against our marriages. Very little in the world around us offers encouragement to *"deny ungodliness and worldly desires and to live sensibly, righteously and godly in the present age"* (Titus 2:12).

Yet we *can* walk in consistent faithfulness to the Lord because He promises: *"No temptation has overtaken you but such as is com-*

mon to man; and God is faithful, who will not allow you to be tempted beyond what you are able, but with the temptation will provide the way of escape also, so that you will be able to endure it" (1 Corinthians 10:13).

So how *do* we remain faithful to our marriage vows when everything around us seeks to tear them apart? How *do* we battle against the temptation to seek another man's attention? What *do* we do when those feelings of enticement arise unexpectedly toward a friend, a long-time acquaintance, or someone new? What can each of us do to keep from becoming another statistic, someone suddenly caught in the downward cyclone of powerful passions toward another man?

> *We need to prepare for the daily battle as well as possible, which means "closing the door" on opportunities for sin.*

Choosing to live the Spirit-controlled life means daily guarding our marriages so that they will continue to honor Him and be lights to the world. We need to prepare for the daily battle as well as possible, which means "closing the door" on opportunities for sin.

In the Old Testament, Nehemiah provides us with a wonderful illustration of barring the gates to keep out sin. After supervising the rebuilding of Jerusalem's walls and encouraging revival in the people's lives, Nehemiah made a quick return trip back to Babylon. But upon returning to Jerusalem, he found the Jews regressing into their old, sinful patterns. God had clearly told the Jews not to buy or sell on the Sabbath, but in Nehemiah's absence, they had started doing so once again.

What did Nehemiah do? Every Sabbath he shut the gates into Jerusalem, effectively "closing the doors" to the city so the Gentiles could not enter in to transact business (Nehemiah 13:15–21).

Nehemiah saw the problem and found a way to shut out the opportunity for sin. What a great picture for us!

How do we "close the door" on infidelity? By protecting our marriages. Usually, once a woman has reached the point of actually pursuing another man, she has already hardened her heart so that counsel and truth often fall on deaf ears. So we need to close the doors of opportunity before we ever reach that point.

Having established godly love as the foundation of our marriage, in these next four chapters we will look at four areas of protection that close the door on infidelity. We will see the vital importance of caring for your marriage, establishing accountability in your marriage, building walls to protect your marriage, and responding to marital temptations.

The Priority of Your Marriage

How easily we can lose our focus on what's important in our marriage! In Luke 10, we see a picture of ourselves in Martha. She had become so bothered with all the tiny details in life that she forgot the Lord God Almighty was sitting in her living room! Similarly, we can become so preoccupied with the little problems in our marriages that we often forget how critically important our marriage is—until tragedy strikes.

Moments of catastrophe suddenly redirect our focus to remember again what is truly important in life. Shortly after the World Trade Center attack, an article by the Family Research Council noted, "In the wake of the terrorist attacks hundreds of couples in Houston decided to dismiss their divorce cases . . . The couples who decided not to divorce saw how small their problems were in comparison to the terrorist attacks. With all of the people who lost their lives, their parents, their children, even big marital problems didn't seem to matter as much."[2]

If we kept in mind how brief our earthly time really is, our priorities would look quite different. We delude ourselves into thinking that our future plans are set and that we know what tomorrow will bring. God warns us, *"Yet you do not know what your life will be like tomorrow. You are just a vapor that appears for a little while and then vanishes away"* (James 4:14).

We never know when events will alter our lives or the lives of those we love forever. On the morning of September 11, 2001, no one anticipated that nearly 3,000 lives would tragically end in the next few moments. Similarly, those unsuspecting people driving across Interstate 40 on May 26, 2002, didn't know that they would be launched into midair to then crash headlong into the Arkansas River because the bridge had collapsed.

If Stottler was lying in a hospital bed, gasping to survive some horrific car accident, all of our petty little arguments would seem utterly insignificant and pointless. Would thoughts of his repetitive singing annoy me? No way! In fact, nothing would thrill me more than to have him suddenly cast off all life-support tubes and burst into twenty-six choruses of "Amazing Grace"!

When we consider the brevity and uncertainty of life, we are far more inclined to refocus on important things. And the *most* important things in life aren't *things*. Next to our relationship with God, our families are the most precious gift we've been given. Consequently, we must determine to keep our marriages the strong priority that God intended.

In Proverbs 31, God paints a portrait of the ideal wife. When we study that chapter, we find that she is simply a woman who sets her priorities according to God's call: God first, then husband, then family, then ministry/work. Although we can easily become buried in the daily "tasks"—even good ones like running carpools and maintaining the home—God clearly calls us to place our husband over events and schedules.

In *The Mystery of Marriage*, Mike Mason writes, "Next to the love of God, the 'one thing' that is by far the most important in the life of all married people is their marriage, their loving devotion to their partner. Nothing on earth must take precedence over that, not children, jobs, other friendships, nor even Christian work."[3]

So how do we keep our marriages as our first priority? While some couples may confront serious issues in their marriage that require professional counseling, the majority simply need to take steps to protect their marriages before marital decay overtakes them. The following seven areas have proven invaluable for Stottler and me.

1. Identify Your Unmet Needs

The man who meets your emotional needs is the one with whom you will fall in love. And if you neglect your marriage, the enemy stands at your door with a line of eligible men just waiting to meet your needs. Dr. Willard Harley writes in *His Needs, Her Needs:*

> In marriages that fail to meet those needs, I have seen, strikingly and alarmingly, how married people consistently choose the same pattern to satisfy their unmet needs: the extramarital affair. People wander into affairs with astonishing regularity, in spite of whatever strong moral or religious convictions they may hold.[4]

That is why it is *absolutely critical* that you begin protecting your marriage by nurturing the relationship with your husband now—because when a vacuum exists, someone *always* pops up to fill the void. In the Caribbean, I spent my free time scuba diving and talking for hours about music and sports with Eric. And sure enough, as I began to enjoy spending time with him the most, he captured my heart.

Most affairs happen with friends or coworkers because they are the ones readily available to know and meet our emotional needs. When we begin to "hang out" with another man by simply spending time pleasurably talking, or jogging, or having lunch together, we begin allowing a man other than our husband to fulfill our needs for companionship.

Once your heart gravitates toward another man with whom you most enjoy spending time, then you start to imagine that your spouse has slighted you. From there it's a short step to thinking you have the right to opt out of your "confining" marriage to be with this other enjoyable person.

To regain that closeness in your marriage, begin by identifying your unmet needs. Of course, your husband isn't designed to meet *all* of your needs. Ruth Bell Graham, wife of evangelist Billy Graham, made this wise statement:

> It is a foolish woman who expects her husband to be to her that which only Jesus Christ Himself can be; always ready to forgive, totally understanding, unendingly patient, invariably tender and loving, unfailing in every area, anticipating every need, and making more than adequate provision. Such expectations put a man under an impossible strain.[5]

Only Christ can meet all of our deepest needs. But as you begin taking steps to protect your marriage, knowing areas of need that your husband *can* meet becomes an important place to start. Do you hunger simply to have your husband's listening ear? Do you miss those days of laughing together? Do you yearn for a night out without the children?

But what if your husband seems incapable of meeting your needs? For example, what if you love extreme sports and classical music, and your husband doesn't possess an athletic or musical bone in his body? I know a couple just like that!

For health reasons, Stottler is unable to participate in high aerobic activities (which somehow doesn't seem to break his heart). And we have already discussed his musical "abilities." These two areas are a *huge* part of my life. So how can he possibly meet my needs? He does so by giving me the freedom and the encouragement to pursue these areas. He also attends every one of my musical performances, always praying for me and supporting me, as well as greatly enjoying the music. And he always encourages me to mountain bike, which I do alone, with another woman, or in a large group.

Many times we need to let our husbands know that we need their support and encouragement because it acts as a safeguard for our marriages. Rather than nag and wheedle them to try and receive their encouragement, we need to explain why it's so important for the marriage's sake. Then leave the results to God.

Your best friend and companion should be your husband. To make that happen, it may mean learning new activities that you can enjoy together. Because Stottler is unable to mountain bike with me, I have taken up hiking. Now when we go camping, though I practically salivate to ride my bike on the winding, wooded trails, I choose to hike with Stottler instead so that we can be together.

But what does a woman do if she finds herself married to a man who would rather talk to their dog than to her? Her natural impulse would be to share her aching heart with another person. But if that other person is the understanding man at work or the kind fellow across the street, she has just opened wide the door for infidelity.

A woman with unmet emotional needs in her marriage is like a pressurized can of feelings just bursting to explode with love toward the first man who seems to meet her deep desires for affection, understanding, and attention. Studies reveal that unfaithful spouses most often cheat because they seek understanding, encouragement, or love. Psychiatrist Dr. Scott Haltzman writes:

> Feeling validated, heard and loved are exactly the same needs that made you fall in love with your spouse to begin with, but as a marriage progresses, you don't feel adored. There are going to be times in every marriage when you don't feel you're getting your needs met. It just feels like everything is wrong in the marriage.[6]

If you find yourself in this situation, instead of confiding your needs to another man, pour out your heart and frustrations to your accountability friend. She not only holds you accountable for your actions, but can also provide encouragement to help you remain faithful through the desert. You may also need to seek the wisdom and counsel of a professional. But don't give up on seeking to rebuild this area with your husband!

Unmet emotional needs may also be an issue for the couple who experiences an empty nest for the first time. If they have failed to maintain their relationship as a priority, they may suddenly look at one another and ask, "Who is this person?" But it's never too late to begin rekindling that intimacy once again, regardless of your age or situation.

2. Spend Exclusive Time Together

What it took to create romance and affection at the beginning of your relationship—exclusive time together—is the exact same thing required to *maintain* those feelings of love and affection.

Think back to those days of dating your husband-to-be. Hours seemed like minutes as you focused on one another in long conversations. You yearned to spend time alone together so you could learn more about each other's interests. Hanging on every word, the simplest of new discoveries brought joy and delight. Then you fell in love, married, and along came the children. Gradually, those intimate, tender hours transformed into diaper-changing, carpool-driving, soccer-watching years. Your marriage slowly slipped into a coma while you frantically chased kids and careers.

Yet you didn't marry with the goal of simply raising children. You married in order to love and serve one another, giving your life to that other individual. And just as we must return to our "first love" of Christ, rekindling that passion and fervency for Him, in our marriages we must also return to our "first love"—and that's *not* the children!

"Children do not require parents' attention 24 hours a day," writes Dr. Harley. "Nor do they suffer when parents are giving each other their undivided attention. It's not the child's fault that parents neglect each other when children arrive—it's the parents' fault when they decide that their children need so much of their time, they have not time left for each other. But the truth is that couples have time for both their children and each other, if they schedule their time wisely."[7] In fact, rebuilding the stability of your marriage is the most important gift you can give to those little eyes that watch and absorb every move Mom and Dad make.

"A relationship is like a fire," says psychologist Shirley Glass. "You can let it go down, but you can't let it go out. Even though you're in another part of the house, you have to go back every once in a while to stoke the coals."[8] No new skills are required to rekindle that ebbing flame of romance. A couple doesn't need to enroll in "Fire Building 101," nor do they need to move to an isolated cabin in the backwoods of Montana. The only requirement to fan the flames of romance is to begin spending exclusive time together again.

My friend Bonnie noticed that in raising her four daughters, a direct correlation existed between time spent with each daughter and her behavior. Whenever one of the girls would act up and begin to cause problems, Bonnie found that almost 100 percent of the time, the child's behavior was directly related to a lack of time she had given that daughter. Whenever she failed to invest time in that relationship, problems developed.

Our marriages are no different. When we fail to invest quality time in the relationship with our spouse, the inevitable result will be problems in the marriage, which can easily lead to infidelity.

After I returned from the Caribbean, one of the first changes Stottler and I made was to institute a "date night." Since then, every Tuesday night is reserved for our exclusive time together, with two parameters: we have to be away from the house, and we can't talk about work. Since we work together, we need time to talk about our personal lives and interests. For most couples, this parameter wouldn't be necessary. However, many couples may need the parameter of not discussing the children, so they get to know one another again.

All the money in the Denver Mint could not replace the value of our date nights! And since we don't have the Denver Mint's money, we seldom do expensive outings. We've had so much fun simply playing games, walking on the beach, enjoying picnics, going to movies, and exploring new areas of a neighboring town.

In *Love Must Be Tough*, Dr. James Dobson notes the importance of building into one another's lives. "When two people love each other deeply and are committed for life, they have usually developed a great volume of understandings between them that would be considered insignificant to anyone else. They share countless private memories unknown to the rest of the world. That is, in large measure, where their sense of specialness to one another originates...Touching and talking and holding hands and gazing into one another's eyes and building memories are as important to partners in their midlife years as to rambunctious twenty year olds."[9]

However you choose to spend time together, have fun. Focus on enjoying and getting to know one another again. As you do, you'll find that your date nights almost always end up with tender times in bed—another vital ingredient for maintaining love in your marriage.

And for these date nights to become a reality, you will need to plan them into your busy lives. I jokingly say that my brain is on paper because I tend to live by my calendar. But I can guarantee that unless you purposefully schedule these exclusive times together on your calendars, they won't just happen.

3. Care About Your Appearance

Caring for your marriage also brings up an important point for busy wives and mothers. What does your husband find when he arrives home at night? Although it may seem like a trivial issue to us, men respond to the stimulus of sight. And if he knows that every night the sight greeting him at home will be a disheveled wife with baby slobber and drool down her shirt, he doesn't have much to look forward to.

Although life with children can create household disasters faster and more destructive than a California earthquake, if possible, attempt to comb your hair, put on a clean blouse, and pick up the major parts of the disaster before he arrives home. He may never witness the instant transformation process, but he *will* be internally grateful to be greeted by an appealing wife.

4. Laugh Together

Laughter has been proven to enhance health and overall well-being. Maybe that's why Bob Hope lived to be a hundred years old!

Stottler and I love to laugh, and we try not to take life so seriously that we can't laugh at ourselves as well. Recently, I was being grouchy and fussy (which is, of course, quite unusual). Stottler called me a "grumpy kitty," which sounded so funny that it made me laugh at myself.

5. Act Like a Duck

Laughter goes along with a principle that I find enormously helpful in our marriage: act like a duck. In other words, let little things roll off your back like water off a duck. Remember, in light of eternity, those little annoyances just don't matter.

> *Let little things roll off your back like water off a duck. Remember, in light of eternity, those little annoyances just don't matter.*

When Stottler splashes water on our just-cleaned bathroom mirror or tracks grass clippings across the carpet after mowing the lawn, I try to remember how insignificant those little frustrations really are. And once I yield the rights to having a clean house back to the Lord, I can practice being a duck by letting those little annoyances roll right off my back. It certainly makes for a far more peaceful household!

6. Harbor No Unresolved Anger

The Lord tells us, *"Be angry, and yet do not sin; do not let the sun go down on your anger, and do not give the devil an opportunity"* (Ephesians 4:26,27). Stottler and I made a decision early in our marriage never to go to sleep with unresolved anger between us. That made for some late nights in those first years of marriage! But that decision kept our disagreements short, allowing our marriage to remain free from the poison of bitterness and unforgiveness.

We also agreed that an argument never gives us the right to have a free-for-all with our words. Dennis Rainey, President of

FamilyLife ministries, recommends "never using the word 'divorce' in the heat of the moment...Research has shown that once a word passes through the lips, it becomes an option."[10]

7. Pray Together

Another important element of our marriage has been praying together. Every night before going to sleep, Stottler and I pray together in bed. We thank the Lord for specific blessings He gave us throughout that day, and we pray for our families. Of course, praying together *before* we get into bed might be preferable because occasionally one of us gets praying and sleeping a bit intertwined.

If your husband will not pray, I would suggest that *you* develop the nightly habit of thanking the Lord for that day's blessings. You could also use that time to pray for your spouse's walk with the Lord.

Before reading the next chapter, I would urge you to please take a look at your marriage and see if it is the priority in your life that God wants it to be. My poor choices in the Caribbean rang a three-alarm fire bell to awaken me to the critical need of proactively protecting my marriage. Is there a warning bell in your life for the need to spend time alone with your husband, learning to laugh and enjoy one another again? Is he your closest friend and companion? Do you need to take steps to close the door on opportunities for infidelity to creep in? You might want to refer to the books listed in the Resources for Chapter 6. These can help you in caring for your marriage.

After establishing the foundation of godly love, the first vital step to protecting your marriage happens as you consistently nurture and care for that relationship with your husband, giving your marriage the place of priority that God intended. You cannot afford to ignore the warning bell! Investing in your marriage is worth every ounce of time and effort.

18

Establishing Accountability in Your Marriage

One summer a few years ago, I found myself standing outside enjoying a warm sun and beautiful scenery in the company of a congenial man. The grass rippled around us as an easy breeze blew past. Not another soul appeared within eyesight, and suddenly I realized that I was taking a bit too much delight in our private conversation. We laughed and talked a few minutes more, then I left to drive home.

As I maneuvered through traffic, my mind began picturing the next time I could talk with this enjoyable friend. In that moment, red flares and blaring sirens erupted inside my head, and I instantly recognized the signs—that sensation of attraction, that enticement of the forbidden. I had been here before.

How easy it would have been to silently nurture those pleasurable thoughts. What difference would it make? Who would know? Who would ever read my mind or be aware of my quickened pulse? And that's the key: If there's something in my life I don't want anyone to know, someone *needs* to know! This is the second important practice of protecting our marriage: accountability.

The Importance of Accountability

God's Word speaks volumes about accountability. Proverbs tells us, *"Listen to counsel and accept discipline, that you may be wise the rest of your days... Cease listening, my son, to discipline, and you will stray from the words of knowledge"* (Proverbs 19:20,27). God knows how desperately we need wise counsel to stay on the path of righteousness.

Accountability, discipline, and correction feel like *bad* things to us, yet God says that those are the very things that lead to godliness, usefulness, and honor. What *feels* right—refusing to seek counsel—leads to shame and poverty of spirit. *"Poverty and shame will come to him who neglects discipline, but he who regards reproof will be honored"* (Proverbs 13:18).

Over and over the Lord warns us against believing we can "go it alone" without the help and wisdom of others. *"He who separates himself seeks his own desire, he quarrels against all sound wisdom"* (Proverbs 18:1). Yet in our human pride, we bristle when corrected. In our natural flesh, we refuse to humble ourselves and admit our frailty and our need. Unfortunately, we often have to learn things the hard way!

As married believers, God gives us a chain of accountability for our protection so that we *can* walk faithfully. We are first accountable to God, then to our husband, then to mature believers.

Accountability to God

When I was about fifteen years old, my family took a short cruise along the Alaskan coast. I marveled at the grandeur and immensity of those glassy icebergs looming above the water. Yet oceanographers tell us that we actually see only a small portion of the berg. Nine-tenths of the giant structure remains hidden deep in the ocean waters.

Our lives can be like those icebergs. We may expose only a shallow facade while attempting to hide the truth of our inner selves, hoping people will never know what's really going on. But God always knows our thoughts and intentions: *"God sees not as man sees, for man looks at the outward appearance, but the LORD looks at the heart"* (1 Samuel 16:7). Although we hide and resist telling others our private struggles, we cannot hide from God.

Accountability to God is inevitable, *"for we will all stand before the judgment seat of God"* (Romans 14:10). Every idle word, every sinful action, every "hidden" thought will one day be judged before God's throne. He will *"bring to light the things hidden in the darkness and disclose the motives of men's hearts"* (1 Corinthians 4:5).

We are all quite capable of committing any sin known to man. Apart from the grace of God, you or I could be the prostitute on the street corner or the lesbian at the gay bar. Although we want to think, "I would *never* do that!" we must remember again that apart from Christ's work within us, we have "no good thing" (Psalm 16:2).

Therefore, we need to maintain an open and transparent heart before the Lord each day. This should become part of our daily time with Him. Spend a few moments of your quiet time asking God to search your heart and reveal any areas of sin that you have tried to hide from Him. Think through your actions over the past twenty-four hours to see if you need to set anything right before Him. Be particularly aware of any act that could have driven a wedge between you and your husband.

After confessing any wrong attitudes or temptations, ask God how you can protect your marriage and your life from these problem areas. Ask Him for wisdom in building and caring for your relationship with your husband. As you consistently practice this accountability time before God, He will be free to point out minor weaknesses in your life that could lead to major problems if left unattended. He will also help you build a far stronger relationship with your spouse.

So we are first accountable to God. And wanting to maintain a consistent, holy walk that pleases Him leads us to the second stage of accountability: with our husband.

Accountability with Your Husband

I heard a speaker say, "The most difficult times in marriage are the years after the wedding."[1] We never outgrow temptation toward another man. Recently, several "giants" in the faith who have reached their later years revealed that they *still* experience temptation toward the opposite sex. No matter how old we are, no matter how much in love we may be, no matter how strong our Christian walk, none of us has received immunity from being attracted to another man.

In an article appearing in the *Kansas City Star*, *Wall Street Journal* editor Jeffrey Zaslow writes, "We assume couples that survive the first few decades have accepted their spouse's quirks and problems and are more apt to live out their lives together ...But that notion is being shattered...More people in their 60s, 70s and 80s are seeking divorce." The article went on to say that a full 10 percent of seniors are now divorced or separated, and that lawyers expect that trend to increase "as divorce-prone baby boomers age."[2]

Choosing to stay faithful in your marriage never becomes a once-for-all settled issue, never to receive testing again. Thus, the No Secrets Policy remains essential. We are far more prone to nurturing sin as long as it remains hidden and unexposed. When we think no one will know, we easily cave into temptation one little decision at a time. Psychologist Ralph Earle says, "The secret is the fertile place for an addiction."[3] As long as our actions remain hidden, those secrets are free to grow and multiply like mold in a damp basement.

When I suddenly encountered that initial spark of emotional allure toward the man I mentioned at the beginning of the chapter, I could have once again silently fed those seeds of interest. I could have allowed my mind to create enticing mental scenarios, fantasizing about the next time we would meet. But having "been there and done that" in the Caribbean, I *knew* the results of such choices! So before any seeds of temptation could be sown and watered, I made a quick decision to pull them out by the roots.

Once Stottler arrived home from work, I prayed for God's strength and words, then exposed my emotions to him. Was it easy? Not on your life! But the moment I revealed my frail heart and wandering emotions, the thrill of the excitement burst, as if a giant pin had been jammed into a balloon. The enticement of the forbidden had lost its allure.

Remember, honesty protects both you and your spouse by letting him know your weaknesses so he is able to help you through the trials. Honesty also shows your commitment to keeping the marriage strong in the face of temptations. And God doesn't say that honesty applies only to a marriage if the husband is a believer. Honesty should be the bedrock for *any* marriage, Christian or not.

God gave us husbands as umbrellas of protection. This idea sends the feminists into spasms. They urge us instead to be strong and independent, in need of no one, proclaiming, "I am woman, hear me roar."[4] Of course, choosing to live in that sort of independent pride will lead to the next song, "I am prideful, see me fall."

I am *not* strong—I'm a weak individual who clings desperately to Christ for *His* strength. And since He has also blessed me with a husband for additional strength and protection, I'll use every means available to ensure that I walk faithfully in Christ. God abhors pride, but honors and rewards humility. It's honest humility that realizes our weaknesses and our needs.

Are my weaknesses easy for Stottler to hear? No, but he realizes that by knowing my frailties, he can pray for me and help guard me against repeating similar mistakes. He would far rather know my weaknesses and be able to help than to blindly assume all is well only to someday discover terrible secrets concealed in the closet!

Stottler realizes that by knowing my frailties, he can pray for me and help guard me against repeating similar mistakes.

Also, you must be prepared to hear secrets that your husband may have hidden from you. This could be just as painful as admitting your own lapses. But just as your husband has helped you with your temptations, you must be willing to help him with his.

When your husband speaks to you, treat him just as you want to be treated in return. Work out between the two of you how you will handle any problems that surface. And be sure when sharing temptations and struggles with one another that your motivation is *never* to manipulate or to make your partner jealous. Nor is that time an excuse for using hurtful words. Share in a way that says you are keeping everything in the open to seek the other's advice, accountability, and prayers to protect your marriage.

Pray together before you end your time. Place each other in God's hands, and ask His protection and guidance for your marriage. And be sure that whatever is revealed remains confidential. Nothing will destroy the No Secrets Policy faster than if you relay one another's innermost thoughts to others.

As Stottler and I remain committed to the No Secrets Policy, it acts as one of our strongest deterrents against temptation. No secrets means sharing *any* pertinent information that affects our marriage. This includes telling Stottler about any actions, and even thoughts, that can be harmful to our marriage, such as mental pictures of spending time with another man, or sensing attraction to a coworker or friend. Knowing I must reveal those mental pictures makes a wonderful deterrent to starting such a train of thought in the first place! Because of this honesty, Stottler and I have built a wall of protection around our marriage that makes it almost impossible for either of us to ever "stumble" into a relationship outside our marriage.

We must be willing to do *whatever it takes* to guard our marriages. That means dealing with even the "little things" that we brush off as unimportant or too inconsequential to bother sharing with each other. Those are the tiny moths that eventually chew holes into the fabric of our marriage. Only as we share our private lives can our relationship become honest and transparent, breaking through those invisible walls that destroy the intimacy we were designed to experience in marriage.

But not only does God hold us accountable and desire that we have accountability with our husbands, He also gives us mature Christian women to uphold us in the storms as well.

Accountability with Mature Christian Women

Every summer, nature's terrifying thunderstorms ravage parts of the central United States. Growing up in Oklahoma, I developed an enormous respect for these powerful house-rattling winds and torrential rains that frequently developed into deadly tornadoes. Each summer we ran for our basement's safety, huddling around a small TV as we listened intently to continuous weather coverage. But one night stood apart.

My brother Steve had received a tiny maple sapling in a paper cup at his kindergarten. He had faithfully planted and nurtured that fledgling tree in the soil beside our house. Responding well to his attention, the maple had reached about four feet by the time that certain night arrived.

One sticky summer evening, an infamous Oklahoma thunderstorm struck in full fury. As a five-year-old, I peered through our side screen door, my eyes the size of dinner plates. I watched in fear as my father braced himself against the gale while holding onto that tender tree. His clothes, drenched in the downpour, whipped around his lean frame. As lightning cracked through the ominous sky and thunder shattered the air, he clutched the tree with one hand while he pounded stakes beside it with the other.

Had it not been for my father's steady support, that maple would have easily become kindling, uprooted and helplessly flung across our yard by the tempestuous winds. But because of his support alongside that tree, it not only survived, but grew to some 25 feet over the following years.

Times occur in each of our lives when we find ourselves like that fragile maple tree, whipped and beaten by the storms. The Lord knows we need the steady support of others to come alongside us and help brace us against the howling winds of temptation. He tells us to *"bear one another's burdens"* (Galatians 6:2). In fact, God says that *not* doing so is foolish: *"The way of a fool is right in his own eyes, but a wise man is he who listens to counsel"* (Proverbs 12:15).

I certainly needed the counsel, admonition, and love of my friends when I contemplated pursuing a relationship with the captain! God tells us that we need one another to help us in a steadfast walk with Christ: *"Two are better than one...for if either of them falls, the one will lift up his companion. But woe to the one who falls when there is not another to lift him up"* (Ecclesiastes

4:9,10). Words fail to express my thankfulness that somewhere back in my early years as a new believer, I had received crucial instruction on setting up accountability with other women. Had I not done so, my life would probably look drastically different right now. But God used my accountability friends to work His truth into my life at a desperate moment.

God designed His church in such a way that He expects us to learn from other believers. He tells us that mature Christian women are to be living examples for us (Titus 2:3,4).

A story I read recently illustrates God's principle of learning from those who are more mature, as demonstrated in the animal kingdom. A mother African elephant recently gave birth in captivity—a rare occurrence. The handlers were elated as this new mother doted on her infant son, showing all the signs of being an ideal parent. Then one morning they found the baby elephant bludgeoned to death by his mother. What happened?

The zoo personnel surmised that because the mother had been taken captive at six months of age and raised in a zoo, she never had the opportunity to learn parenting skills from the other females in a normal elephant society. "In the wild, a female elephant grows up with her mother and aunts, watching as they give birth roughly every four to five years and observing how they care for their young. In fact, females in the wild assist one another during birth, and later engage in a form of collective baby-sitting ...in which they protect, play with and sometimes even nurse the other's offspring. Wild elephants have even been observed crowding a reluctant mother, forcing her to be still so her calf can nurse, or disciplining mothers that are too rough with a baby."[5]

Just as God designed elephants to learn from one another, so He designed us to learn from other mature believers. *"He whose ear listens to the life-giving reproof will dwell among the wise"* (Proverbs 15:31).

We become like the people with whom we spend time, whether for good or for ill. God warns us, *"Do not be deceived: 'Bad company corrupts good morals'"* (1 Corinthians 15:33). If I spend my time around those possessing no godly perspective and who fail to base their decisions on the wisdom of Scripture, I *will* pick up their attitudes and actions. However, if I choose to spend time around those who seek the Lord's wisdom and who depend on the Spirit's guidance through prayer, then my life begins to imitate them.

At all walks of life, we need one another to hold us to God's path and to help keep our feet from straying. Family ministry specialist Kent Choate says that young couples who are in an accountable relationship with another couple "have a far better chance of staying together than those who are not; in fact, it increases their chances by almost 80 percent."[6] Accountability is worth it!

When we know that an accountability friend will be asking us hard questions, we help close the door on anything that can invade the sacredness of our marriage, whether that be choosing a poor movie or pursuing another man. Yet even though God speaks so clearly on our need to uphold one another, few believers willingly commit themselves to this crucial act of obedience. Patrick Morley writes in *The Man in the Mirror* that where accountability has been promoted to men, "no more than 15 percent of the men have taken the action step and stuck with it."[7] Why? Why wouldn't we instantly leap to obey that which makes such a profound difference in our lives and marriages?

Because of that recurring problem of *pride*. Pride makes us want to look good before others. Pride makes us want to appear strong and spiritual. Consequently, we fear exposing our innermost thoughts and private struggles. We fear what others will think of us more than we fear falling into sin.

But once again, pride can be overcome by simple steps of humble obedience. As we recognize our capability to fall into any sin and acknowledge our need for accountability, we must then take immediate steps to set up that accountability.

Setting Up Accountability

When setting up accountability, choose one or two mature Christian women with whom you can bare your soul and learn from their wisdom. Confiding your struggles to a person of the opposite sex invites disaster. Consistent accountability needs to be with a mature Christian *woman* whose walk with the Lord has been proven faithful.

If you are seeking counsel from a male pastor, I would *strongly* suggest that you either have another woman go with you, or you ask that the door to the counseling room remain ajar. Far too many examples exist of tenderhearted pastors who have fallen into an affair while counseling a distressed woman. If possible, the best scenario would be to seek counsel from the pastor's *wife*. Please do not take this lightly.

As you set up accountability, prepare a list of specific questions that your female accountability friend will ask you each time you talk. Select specific questions like: "Have you struggled with any impure thoughts this week? Tell me briefly about them. And what have you done to take those thoughts captive to the obedience of Christ?" Then make the final question of your meeting, "Have you lied to me about anything during this time?" Ouch!

For accountability to work, our attitude must be right. We must be teachable, vulnerable, honest, and dependable.

Be Teachable

For an alcoholic to begin recovery, she must first admit her need. We are no different. Recognizing that we are in a spiritual battle and that we need the strength, counsel, and wisdom of others makes us teachable. *"For by wise guidance you will wage war, and in abundance of counselors there is victory"* (Proverbs 24:6). Of course, the guidance and counsel of others must always match Scripture, so I encourage you to always check others' advice against the Word of God.

Be Vulnerable

Through the years, I have built such a level of trust with Bonnie and Holly that I know they will love and guide me through any dumb thing I may do. But that level of trust starts with vulnerability. I willingly commit to share with my accountability partners anything about the areas in which they are holding me accountable.

Be Honest

Along with vulnerability comes honesty. Yes, gut-level honesty hurts. Yes, our failures are embarrassing. Yes, it often feels painful, like exposing raw areas to the sting of antiseptic. Yet how else can those areas be healed? When Holly spoke harshly (in love) to me concerning my relationship with Eric, her words pierced and stung. Yet because I willingly told her the truth and by God's grace finally responded in obedience, Stottler and I now delight in a fantastic marriage and are able to minister to other hurting couples. Imagine how I would have removed myself from God's service and will if I had refused to be honest with Holly, and consequently had left Stottler to pursue my own selfish desires!

Be Dependable

Teachability, vulnerability, and honesty are useless without dependability. Set a regular weekly time to talk either in person or over the phone, and stick with it. Don't make excuses. Excuses are the red flare that spells out s-e-c-r-e-c-y. Remember, if secrets exist in your life that you don't want anyone to know, someone *needs* to know.

Accountability can be the difference between an entire life of usefulness or uselessness. Do you want your life to be used for the Lord's purposes? Do you want to make a difference in your short time here on earth? If so, determine to remain transparent before the Lord, commit to the No Secrets Policy with your husband, and set up accountability with another woman. Charles Swindoll sums it up: "People who really make an impact model accountability."[8]

Once you have determined to implement these first two marital building blocks (caring for your marriage and establishing accountability in your marriage), then you're ready to move into the final two areas. These have not only enhanced the walls of protection around my marriage, but they have also brought dramatic changes to my entire life!

19

Building Walls to Protect Your Marriage

braham and his three illustrious guests lounged under the broad tree, its spreading branches providing shade from the intense heat of the day. As they dined on choice beef, breadcakes, and curds, activity surrounded them. Camels, sheep, and cattle ambled about, and servants scurried to meet their needs. Yet Abraham's attention remained solely riveted upon one of his visitors—the Lord God Himself! With awe he listened as the Lord unfolded His upcoming plans for the birth of Isaac and the destruction of Sodom and Gomorrah. The afternoon seemed to pass in a few fleeting moments, and then his visitors were gone. But Abraham's heart continued to pound within him. He had spoken with God!

This was not the first time that God had visited Abraham. He had appeared twice before and had also clearly spoken on three other occasions. Now the Lord had spent an entire afternoon with him, discussing great and awesome plans that only He could do.

Shortly thereafter, Abraham and Sarah journeyed south into the territory of the godless Philistines. Sarah possessed great beauty, and they feared the heathen Philistine king might desire her. So to save his own neck, Abraham declared that Sarah was his sister—and consequently, King Abimelech took her into his harem (Genesis 18–20)!

How on earth could Abraham talk face to face with God, witness His miraculous works, know of His awesome plans, and then turn around and deny God's ability to protect Sarah and him from a heathen king? How could he *do* that?

Over and over God gives us examples of people who started well, only to wind up in sin and its disastrous consequences. Just as Abraham gave his wife away to a heathen king right after meeting *face to face* with the Lord, I know how quickly I can turn my back on God and give in to temptation.

To stand firm in the battle for our marriages, we must be prepared. We can never assume that having a good marriage shelters us from temptation. In this age of "anything goes," the wise woman will purposefully build walls around her marriage ahead of time to help close the door on opportunities for temptation.

We have discussed the need to love with Christ's love, to care for our marriage, and to establish accountability. Now let's look at eight areas in which we can develop habits that build walls of protection around our marriage.

1. Protecting Your Marriage through Daily Times with God

I cannot emphasize strongly enough that your personal, daily time with the Lord builds an enormous wall of protection around your marriage. Time with the Lord each day immediately impacts your relationship with your spouse. When you fail to meet with God, your heart becomes hardened to the Lord and to His truths. And once the snowball of sin begins rolling, your marriage is instantly endangered. But as you cling to Him each day, you will confess sin and continue to grow in Christ's likeness. As you keep God in His rightful place, not only will your marriage experience dramatic differences, but *all* of your relationships will be affected.

2. Protecting Your Marriage by Safeguarding Your Relationships with Other Men

The best way to prevent problems from happening in the first place is to avoid being in potentially compromising situations. Some of the following parameters may sound like something out of the 1950s, but the divorce rate then wasn't 50 percent either! So we would be wise to return to some "old-fashioned" practices.

I have learned the wisdom of bringing Stottler into all my friendships with other men. A few years ago, God brought an opportunity for me to help exercise horses at a nearby ranch. Suddenly, I was thrust into an arena full of fun-loving, athletic cowboys. Knowing the potential to feel drawn to men of like mind in an enjoyable setting, I immediately began practicing some safeguards.

The best way to prevent problems from happening in the first place is to avoid being in potentially compromising situations.

Whenever I meet a new fellow at the ranch, within one or two sentences I mention that I am married by simple references such as, "Stottler and I live just down the highway." If the conversation continues, all references to my life include the word "we," letting him know that my husband plays an integral part in my life. And periodically, Stottler will come out to the ranch not only to participate in this part of my life, but also to make his presence known among the men there.

As a rule, if a man continues to be part of my life, then I seek to build a friendship with his wife. I recommend this *very* highly whenever possible. I also introduce them to my husband.

I am aware that some relationships pose more potential danger than others. Not only can a growing friendship with another man easily turn into temptation (most affairs start from a friendship), but friendship with a *Christian* man carries extra explosives. Don't buy into the delusion that friendship with any Christian man is "safe." Actually, the fact that he is a wonderful Christian man makes him a much *greater* attraction because our spirit bonds to other believers in a far deeper way than to nonbelievers.

Another practice I employ is one I picked up from observing a friend. I call it "the invisible wall." After college, I became increasingly involved at my church and began developing a friendship with the pastor. Not only did he immediately bring his wife into our interactions, but I sensed that he kept an "invisible wall" between us. Although we became close friends, I never doubted that a barrier existed that he would not cross. Consequently, an improper relationship with him never entered my mind.

Today, I practice what that pastor modeled. Men can sense when a woman opens the door a crack. Whether it's a second look, lingering eye contact, a facial expression that says, "You're really important to me," a wink, or a special compliment, these all communicate, "Maybe there's potential for something more here." Instead, to establish an unbreachable boundary, we need to create an invisible wall that says, "I can be your friend, but I love my husband, so don't even *think* of crossing this boundary, buddy."

A good way to reinforce that invisible wall is by not engaging in personal conversations unless your husband is with you. If you find yourself alone with another man and the conversation swings toward the personal, politely end the conversation and leave. That sends a powerful message!

Even if you and your husband enjoy spending time with another couple, you should always maintain that invisible wall by never exchanging furtive glances with the other man. I know of an affair that began when two couples met socially, and the unfaithful partners shattered the wall between them by simply glancing at one another while their spouses sat unaware. Once the barrier evaporated, they were off and running.

And speaking of signals that open the door for problems, touching another person communicates a world of unspoken thoughts. For some people, the emotions communicated by touch are highly charged. Therefore, avoid front hugs and kisses of any kind. If you feel it necessary to hug another man, simply give a quick, loose hug from the side. And stiff-arm any attempts at kisses, unless you're in an international situation where it's the cultural norm. Even then, never kiss on the lips.

For those with twinkle toes, dancing with another man is definitely out. I'm sorry, but as a musician, I know the powerful effect that music has upon our souls. And when you put two emotionally heightened bodies together, the internal fireworks could illuminate New York City!

You should never spend time alone with a man other than your husband. This includes sports activities. Many an affair has started with the "harmless" act of a pleasant evening jog together. If your husband can't participate in the activity with you, do it alone, do it in a group (preferably of women), or not at all.

It's important that you know your own tendencies. I have seen firsthand that I can be attracted to a man with like interests. Knowing that vulnerability, I can then make wise decisions. For instance, I have always yearned to participate in a cattle drive. (Strange, I know.) Various opportunities exist around the country, but at an expensive price. Therefore, both Stottler and I can't afford to go at once. One day we began discussing the option of me going without Stottler. Immediately, I realized this would put me alone for a week with athletic men who shared my love of horses and the outdoors. Quickly, I decided not to place myself in such a potentially vulnerable position.

Walking with the Lord and protecting our marriage may require us to sacrifice some of our dreams in order to remain faithful. That's what "taking up your cross" is all about (Matthew 16:24). Yet compared to *Christ's* sacrifice, our "sacrifices" are quite minute. And the blessings He pours upon us for walking faithfully far outweigh anything we may give up!

> *A wise woman establishes rules for herself now that hinder her from improper actions with another man in the future.*

A wise woman establishes rules for herself *now* that hinder her from improper actions with another man in the future. By not spending time alone with another man, you not only protect your marriage, but you also avoid the appearance of evil by *"giving no cause for offense in anything"* (2 Corinthians 6:3). The bottom line comes down to this: *When in doubt, don't.* If you question whether God would approve of some interaction with another man, *don't do it.* Pay attention to the red flags in your spirit. God graciously gives us those warnings for our own protection. And by incorporating these parameters in all of our relationships with other men, we greatly fortify the protective walls around our marriage.

3. Protecting Your Marriage through Boundaries in the Workplace

The most frequent point of initial contact for affairs is in an office. And as more and more women enter the workplace, the number of women involved in extramarital affairs continues to rise. As always, the person with whom you spend the most quality time will be the one who captures your heart. And the average work environment sets up the opportunity for affairs beautifully.

At work, a woman finds herself surrounded by like-minded men focused on the same important task. Everyone appears well groomed and looking their best. Each day, the job seems significant and challenging, compared to the routine at home of disciplining wayward children, cooking endless meals, and changing stinky diapers.

To make matters worse, many corporations now include "team building" activities that throw male and female coworkers into intimate, trust-building situations. If you travel with an attractive male coworker to an office retreat, share your feelings and thoughts, and practice building one another's esteem, then *of course* you will feel attracted to this man!

In any type of relationship, whether business or casual, a wise woman will protect her marriage by not spending time alone with another man. This includes riding in a car alone together, sitting together on a business flight, enjoying long phone conversations, and meeting a male coworker outside the office.

But someone may complain, "What if we need to finalize some work while on the plane?" You can *always* find alternatives. If you set your boundaries, you can always find ways to work together in a public airport lobby, or finish the work at the office *before* you leave. And if your job demands that you meet with men, always meet in groups or include another person. Although your coworkers may tease you or scoff at you, people respect someone who refuses to compromise. However, whether they respect you or not, your wise actions bring joy to the heart of God and protect your own marriage.

If ever a situation needed solid protective walls firmly entrenched around it to prevent infidelity, the workplace is it. Such protection requires *predetermined* decisions, all maintained through accountability to your husband and to other women. The practices of establishing an invisible wall and refraining from personal contact and conversations with other men are utterly critical. Without predetermining to follow these safeguards, you will effectively set yourself up to fall.

4. Protecting Your Marriage through Discretion in Clothing

As I picked up the phone, a tearful voice on the other end began to pour out her heart. She had just discovered her husband's involvement with pornography. My heart bled for her as we talked and prayed together. Shortly thereafter, the couple sought counseling in their city, and by God's grace, his life choices began to change.

Several months later, they came to visit Stottler and me, bringing their two small boys. We walked along the beach, digging our toes into the soft sand as we talked about life and its challenges.

As the sun began to fade, we headed back to the car. Strolling along the sidewalk, we walked past the lingering sunbathers soaking up the final rays. As I glanced around, there to my horror lay a woman face down wearing nothing on top and a mere string on the bottom! I desperately glanced back to see if my friend's husband, along with their two young sons, would see this spectacle of flesh. Given his particular struggle, this was *not* the picture he needed to see! Fortunately, the boys scampered on the far side of him, keeping his eyes diverted in the other direction. I heaved an enormous sigh of relief.

Not that most of us are tempted to wear a thong bikini to the beach, but the way we dress reveals an enormous amount about us (no pun intended). What do we want people to notice? What is the reaction we seek from men? We never know if some man around us is struggling with his thought life.

Men become easily aroused sexually by the stimulation of sight. Therefore, what we wear is *very* important. To attract men to you sexually by the clothing you choose is to defraud them because you cannot (or should not!) fulfill the desire you arouse. *"For this is the will of God... that each of you know how to possess his own vessel in sanctification and honor... and that no man transgress and defraud his brother in the matter"* (1 Thessalonians 4:3–6).

Discretion is important not only in our choice of clothing, but in *all* of our conduct. God tells us how He views a woman who has no discretion: *"As a ring of gold in a swine's snout, so is a beautiful woman who lacks discretion"* (Proverbs 11:22).

Stottler doesn't watch many movies, therefore he isn't familiar with most of today's "stars." But he does know about one beautiful leading lady who dresses provocatively and who lived immorally with a man while publicly bragging about having their first child together. Since Stottler doesn't know her name, every time she appears on TV he asks, "Isn't that the pig with the golden ring in her nose?" He doesn't mean it unkindly—he just sees her from God's perspective.

God calls us to act with *"purity and reverence"* (1 Peter 3:2, NIV), adorning ourselves *"with proper clothing, modestly and discreetly"* (1 Timothy 2:9). The reason we are to do these things is to *"encourage one another and build up one another"* (1 Thessalonians 5:11). We can't very well build up others if we are causing them to stumble by what we wear and how we act! Save the cleavage for your husband. He is the only one who should have the privilege of seeing and responding to your sexuality.

5. Protecting Your Marriage by Guarding Your Eyes and Ears

We women love romantic movies and TV shows. But along with those romantic stories usually come glamorized sensuality, infidelity, and adultery. As we pour these images into our minds, our sensitivity to sin becomes dulled, making us vulnerable to *"the lust of the flesh and the lust of the eyes"* (1 John 2:16).

When we absorb Hollywood's portrayal of love, we begin to place unreal expectations on our spouse. No marriage remains glamorous and romantic at every moment.

A survey by sociologist David Popenoe of Rutgers University reveals that many Americans have adopted the Hollywood version of finding one's ideal "soul mate." Popenoe says that such expectations can spell doom for marriages: "It really provides a very unrealistic view of what marriage really is. The standard becomes so high, it's easy to bail out if you didn't find a soul mate." Sociologist Heather Helms-Erikson agrees that couples should never expect a lasting romantic high: "Ten years into a marriage, you don't have that anymore. You notice someone else and think, 'Maybe *this* person is my soul mate.'"[1]

Besides placing false expectations on marriage, sexually explicit Hollywood stories rarely portray reality. When was the last time you saw a movie that showed a family's destruction and heart-wrenching agony due to an affair? When has a show ever examined the lifelong effects of a mother's infidelity on her children? When have you seen a program showing one out of five characters contracting genital herpes after having casual sex, like they do in real life? When did a movie ever show a woman confronting life-altering choices brought about by a pregnancy from an affair?

Sensual music can also warp our perspective on love and marriage. Every performer in the music industry knows how to craft songs and arrangements to evoke particular moods.

Mark 4:24 tells us to *"take care what you listen to."* Any movie or music containing an immoral or ungodly message should never enter our ears. But we must also be wise about how certain "clean" shows and music affect us. When I find that some romantic movie rekindles images of the Caribbean, I turn it off. Although we are *"dead to sin, but alive to God in Christ Jesus"* (Romans 6:11), those old sin patterns within us can easily be stirred to life!

Also, many Christian women spend their free time devouring novels filled with various forms of immorality. And if reading a Christian romance novel also sparks improper romantic images or ideas, it's best not to read that as well.

As for all of the Christian life, the key to guarding our eyes and ears is for each of us to remain sensitive to the Holy Spirit. We must take care to not engage in *anything* that draws our thoughts and hearts away from the Lord and from our husbands. By guarding what we see and hear, we keep impurity out and strengthen the walls around our marriage.

> *Many Americans have adopted the Hollywood version of finding one's ideal "soul mate." Such expectations can spell doom for marriages.*

6. Protecting Your Marriage by Guarding Against the Lure of the Internet

Not long ago, a married acquaintance of mine met a man in another state through an Internet chat room. As the relationship progressed, they soon yearned to meet. Teresa then asked her husband for money "to attend a conference" in a distant state. Since Teresa said that her coworker was going too, the arrangements sounded fine to her husband.

One day while Teresa was "at the conference," her husband called the store where she worked. Who should answer the phone but the friend who was supposedly traveling with her! When Teresa returned, she admitted to her husband that she had traveled to meet her Internet "friend." Within a month, she and her husband were separated, and she had begun divorce proceedings. Their marriage ended, and so did the Internet relationship. The ensuing destruction in their children's lives defies description.

We have discussed the ease with which Internet access allows pornography into our homes. But just as luring, and far more subtle, lurks the danger of those enticing chat rooms—someplace to vent our 40,000 daily words!

E-mail and chat rooms may appear harmless, but the number of women naively falling into affairs because of their hunger for communication has skyrocketed! Psychologist Dr. David Greenfield found in a survey of more than 18,000 people that "a major reason individuals go online is to find intimacy."[2]

Teresa's story is certainly not unique. Many marriages have been destroyed through a "harmless" relationship that began over the Internet and ended up in a motel room. At every moment, thousands of strangers wait in chat rooms to "meet the needs" of downhearted women. And thousands of women are longing to have someone do just that.

Yale psychologist Janis Abrahms Spring, author of *After the Affair*, says, "Whenever I give a workshop, I always ask how many of the counselors in the room are dealing more and more with affairs that began on the Internet. And almost every hand goes up."[3] Houston attorney J. Lindsay Short, president of the American Academy of Matrimonial Lawyers, says that he and his co-workers are witnessing a "dramatic increase" in divorce cases involving Internet affairs. He says that people "believe it to be safe to have these Internet discussions. Over time, they think they know this person, and from there, it's a pretty easy step to pick up the phone and make a call."[4]

Chat rooms and e-mails particularly entice women because they seem to satisfy our need to share our heart with an understanding man. If a woman's emotional needs are not being met at home, she can easily find thousands of "available" men online who hunger to supposedly fulfill her desires. Al Cooper, staff psychologist at Stanford University, said, "We see women all the time who may not feel that attractive, but they get 20 guys going after them at a time in a chat room, e-mailing them instantly. That's affirming to a woman, and it's hard to match when your husband is in the next room drinking a beer, maybe asking you if you're going to exercise next week because he thinks you're overweight."[5]

When a woman gets to "know" some man through the Internet, he becomes the fantasy "perfect male," meeting all of her emotional needs, giving kind and clever responses, enjoying her company, being available at all times. What marriage relationship can compete with that? When emotionally involved with an unseen "perfect" man, a woman will start comparing him against her less-than-perfect husband full of flaws and mistakes. She then begins placing completely unrealistic demands and expectations on her spouse and on their marriage.

When two Internet "lovers" do meet, their fantasy must eventually burst. The ideal must give way to the real. Unfortunately, by the time the two meet and discover that love in the real world requires sacrifice and honesty, the marriage may have already been lost.

Any married woman seeking to fulfill her needs over the Internet must realize that her pursuits will lead only to heartache and enormous disappointment. Genuine godly love—the desire of every heart—can be found only in a committed relationship based on unconditional love.

And though an Internet love relationship may be based on fantasy, virtual infidelity causes actual pain. The devastation to the spouse can be just as painful as if the partner had been involved in a sexual affair. The broken trust and the regrets are just as difficult to repair.

Secrecy in a marriage *always* brings damage. It creates an emotional separation between the couple and builds barriers to overcome. It denies the spouse the intimacy that should have been theirs.

We must also be wise in our use of e-mail at home or work. In my work, I must frequently correspond by e-mail with godly Christian men. Recently, I was writing back and forth about business with a kind Christian man I had met at a conference. My "invisible wall" went up. As we wrote, I noticed that his conversation became a bit more personal. So in my reply e-mail, I asked him if he had ever met my husband and wrote a short synopsis of Stottler's attributes. (It was a challenge to make it short!) I also copied Stottler on the e-mail so he would be aware of these transactions and so the other man would see that my husband was receiving our e-mails as well. The return reply from the gentleman came back short and concise. My point had been made, and my marriage walls had received fortification.

One of the best guards against infidelity comes from having your emotional needs met within your marriage.

If you have already begun an improper relationship over the Internet, it needs to end immediately. You cannot worry about hurting the other man's feelings; do what's right! The No Secrets Policy needs to be practiced so that your husband knows what has transpired, knows your vulnerabilities, and knows how to pray for you. You should also begin identifying the needs you hoped to have met through this online relationship, and begin working as a couple to meet those needs.

If using the Internet becomes too great a temptation toward re-contacting someone or rekindling improper feelings, then *stay off the computer* until your heart mends. To heal from any type of infidelity requires time and absolute isolation from the individual. There are no shortcuts.

With the Internet providing such easy access to a world of fantasy relationships, we need to carefully guard our marriage relationship. As Internet pioneer Clifford Stoll says, "Life in the real world is far more interesting, far more important, far richer than anything you'll ever find on a computer screen."[6]

7. Protecting Your Marriage by Spending Time Together

One of the best guards against infidelity comes from having your emotional needs met within your marriage. That means *sticking to the plan* of spending time alone together each week! Unless we purposefully protect that time, all of life's little "urgent" needs will undermine our marital intimacy like termites that slowly eat away the foundation of a house. What can be more urgent than protecting your marriage?

8. Protecting Your Marriage through Accountability

As we've seen, the No Secrets Policy and accountability to a mature godly woman are invaluable. If I had not laid a foundation of honest accountability through years with Bonnie and Holly, I seriously doubt I would have made it through my Caribbean ordeal. Accountability may be the key issue that makes or breaks our faithfulness to God and to our spouse.

These eight crucial practices *will* strengthen and fortify the walls around your marriage. God may also show you other safeguards that are equally as important for your life and your particular vulnerabilities.

So how are you doing in protecting your marriage? Are you spending daily time with the Lord? Will you practice building an invisible wall in your relationships with other men, as well as begin implementing these other protections?

We have now built the first three walls around our marriage by caring for our marriage, establishing accountability in our marriage, and establishing the eight areas of specific protection around our marriage. Now let's look at the final part of the wall that deals with how we are to respond to marital temptations that inevitably arise.

20

Responding to Marital Temptations

R ita considered herself to be an average wife and mother. As she examined her ordinary life, nothing seemed too outstanding, or too terrible. She found the daily challenge of juggling two teenagers' schedules, the needs of her husband, and the demands at home to be exhausting, yet rewarding. But once a week she took a break from the routine and escaped to volunteer at the church library.

As she sorted books and catalogued new entries, one of the pastoral staff dropped by to chat and offer thanks for her service. She especially enjoyed these moments of talking with another adult, and this pastor always extended her exceptional kindness.

As they visited, she suddenly felt her heart begin to beat faster. Rita gazed at the pastor, and for the first time noticed his sparkling blue eyes and warm smile. As he prepared to leave, she yearned for their conversation to continue. She had never felt this sensation before. As she watched him depart down the hall, a silly grin broke out on her face. Returning to her filing, she noticed that her mind continually reverted back to their interaction.

We've seen how fortifying the walls around our marriage helps close the door on opportunities for temptation. Yet many a battle has been lost when the enemy finds a tiny breach in the wall. Even though we prepare as well as possible, at times we may find our heart suddenly drawn to someone, and we begin picturing ways to be together.

Responding Rightly in the Midst of Temptation

If you find yourself in a situation where your heart is drawn to another man, are there ways to keep that relationship from developing into something improper? Absolutely! We now turn to building the fourth wall of protection around our marriage: how to respond rightly when feelings of attraction suddenly burst into our heart. Let's look at eight things we must not do when attracted to another man.

1. Don't Divulge Your Feelings

When the thrill of forbidden attraction arises, we instinctively want to share those feelings with the enticing individual. *Never tell the other man how you feel about him!* Those few words open the floodgate for infidelity. Once the dam has broken, it's hard to stop the town from flooding. Even if the man never thought of you in this manner before, he may now begin to consider the possibility of an affair and will forever view you differently.

I spent weeks nurturing and contemplating my feelings toward the captain. Then one perfect afternoon under a brilliant sun, we lounged alone on the boat deck at a charming port in Guadeloupe. Our conversation began casually, but I maneuvered the topic so I could finally convey my pent-up feelings. Although a connection had existed between us from the start, Eric had considered me "untouchable" because of my marriage and ministry. Now the door had suddenly swung open and the forbidden fruit beckoned.

Dr. Willard Harley believes that "from the moment he knows she loves him, their friendship should end . . . This may seem very harsh and unrealistic, but the alternative to ending such a friendship is to create a huge risk of having an affair."[1]

Ask God to *"set a guard, O LORD, over my mouth; keep watch over the door of my lips"* (Psalm 141:3). *Don't* share your emotions with the other man, but *do* share them with your husband.

2. Don't Keep Secrets

When you feel drawn to another man, you will want to begin confiding things to him, sharing your feelings, your dreams, and your inner thoughts. When this happens, you will automatically hide that relationship from your husband. An attraction can quickly evolve into emotional infidelity when elements or actions exist within the relationship that you wouldn't want your husband to know. That relationship then becomes a replacement for your own marriage.

Consider the woman who bares her soul to the gentleman she finds attractive next door. Once her husband arrives home from work, she no longer feels the need to share with him. The same holds true for the working woman who frequently eats lunch with the enjoyable male coworker. Laughing, sharing, confiding over these meals, she no longer shares those parts of her life with her husband. And as these times of sharing continue, the emotional entanglement grows deeper.

Over and over again, researchers find that *emotional* infidelity devastates a marriage as much as or even more than physical infidelity. Therapist M. Gary Neuman says:

> We can't fool ourselves into believing that we can have intimate relationships at work and still have a great relationship

at home. My message is that if you want to infuse passion and have a buddy for the rest of your life, you have to keep that emotional content in your marriage. Otherwise, it's not going to happen . . . If you put the majority of your emotions in the hands of someone other than your spouse, you're still short-changing your spouse.[2]

Emotional infidelity can quickly lead to physical adultery. As your lives become emotionally intertwined, it's a short hop into bed. You never intended for it to happen, you never thought it would happen, but it's the normal progression of any emotional entanglement.

Secrets in your life should always raise an enormous red flag signaling a problem. Remember, if something exists in your life that you don't want anyone to know, someone *needs* to know. The moment you sense that your husband wouldn't approve of a relationship that you are developing, the No Secrets Policy should jump to mind. The wise woman will stop a problem before it can ever take root.

3. Don't Be Lured in by the Adrenaline Rush

A sister to secrecy is the excitement of the forbidden. Certain personalities are drawn to the adrenaline rush of "hanging over the edge." Pursuing forbidden fruit becomes a game—albeit a very sick and dangerous one, similar to Russian roulette. The lure and thrill of "getting away with it" can feel as exhilarating as being a counterintelligence spy for a foreign government.

Once I had reached the point of purposefully pursuing Eric, I felt that rush of excitement, not only from the tingle of "being in love" (a totally selfish "love"), but also from the adrenaline rush of being involved in something forbidden. Once I reached that point, even telling Stottler failed to completely thwart that excitement. That's why it becomes so critical to practice the No Secrets Policy at the *first* sign of attraction to another man.

The woman drawn to the adrenaline rush of a secret allure needs to tell her husband of this tendency so that he can be aware of possible dangers, as well as hold her accountable when she is tempted. Stottler is keenly aware of my love for adventure and excitement, and therefore he is sensitive to areas of danger for me. This acts as a wonderful form of accountability in my life.

If you recognize yourself in this particular issue, do not treat it lightly! Tell your husband immediately of your tendencies and talk through potential "danger zones" (such as spending time around athletic, adventurous guys) so that he will understand how to help you make wise decisions that protect and fortify the walls around your marriage. If he fails to understand this tendency in your life, he may tend to downplay the importance of the temptations you reveal to him.

4. Don't Give in to Curiosity

Zoos in many foreign countries allow you to wander quite close to the caged animals. As I gazed at the cute raccoons in a small Argentine zoo, my curiosity about their amazingly dexterous hands rose to the surface. Never had I been close enough to examine their tiny fingers. So to lure one closer, I pushed the long strap of my purse handle between the bars.

Faster than I could blink, one of the raccoons leaped upon that handle and grasped it in his claws. I instantly realized that my purse was thin enough to slide into his cage, so I began attempting to yank it free. But the harder I pulled, the more determined that raccoon became to keep his new treasure.

A regular tug-of-war ensued until finally the purse strap broke and I fell back on the grass with the purse on top of me. My curiosity had almost cost me all of my money and my passport!

When facing temptation, curiosity can be far more costly than a purse. In Proverbs 7, God gives us a picture of a curious man meeting a married woman. *"All at once he followed her like an ox going to the slaughter, like a deer stepping into a noose till an arrow pierces his liver, like a bird darting into a snare, little knowing it will cost him his life"* (Proverbs 7:22,23, NIV).

You may have allowed a growing interest to develop between you and some soccer-father. Then one afternoon he invites you to go for coffee. You agree. *What's the harm? We're only going to get coffee in a public place*, you think.

When we feel attracted to another man, not only should we never tell him, but we should never show it through our eyes or gestures.

I'll say it again: *Never underestimate the power of attraction!* Curiosity should be a red flag warning of potential danger. It's tempting to think that toying with sin won't be the same as actually sinning, but God tells us, *"The devising of folly is sin"* (Proverbs 24:9, emphasis added).

When a man catches our interest, we must never toy with curiosity. That's like going to the grocery store hungry. You don't *plan* on buying that box of Entenmann® cookies or the gallon of Breyers® mint chocolate chip ice cream or the cream puff at the bakery—but you set yourself up!

The same happens when you are curious about spending time with another man. If you wind up in his bed, it's not because you were magically transported there by little green demons. Out of curiosity, you chose to visit that man's home! What did you think was on his mind?

God warns us not to go near the temptation: *"Avoid it, do not pass by it; turn away from it and pass on . . . Watch the path of your feet and all your ways will be established. Do not turn to the right nor to the left; turn your foot from evil"* (Proverbs 4:15,26,27).

5. Don't Flirt

Seeing her boss across the room, Gloria again felt a rush of excitement surging through her. That particular afternoon she had foolishly lingered after all of her coworkers had gone home. Alone in the building with her boss, she knew she shouldn't share her feelings—that seemed far too forward. But as they casually joked about work, she gave him a quick wink. It seemed harmless enough, though a world of emotions lay behind that gesture. For an instant their eyes locked, and they both knew the wall had been broken.

What constitutes flirting? It can be as casual as a sideways glance, a touch, a tone of voice, or a lingering look, to something as blatant as suggestive mannerisms, winking, or blowing kisses. All of these open a wide door for infidelity, because when a woman flirts with other men, she will begin comparing their positive reactions against her husband's routine behavior. And the husband will always fall short.

Oh, the torrent of feelings that can be conveyed through a single look! That is why God says, *"The eye is the lamp of your body; when your eye is clear, your whole body also is full of light; but when it is bad, your body also is full of darkness"* (Luke 11:34). Therefore, when we feel attracted to another man, not only should we never tell him, but we should never show it through our eyes or gestures.

Why are women so prone to flirting? Many girls learn to flirt early in life to gain the attention they failed to receive from their fathers. In America, about 20 million children under age eighteen live with only one parent, the majority (84 percent) living with their mothers.[3] On top of that, Dr. James Dobson says, "Within three years of the divorce, half of the fathers never see their children."[4] Consequently, many young girls yearn for the attention that God designed them to receive from Dad. Not receiving that attention leads them to look elsewhere for affection, developing habits that attract other men's attention.

Women also flirt to receive praise and validation from others. It feeds our ego to have some kind man shower us with his attention. But no other person, male or female, can ultimately fulfill our needs for self worth. That must come from God.

If you lacked the attention of your father and now find yourself drawn to other men, seeking to fill that void through their attention, please see the Resources for an excellent book on this topic. You will also find recommendations of several studies to help you understand your inestimable worth in Christ. If these are issues in your life, *please* seek the counsel needed to heal these areas and to find your fulfillment in Christ. Otherwise, you may struggle with attraction to other men the rest of your life.

6. Don't Fantasize

The missions committee meeting dragged on, but Maria's mind wandered far from the stuffy church basement room. She and her husband had been working closely with various committee members to plan the upcoming trip to Guatemala. But these last several days, she had found herself continually creating reasons to call one particular member—Carlos. Now she sat daydreaming about their next interaction, enjoying the tingle of excitement that these mental pictures produced.

Each day we all experience an amazing amount of what I call "dead brain time." During these moments, our thoughts wander and can easily create mental images of another man to whom we have felt drawn. These mental pictures can come upon us so quickly that we find ourselves dwelling on something before we realize it. Like favorite movie reruns, we replay enticing scenes over and over in our minds, thinking they will do us no harm.

But thoughts are *always* the first step toward actions. No infidelity ever occurred without the parties first fantasizing about it. And unless we consistently put on the helmet of salvation, daily *"taking every thought captive to the obedience of Christ"* (2 Corinthians 10:5), we can easily find ourselves headed toward acting out those supposedly "harmless" thoughts.

Guarding our thoughts also includes the area of our prayer life. Let me explain. Any person to whom you feel attracted becomes an important part of your life. And since you care about him, you naturally care about his spiritual well-being and often want to pray for him. I highly recommend *not* praying for that individual. By praying for someone to whom you have felt attracted, you constantly imprint him upon your conscious mind, making him a continued part of your life. Instead, ask one of your accountability partners to pray on your behalf. God is certainly big enough to handle that man's needs without requiring your prayers to do so!

7. Don't Give in to Rescue Tendencies

Lisa stood beside the ice rink, watching in misery as her determined young daughter struggled to master a jump. Up she would go, only to repeatedly crumble in a heap on the unforgiving ice. Lisa's heart bled for her precious child.

Suddenly, Tom appeared beside her, observing his daughter's skating as well. They had talked many times at these weekly lessons, but today Tom seemed distraught. Lisa's heart, already tender from her daughter's struggles, instantly felt compassion toward Tom as he poured out his sad plight. She felt drawn to help him and offered to talk anytime he needed a listening ear.

Tom did bend her ear, at first calling occasionally when Lisa's husband was away at work. Soon the calls came every day. Then the two began to meet. Then . . .

If a distressed man comes to you for counsel, painting a verbal picture of his pathetic situation, your tender heart may find it difficult not to rescue this poor soul from his misery. But it is crucial to realize how easily these counseling sessions can lead to an affair.

If you recognize this tendency in your life, determine to respond in a way that will not lead to compromise. Guard your heart by sending all hurting men to a pastor, counselor, or therapist. Do *not* become a listening ear to another man's woes. Otherwise, you can easily jeopardize your marriage. And as always, tell your husband of your tendencies.

8. Don't Doubt Scripture or God

Working closely with John every day, Felicia had allowed her heart to fall for this alluring man. She often lingered after work, making excuses to her angry husband about why she arrived home late.

That Sunday as she sat in church, Felicia began to wonder if God really would frown upon her secret desire to escape her unfulfilling marriage to be with someone who brought joy and laughter back into her life. How could God be so cruel as to deny her happiness? Besides, the Bible was written so long ago. Surely its words didn't really apply to modern society anymore, did they?

As we've discussed, doubting God affects *everything else* we believe and do. So can we never question Scripture? God gave us minds, and I for one love to search and study the Word to try and fully understand all I can in the Bible. Do I understand it all? Of course not! God is so huge and His ways are so completely different from mine that I will need all of eternity to learn about Him.

However, when we fail to comprehend what He tells us, we still must choose to believe that His Word is 100 percent accurate. If we don't, we will end up creating a new "moral code" that allows for the sin we hope to justify. Just look at the person mired in homosexuality who claims that he or she follows the Bible, or those who justify killing unborn babies.

Doubting God and His Word can lead to the justification of any sin you choose to pursue—and consequently to your life's destruction (2 Peter 3:16). Whether we fully understand His Words at the time or not, they are given for our guidance and protection, to keep us from *"the sin which so easily entangles us"* (Hebrews 12:1).

For the protection of our marriage, we must recognize these eight situations and choose to respond in a godly manner in the midst of the temptation. In doing so, we will extinguish the sparks of attraction before they can erupt into a consuming inferno.

Seven Immediate Steps for Responding to Marital Temptation

As we know, attraction to another man can happen to anyone, anywhere, anytime. Therefore, this statement bears repeating over and over: *Never underestimate the power of attraction!*

The foolish woman says to herself, "Oh, this is such a little thing. These feelings won't amount to anything. Nothing will ever happen here." That's what I thought on the boat! God tells us that we are fools to think our feelings will ever make a right choice. *"He who trusts in his own heart is a fool, but he who walks wisely will be delivered"* (Proverbs 28:26).

So how do we "walk wisely" the *moment* our heart suddenly feels drawn to another man?

1. FLEE! Get away from the person!

If your pulse suddenly quickened while talking with another man, immediately end the conversation and leave! If your boss just winked at you and your heart rate instantly spiked, walk away! Don't give in to the flesh and further the opportunity to open the door wider.

God provides us with very clear instructions when it comes to sexual temptation: *"Yet the body is not for immorality, but for the Lord; and the Lord is for the body...**Flee immorality***" (1 Corinthians 6:13,18, emphasis added). God *never* tells us to stand and fight physical attraction. He says to "get out of Dodge!" *"A prudent man sees evil and hides himself, the naive proceed and pay the penalty"* (Proverbs 27:12).[5]

2. Pray for God's perspective on infidelity and your marriage.

When your emotions suddenly flutter with improper passion, immediately seek the Lord's presence and stand there until the whirlwind of feelings passes and you once again have His perspective on infidelity and marriage. *"The name of the LORD is a strong tower; the righteous runs into it and is safe"* (Proverbs 18:10).

3. Resist the devil.

James tells us to *"resist the devil and he will flee from you"* (4:7). When I experience feelings that I know are not from the Lord, I say aloud, "Satan, I resist you in the name of the Lord Jesus Christ." I still marvel at how well this works! Of course, it's simply obeying what the Lord tells us to do, so I shouldn't be surprised.

4. Tell your husband.

Transparency with your husband puts a deadbolt on the door to infidelity. Not only does telling him pour ice water on your elevated pulse, but it allows him to be aware of the situation, to hold you accountable, and to pray. I can never overemphasize the value of this act.

5. Tell your accountability partner.

God reminds us that *"where there is no guidance the people fall, but in abundance of counselors there is victory"* (Proverbs 11:14).[6] Request that your accountability friend ask you specific questions, such as: "Have you given this other man any indication that you find him desirable?" "Have you been alone with him?" "Have you continued to inform your husband about any impure thoughts or improper actions?"

6. Replace enticing mental pictures of another man with Scripture.

Initial temptation is not sin. But once we begin dwelling on those enticing feelings and start creating mental pictures, then we have passed from temptation into sin. *"Then when lust has conceived, it gives birth to sin; and when sin is accomplished, it brings forth death"* (James 1:15).

God promises us the power to resist all temptation (1 Corinthians 10:13), but we must choose to practice living by His Spirit's power by *"taking every thought captive to the obedience of Christ"* (2 Corinthians 10:5). The moment enticing thoughts of another man come to mind, meditate on God and His Word. During the temptation, if you don't have access to a Bible, quote any Scripture you have learned. (This is a good reason to memorize the Word!)

7. Do whatever it takes!

God tells us, *"Marriage is to be held in honor among all, and the marriage bed is to be undefiled"* (Hebrews 13:4). Therefore, we must be willing to *do whatever it takes* to keep our marriage pure and undefiled. And "whatever it takes" may mean making some difficult decisions.

If working or living near someone has already led to infidelity, or most likely will, then it's better to leave that job and move away rather than to destroy your marriage and your family. Does that seem unreasonable? "What about disrupting the children's schooling?" someone cries. To that question, I would ask: "What about the far *greater* devastation to your children's lives if you commit adultery, thereby poisoning your marriage and the entire stability of your family?" Far more important than what school your children attend is for them to have parents who live in committed harmony.

In God's eyes, it is of far greater value to quit your job and lose your pension in order to remain faithful than to foolishly remain in a tempting situation and fall into sin. The Lord values the faithfulness of a godly McDonald's employee in Backwoods, Wyoming, *far* above the prestige of a San Francisco corporate woman secretly mired in an affair with her boss.

In fact, position and riches are of no value to the Lord! *"That which is highly esteemed among men is **detestable** in the sight of God"* (Luke 16:15, emphasis added). Our *first* priority is faithfulness to God, then to our husband, then family, and *lastly* to our job.

Are you willing to do *whatever it takes* to keep your marriage pure? Will you begin now to practice the seven steps to extinguish any sparks of attraction you may suddenly feel, as well as practice the other safeguards?

As you incorporate these principles into your life, the Lord *will* give you the strength to overcome every temptation! In Him you *can* have the victory, because He alone *"is able to keep you from stumbling, and to make you stand in the presence of His glory blameless with great joy"* (Jude 24). Praise God!

21

View from the Top

On one of those perfect sunny days when the air feels warm, the breeze blows gently, and life seems lazy, to me there is nothing better than an exhausting ride on a single-track, mountain bike trail. Splashing across ravines of bubbling water, darting through shaded stretches of tall trees, then churning up the final steep grade to reach a breathtaking view at the top gives me inexpressible delight.

One trail near our home provides a perfect workout. It repeatedly climbs to a high peak, only to drop back to the valley floor. All the way up, then all the way back down again, only to repeat that arduous climb several more times. Toward the last hill, my leg muscles scream for relief, and my lungs threaten to burst through my chest.

But on the top of that final climb sits one of my favorite spots in all of Southern California. At the peak of the hill, a solitary bench rests peacefully below a towering California pepper tree. From that vantage point, my eyes can gaze down the broad green valley leading to glorious mountains beyond. Or I can collapse in joy on the bench while reveling in the sweeping Pacific coast before me. The sheer beauty of that view and the moment of utter contentment it provides motivate me to keep pedaling during every ounce of the torture necessary to arrive at that point.

Like that bike ride, life is full of peaks and valleys. The daily, hourly choices of making right decisions to climb the hill called "righteousness" can be difficult. It's often hard to turn away from an enticing temptation. Sometimes it really hurts! But in the end, it's definitely worth the *"prize of the upward call of God in Christ Jesus"* (Philippians 3:14).

> *If we women refuse to participate in infidelity and instead choose to live lives marked by godly integrity, think of the impact we could have!*

Not only do we have our future rewards to look forward to, but God also blesses our faithful obedience in this life beyond description. They may not be material blessings, but the joy of complete peace with the Lord, harmony with others, and a marriage that honors God and brings joy to His heart make every right choice worth the effort.

And our choices have far-reaching effects. A few years ago, a U.S. congressman proposed House regulations that would prohibit congressmen from having sex with their interns.[1] Of course, if their own marriage vows weren't restraining them, I'm not too sure that any law would have a much greater effect!

But what *would* have an effect is for the female interns to refuse to participate. It always takes two to tango. For a congressman to have an affair with his intern, she must agree to do so. For a pastor to divorce his wife and marry the church organist, she has to consent. For a businessman to secretly rendezvous with a married female coworker, she must agree to meet with him.

But if we women refuse to participate and instead choose to live lives marked by godly integrity, think of the impact we could have! Our decisions of marital faithfulness could bring dramatic change to the divorce statistics! No longer would the church look exactly like the nonbelieving world. No longer would nonbelievers wonder if Christianity makes any difference in a person's life. No longer would so many lives be fractured and homes torn asunder.

Just as Isaiah called, *"Rise up you women who are at ease, and hear my voice; give ear to my word, you complacent daughters"* (32:9), we need to rise up today and be the light of Christ to *our* generation. And as we, the women of His church today, begin choosing to live in daily dependence on Him, living out His integrity in every aspect of our lives, what a difference we could make! With Christ radiating through us, we could begin to see dramatic differences in our marriages, in the church, and in our entire society like nothing seen before!

Praise to our God who alone can do such wondrous things! *"Blessed be the LORD God, the God of Israel, who alone works wonders. And blessed be His glorious name forever; and may the whole earth be filled with His glory. Amen, and Amen"* (Psalm 72:18,19).

Resources to Help You Build Your Marriage

Chapter 6: Resources to help build a godly marriage

Loving Your Husband by Cynthia Heald
His Needs, Her Needs by Dr. Willard F. Harley, Jr.
His Needs, Her Needs for Parents by Dr. Willard F. Harley, Jr.
Love for a Lifetime by Dr. James Dobson
What Wives Wish Their Husbands Knew About Women by Dr. James Dobson
Staying Close by Dennis Rainey
One Home at a Time by Dennis Rainey
Strike the Original Match by Charles R. Swindoll
The Mystery of Marriage by Mike Mason

Chapter 6: Resources to help recover from an affair

Love Must Be Tough by Dr. James Dobson
Surviving an Affair by Dr. Willard F. Harley, Jr., and Dr. Jennifer Harley Chalmers
Torn Asunder by Dave Carder

Chapter 11: Reference books and Bible studies I like

My favorite Bible:

The Ryrie Study Bible, New American Standard Version (personal preference)

Books on the Attributes of God:

GOD: Discover His Character by Dr. Bill Bright (my highest recommendation)

Knowing God by J. I. Packer (another winner)

The Knowledge of the Holy by A. W. Tozer (also great)

The Attributes of God by A. W. Pink

Read Through the Bible in a Year:

I like to read through all the books chronologically by date so that it is easier to follow the historical events as they unfolded. Numerous Bibles are arranged so that you read through all the Scriptures in a year's time. Also, in the additional pages of many study Bibles, you will find a "calendar" for reading through the Bible in a year.

Individual Commentaries on each book of the Bible:

My favorite commentaries on books of the Bible are by Warren Wiersbe.

Topical and general Bible studies I have loved:

Loving Your Husband by Cynthia Heald (my highest recommendation)

Ten Basic Steps Toward Christian Maturity by Campus Crusade for Christ (ten studies covering topics such as the Uniqueness of Jesus, the Holy Spirit, Prayer, Obedience, Witnessing, etc.)

Reference Tools:

An exhaustive concordance (get one that matches the Bible translation you use)

A parallel Bible (includes several different translations side by side)

A Harmony of the Gospels, published by Moody Press (helps you read through all four Gospels together)

The Zondervan Pictorial Encyclopedia of the Bible

Bible commentaries, such as *The Wycliffe Bible Commentary* (my favorite)

Systematic Theology, An Introduction to Biblical Doctrine by Wayne Grudem (an excellent insight into almost any theological question you may have)

Evangelical Dictionary of Theology, edited by Walter A. Elwell

Vine's Expository Dictionary of Old and New Testament Words

Bible Study Groups:

"Precept Bible Studies" by Kay Arthur, Bible Study Fellowship, and Beth Moore's Bible studies are three excellent group studies that can be found in many local churches. I highly recommend all of them.

Devotionals:

My Utmost for His Highest by Oswald Chambers (Can a devotional be better than this? Still, it is most important to spend time reading *God's* words rather than just man's.)

Chapter 15: Resources to recover from pornography addiction

Book:

No Stones—Women Redeemed from Sexual Shame, by Marnie C. Ferree

Internet Filtering Software:
Integrity Online: www.integrity.com
Setting Captives Free: www.settingcaptivesfree.com/home/
    scf_isp.php
Christian Living: www.christianliving.com

Ministries:
Pure Intimacy (Focus on the Family): www.pureintimacy.org
Woodmont Hills Counseling Ministry (Marnie Ferree):
    (866) 464-4325, www.bethesdaworkshops.org

Chapter 20: Resources for dealing with an absent father

Your Parents & You by Robert S. McGee, Pat Springle, and Jim
    Craddock (This is an excellent book if you missed receiving
    your father's attention while growing up. Though it is cur-
    rently out of print, copies are available at www.amazon.com.)
Father Care booklet by Jim Craddock. Available from SCOPE
    Ministries, 700 NE 63rd, Oklahoma City, OK 73105 (405)
    843-7778.

Chapter 20: Resources for understanding your worth in Christ

The Search for Significance by Robert S. McGee
Experiencing God by Henry T. Blackaby and Claude V. King
Lifetime Guarantee by Dr. Bill Gillham
Living Free in Christ by Neil T. Anderson (out of print but avail-
    able at www.amazon.com)
Handbook to Happiness by Charles R. Solomon (out of print but
    available at www.amazon.com)
Sidetracked in the Wilderness by Michael Wells (out of print but
    available at www.amazon.com)

Notes

Chapter 2

1. Constance T. Gager and Laura Sanchez, "Two as One? Couples' Perceptions of Time Spent Together, Marital Quality, and the Risk of Divorce," July 29, 2002 <www.swarthmore.edu/SocSci/cgager1/couples.html>.
2. The Barna Group, "Born Again Adults Less Likely to Co-Habit, Just as Likely to Divorce," August 6, 2001 <www.barna.org/FlexPage.aspx?Page= Topic&TopicID=20>.
3. The Barna Group, "Christians Are More Likely to Experience Divorce than Are Non-Christians," December 21, 1999 <www.barna.org>.
4. Barna, "Born Again Adults."
5. B. A. Robinson, "U.S. Divorce Rates: For Various Faith Groups, Age Groups, & Geographic Areas," April 27, 2000 <www.religioustolerance.org/chr_dira.htm>.
6. Dr. James C. Dobson, *Love Must Be Tough* (Nashville: Thomas Nelson, Inc., 1996), 147.
7. Dennis Rainey, *Staying Close* (Dallas, TX: Word Publishing, 1989), 81.
8. Patrick Kampert, "Virtual Infidelity: In Causing Pain, It's the Real Thing," *The Chicago Tribune, Chicagoland Final* (February 3, 2002): Health & Family section, 1.
9. Bill Gothard, *Institute of Basic Youth Conflicts*, notebook from 1975 seminar, Moral Freedom, 2.
10. Mark O'Keefe, "Women Account for Hefty Portion of Web Porn Viewing," October 31, 2003 <www.newhousenews.com/archive/okeefe103103.html>.

11. Dr. Willard F. Harley, Jr., "Coping with Infidelity: Part 2, How Should Affairs End?" <www.marriagebuilders.com/graphic/mbi5060_qa.html>.

12. Dr. Willard F. Harley, Jr., *His Needs, Her Needs* (Grand Rapids, MI: Fleming H. Revell, 2001), 20.

Chapter 3

1. Charles Ryrie, *The Ryrie Study Bible* (Chicago: Moody Press, 1978), 11.

2. Pat Centner, "Divorce in a Consumer Culture," *American Family Association Journal* (March 2002): 18.

3. Susan Graham Mathis, "One Amazing Lady: Kay Coles James," *Focus on the Family* (October/November 2003): 5.

4. Dr. Bill Bright, "Insights from Bill Bright: Reflections from the Founder of Campus Crusade for Christ," October 20, 2002 <www.crosswalk.com/faith>.

5. Also see Titus 2:4; Genesis 2:18; and Ephesians 5:33.

6. Susan T. Foh, *Women and the Word of God: A Response to Biblical Feminism* (Phillipsburg, NJ: Presbyterian and Reformed Publishing Co., 1979), 186. Quoted by Cynthia Heald, *Loving Your Husband* (Colorado Springs, CO: NavPress, 1989), 61.

7. I highly recommend Cynthia Heald's book, *Loving Your Husband*, for gaining a biblical perspective on our role as wives.

8. Dr. Willard F. Harley, Jr., "What to Do with an Unfaithful Wife" <www.marriagebuilders.com/graphic/mbi5033a_qa.html>.

9. Dr. Willard F. Harley, Jr., "How to Survive Infidelity" <www.marriagebuilders.com/graphic/mbi5525_qa.html>.

10. Dr. Willard F. Harley, Jr., "Coping with Infidelity: Part 4, Overcoming Resentment" <www.marriagebuilders.com/graphic/mbi5062_qa.html>.

11. Ron Auch, *Prayer Can Change Your Marriage* (Green Forest, AR: New Leaf Press, 1996), 155. Quoted by Julia Rossen, "Christian Divorce Statistics," October 16, 2003 <www.vvcc.org/vision/homefront/divorce.htm>.

12. Charles Colson, "Marital Safety Nets: Community Marriage Policies," BreakPoint with Charles Colson, commentary #020225, February 25, 2002 <www.pfmonline.net/transcripts.taf?_function=detail&Site=BPT&ID=2434&_UserReference=8AD6D244235801304083FDC0>.

13. Linda J. Waite, et al., "Does Divorce Make People Happy? Findings from a Study of Unhappy Marriages" (July 11, 2002) <www.americanvalues.org/html/r-unhappy_ii.html>.

14. Kathleen Kelleher, "Birds and Bees: The Upside of Down Marriages," Part 5, *The Los Angeles Times* (July 22, 2002): 2. Quoted by Dr. James Dobson, *Family News from Dr. James Dobson* (September 2002): 1,2.

15. Linda J. Waite, et al., "Does Divorce Make People Happy? Findings from a Study of Unhappy Marriages" (July 11, 2002): 5,12. Quoted by Dr. James Dobson, *Family News from Dr. James Dobson* (September 2002): 1.
16. Lee Robins and Darrel Regier, *Psychiatric Disorders in America: The Epidemiologic Catchment Area Study* (New York: Free Press, 1991), 64. Quoted by Glenn T. Stanton, "Fact Sheet on Divorce in America" <www.smartmarriages.com/divorce_brief.html>.
17. Randy M Page and Galen E. Cole, "Demographic Predictors of Self-Reported Loneliness in Adults," *Psychological Reports* (1991) 68:939-45. Quoted by Glenn T. Stanton, "Fact Sheet on Divorce in America" <www.smartmarriages.com/divorce_brief.html>.
18. Dr. Anne-Marie Ambert, "Contemporary Family Trends, Divorce: Facts, Causes and Consequences," The Vanier Institute of the Family, York University, 2002 <www.vifamily.ca/library/cft/divorce.html>.

Chapter 4

1. Shirley Glass, "Shattered Vows," *Psychology Today*, July-August 1998 <www.findarticles.com/cf_dls/m1175/n4_v31/20845729/p1/article.jhtml>.
2. Ibid.
3. Avis Gunther-Rosenberg, "A Marriage Guru Looks at Unfaithfulness," *Providence Journal* (May 15, 2002): G7,12.
4. Ibid.
5. Ibid.
6. See Proverbs 7:10,11,13,19; 9:13.

Chapter 5

1. See Proverbs 1:28–33; Jeremiah 15:6; 2 Timothy 2:24–26; James 5:19,20; 1 Corinthians 5:5; 11:30.
2. Also see Leviticus 19:12; Psalm 76:11; 116:17,18; Proverbs 20:25; Jonah 2:9.

Chapter 6

1. See Ephesians 5:22–33; Colossians 3:18; Titus 2:5; 1 Peter.3:1–7.
2. Dr. Willard F. Harley, Jr., "A Summary of Dr. Harley's Basic Concepts" <www.marriagebuilders.com/graphic/mbi3550_summary.html>.
3. Dr. Willard F. Harley, Jr., "Honesty and Openness (Part 1), Letter 2" <www.marriagebuilders.com/graphic/mbi5015b_qa.html>.
4. Lawrence J. Crabb, Jr., *The Marriage Builder* (Grand Rapids: Zondervan Publishing House, 1982), 63. Quoted by Cynthia Heald, *Loving Your Husband* (Colorado Springs, CO: NavPress, 1989), 37.

5. Bill Gothard, "Our Most Important Messages Grow Out of Our Greatest Weaknesses," *Institute in Basic Youth Conflicts*, Supplementary Alumni Book Vol. 5, 1979, introduction page. Also see 2 Corinthians 12:9; Ephesians 3:16–20.

Chapter 7

1. Patsy Clairmont, Barbara Johnson, Marilyn Meberg, and Luci Swindoll, *Joy Breaks: 90 Devotions to Celebrate, Simplify, and Add Laughter to Your Life* (Grand Rapids: Zondervan Publishing House, 1997), 217,218.
2. "Lookin' for Love," recorded by Johnny Lee, 1980.
3. "I Come to the Cross," by Bob Somma and Bill Batstone, Maranatha Music and Meadowgrass Music Inc., 1996.
4. Also see Romans 8:9–11; 1 Corinthians 6:19.

Chapter 8

1. Also see 1 Chronicles 10:13; Jeremiah 15:6; James 5:19,20.
2. Martin Luther, *Luther's and Zwingli's Propositions for Debate: The Ninety-Five Theses of 31 October 1517 and the Sixty-Seven Articles of 19 January 1523*, in the original version and contemporary translations, with a new English translation, introduction, and bibliography by Carl S. Meyer (Leiden, The Netherlands: E. J. Brill, 1963), 2,3.
3. Bill Bright, *Have You Made the Wonderful Discovery of the Spirit-Filled Life?* (Orlando, FL: NewLife Publications, 1995), 15.
4. "Clear Conscience" pamphlet, Life Action Ministries, January 1, 2000 <www.lifeaction.org/Articles/viewarticle.asp?id=1031103317>.

Chapter 9

1. Paul Hattaway, *The Heavenly Man* (London: Monarch Books, 2002), 56.

Chapter 10

1. J. I. Packer, *Knowing God* (Downers Grove, IL: InterVarsity Press, 1973), 34.
2. Bill Bright, "Ten Keys to Anointed Leadership," *Fuller Focus*, Fuller Theological Seminary (Fall 2001): 1.
3. See 1 Timothy 4:8.
4. John Stott, *Romans* (Downers Grove, IL: InterVarsity Press, 1994), 323,324.
5. See Romans 15:4,5.

6. Jack Graham, "SBC President Asks Southern Baptists to Salt Decaying Culture," *Baptist Messenger* (June 26, 2003): 14.

7. Barna Research Group, "Born Again Adults Less Likely to Co-Habit, Just as Likely to Divorce," August 6, 2001 <www.barna.org/FlexPage.aspx?Page=BarnaUpdate&BarnaUpdateID=95>.

8. See Matthew 27:20–26; Acts 5:1–11; 2 Samuel 11.

9. Joni Eareckson Tada, talk at Colorado State University, Campus Crusade for Christ staff training, July 24, 2001.

10. "Come, Thou Fount of Every Blessing," words by Robert Robinson, 1758, tune Warrenton, *The Sacred Harp*, 1844.

Chapter 11

1. Don Stewart, *The Bible* (San Bernardino: Here's Life Publishers, 1983), 14.

2. Andrew Murray, *With Christ in the School of Prayer* (Old Tappan, NJ: Fleming H. Revell Co., 1965), 126.

3. Henry Blackaby, "Who Holds the Future?", *Current Thoughts & Trends*, vol. 16, no. 1 (January 2000): 2.

4. "Barna study: Christians losing their influence in America," *Baptist Messenger* (September 25, 2003): 9.

5. Paul Hattaway, *The Heavenly Man* (London: Monarch Books, 2002), 297.

6. A. W. Tozer, *The Knowledge of the Holy* (San Francisco: Harper & Row Publishers, 1961), 1.

7. For those who are curious, my bumper sticker quotes Mother Teresa: "It is a poverty to decide that a child must die so that you may live as you wish."

Chapter 12

1. The Barna Group, "Faith Commitment" <www.barna.org/cgi-bin/PageCategory.asp?CategoryID=19>.

2. See Psalms 3, 10, 13, 55, 60, 77.

3. Charles Spurgeon, *The Power of Prayer in a Believer's Life*, compiled and edited by Robert Hall (Lynnwood, WA: Emerald Books, 1993), 15.

4. In the novel *Blessed Child*, I found the example of the main character's communication with God to be enormously helpful as I go to meet with the Lord. Bill Bright and Ted Dekker, *Blessed Child* (Nashville: Word Publishing, 2001).

5. For example, see Psalm 29:2; 99:3; 111:9; 148:13; Matthew 6:9.

6. Also see Proverbs 28:9 and James 4:17.

7. Charles Ryrie, *The Ryrie Study Bible* (Chicago: Moody Press, 1978), 1787.

8. To see examples of God's specific answers to prayers, see 1 Samuel 23:1–5,9–13; 2 Samuel 2:1; 1 Chronicles 14:8–17; Acts 9:10–18; 10:1–48; 13:2; 2 Corinthians 12:7–9.

Chapter 13

1. For a contrast between incomplete obedience and complete obedience, see the difference between King Saul (1 Samuel 15) and Joshua (Joshua 11:15).
2. See 1 Corinthians 11:1; Galatians 4:12; Philippians 3:17; Hebrews 6:12; 13:7.
3. Also see Psalm 40:4; 84:5,12; 89:15; 106:3; 112:1; and 119:1,5.
4. Also see Psalm 19:11; Proverbs 13:13; 1 Corinthians 3:14; Revelation 11:18.
5. Warren Wiersbe, *Be Confident* (Colorado Springs, CO: Chariot Victor Books, 1982), 16.

Chapter 14

1. The Barna Group, "Survey Shows Faith Impacts Some Behaviors But Not Others," October 22, 2002 <www.barna.org/FlexPage.aspx?Page= BarnaUpdate&BarnaUpdateID=123>.
2. Henry Blackaby, "Who Holds the Future?", *Current Thoughts & Trends*, vol. 16, no. 1 (January 2000): 2.
3. Idea taken from Randy Presley, *Baptist Messenger*, Special Edition for Trinity Baptist Church (May 1, 2003): 1.
4. Charles H. Spurgeon, *The Treasury of David*, vol. II, part 2 (McLean, VA: MacDonald Publishing Co., n.d.), 240. Quoted by Cynthia Heald, *Loving Your Husband* (Colorado Springs, CO: NavPress, 1989), 103.
5. Cynthia Heald, *Loving Your Husband* (Colorado Springs, CO: NavPress, 1989), 100.
6. Brad Kallenberg, "Embers of Faith," *Worldwide Challenge* (July/August 2001): 45.
7. Byron Paulus, *Revival Report*, Life Action Ministries (November 2001): 3.
8. Warren Wiersbe, *Be Victorious* (Colorado Springs, CO: Chariot Victor Books, 1985), 33.

Chapter 15

1. Joel Belz, "Why Do We Tolerate Simulation When the Real Thing's Not Allowed?" *World* magazine, August 23/30, 1997. Quoted in *American Family Association Journal* (Nov./Dec. 1997): 19.
2. Anthony Jordan, "Television Garbage," *Baptist Messenger* (January 18, 2001): 3.

3. The Barna Group, "Christians Embrace Technology," June 12, 2000 <www.barna.org/FlexPage.aspx?Page=BarnaUpdate&BarnaUpdateID=64>.

4. "Zogby Survey Reveals a Growing Percentage of Those Seeking Sexual Fulfillment on the Internet," March 2000 <www.pureintimacy.org/news/a0000031.html>.

5. Ramona Richards, "Dirty Little Secret," *Today's Christian Woman*, Sept./Oct. 2003 p. 58 <www.christianitytoday.com/tcw/2003/005/5.58.html>.

6. Mark O'Keefe, "Women Account for Hefty Portion of Web Porn Viewing," October 31, 2003 <www.newhousenews.com/archive/okeefe103103.html>.

7. Richards, "Dirty Little Secret."

8. Frank Rich, "Naked Capitalists," *The New York Times Magazine*, vol. 150, no. 51759 (May 20, 2001): 50.

9. Richards, "Dirty Little Secret."

10. Ibid.

11. "Subtle Dangers of Pornography," July 1997 <www.pureintimacy.org/online1/essays/a0000008.html>.

12. Richards, "Dirty Little Secrets."

13. C. S. Lewis, *The Joyful Christian* (New York: Macmillan Publishing Company, 1977), 199.

14. Charles Colson, "Spiritual Crack Cocaine: The Rise of Cybersex Addiction," March 31, 2000 <www.pureintimacy.org/news/a0000030.html>.

15. Richards, "Dirty Little Secrets."

Chapter 16

1. Shirley Glass, "Shattered Vows," *Psychology Today*, July-August 1998 <www.findarticles.com/cf_dls/m1175/n4_v31/20845729/p1/article.jhtml>.

2. "You've Lost That Lovin' Feelin'," by Barry Mann and Cynthia Weil, recorded by The Righteous Brothers, 1964.

3. Arthur H. DeKruyter, *Family Concern*, J. Allan Petersen, ed., vol. 10, no. 3 (1986). Quoted by Cynthia Heald, *Loving Your Husband* (Colorado Springs, CO: NavPress, 1989), 60.

4. Eleanor Doan, *Speaker's Sourcebook* (Grand Rapids, MI: Zondervan Publishing House, 1960), 157.

5. Dr. James C. Dobson, *Love Must Be Tough* (Nashville, TN: Thomas Nelson, Inc., 1996), 96.

6. Don Meredith, *Becoming One: Planning a Lasting, Joyful Marriage* (Nashville, TN: Thomas Nelson Publishers, 1991), 173. Quoted by Cynthia Heald, *Loving Your Husband* (Colorado Springs, CO: NavPress, 1989), 95.

7. Dr. Willard F. Harley, Jr., "Caring for Children Means Caring for Each Other" <www.marriagebuilders.com/graphic/mbi8112_care.html>.

8. Dr. Neil Clark Warren, "The Cohabitation Epidemic," *Focus on the Family* (June/July 2003): 10.

9. Al Janssen, "The Perfect Model for Marriage," *Focus on the Family* (February 2002): 3,4.

Chapter 17

1. Kelvin Moseley, "What Is Life Like?" *Baptist Messenger* (February 21, 2002), 12.

2. Bridget Maher, "Marriage: The Tie That Binds Us," Family Research Council, January 2, 2002 <www.frc.org/get/pv01j14.cfm>.

3. Mike Mason, *The Mystery of Marriage* (Portland, OR: Multnomah Press, 1985), 99. Quoted in Cynthia Heald, *Loving Your Husband* (Colorado Springs, CO: NavPress, 1989), 53.

4. Willard F. Harley, Jr., *His Needs, Her Needs* (Grand Rapids, MI: Fleming H. Revell, 2001), 20.

5. Ruth Bell Graham, *It's My Turn* (Old Tappan, NJ: Fleming H. Revell, 1982), 33. Quoted in Cynthia Heald, *Loving Your Husband* (Colorado Springs, CO: NavPress, 1989), 16.

6. As quoted by Avis Gunther-Rosenberg, "A Marriage Guru Looks at Unfaithfulness," *Providence Journal* (May 15, 2002): G7,12.

7. Dr. Willard F. Harley, Jr., "Caring for Children Means Caring for Each Other" <www.marriagebuilders.com/graphic/mbi8112_care.html>.

8. Shirley Glass, "Shattered Vows," *Psychology Today* (July–August 1998) <www.findarticles.com/cf_dls/m1175/n4_v31/20845729/p1/article.jhtml>.

9. Dr. James C. Dobson, *Love Must Be Tough* (Nashville, TN: Thomas Nelson, Inc., 1996), 218,220.

10. As quoted by Michael Fousst, "Relationship with Spouse Called Seminarians 'Most Important Sermon,'" *Baptist Messenger* (August 1, 2002): 10.

Chapter 18

1. Bob Horner, emcee at Campus Crusade for Christ staff meetings, Colorado State University, Fort Collins, CO, July 21, 2003.

2. Jeffrey Zaslow, "The Gray Divorcee," *The Kansas City Star* (July 21, 2003): D1.

3. Focus on the Family Ministry Outreach, "Help for Struggling Christian Leaders" <www.pureintimacy.org/online1/essays/a0000016.html>.

4. "I Am Woman," by Helen Reddy and Ray Burton, EMI, 1972.

5. Kara Platoni, "Great Expectations," *Smithsonian* (June 2003): 61.
6. Bob Nigh, "Oklahoma Front Runner in Marriage Issues; Churches Have Work to Do," *Baptist Messenger* (August 1, 2002): 1.
7. Patrick M. Morley, *The Man in the Mirror* (Brentwood, TN: Wolgemuth & Hyatt, Publishers, Inc., 1989), 285.
8. Charles R. Swindoll, *Living Above the Level of Mediocrity: A Commitment to Excellence* (Waco, TX: Word Books, 1987), 123.

Chapter 19

1. Family Research Council, "Culture Facts," June 28, 2001 <www.frc.org/get/cu01f5.cfm>.
2. Pure Intimacy <www.pureintimacy.org>.
3. As quoted by Patrick Kampert, "Virtual Infidelity: In Causing Pain, It's the Real Thing," *Chicago Tribune* (February 3, 2002): Chicagoland Final, Health & Family section, 1.
4. Ibid.
5. As quoted by Mark O'Keefe, "Women Account for Hefty Portion of Web Porn Viewing," October 31, 2003 <www.newhousenews.com/archive/okeefe103103.html>.
6. As quoted by Steve Watters, "Can Intimacy Be Found Online?" 1999 <www.pureintimacy.org/online2/essays/a0000013.html>.

Chapter 20

1. Dr. Willard F. Harley, Jr., "Coping with Infidelity: Part 1. How Do Affairs Begin?" <www.marriagebuilders.com/graphic/mbi5059_qa.html>.
2. As quoted by Peter Jensen, "Emotional Infidelity: Cheating Isn't Just Sneaking Out to a Hotel Room with the Office Hottie," *The Baltimore Sun* (February 24, 2002): 1N.
3. Smart Marriages Archive, "Marrieds Remain Majority. But Percentage Continues to Decline," January 7, 1999 <www.divorcereform.org/mel/rmarriage02.html>.
4. Dr. James C. Dobson, *Love Must Be Tough* (Nashville, TN: Thomas Nelson, Inc., 1996), 232.
5. Also see Proverbs 10:9; 14:16; 16:17.
6. Also see Proverbs 10:17; 12:1; 19:20.

Chapter 21

1. Walter Scott, "Walter Scott's Personality Parade," *Parade Magazine* (September 9, 2001): 2.

JUDY STARR has worked full-time on the staff of Campus Crusade for Christ since 1987. She discipled college women at universities in Indiana and Louisiana, then developed and directed the evangelism and discipleship training program at The JESUS Film Project in California. For the past ten years, she and her husband, Stottler, have ministered in more than forty countries, giving people in Latin America and Asia the opportunity to know Christ. She also continues to speak to women on evangelism, discipleship, and world religions. Her passion is to see women develop an intimate, daily fellowship with the Lord that transforms their lives, bringing change to their marriages, families, and nation.

If you would be interested in having Judy speak at or lead a one- to two-day retreat or workshop helping women grow in their relationship with the Lord, please contact her at:

(949) 361-7575
or
jstarr@ccci.org